ADVANCES IN
LIBRARY ADMINISTRATION
AND ORGANIZATION

Volume 12 • 1994

ADVANCES IN LIBRARY ADMINISTRATION AND ORGANIZATION

Editors: GERARD B. McCABE
Director of Libraries
Clarion University of Pennsylvania

BERNARD KREISSMAN
University Librarian, Emeritus
University of California, Davis

VOLUME 12 • 1994

 JAI PRESS INC.

Greenwich, Connecticut   London, England

CONTENTS

INTRODUCTION   vii
  Gerard B. McCabe and Bernard Kreissman

OWNERSHIP OR ACCESS? A STUDY OF COLLECTION
DEVELOPMENT DECISION MAKING IN LIBRARIES
  Sheila S. Intner   1

A STUDY OF THE FIT BETWEEN THEORETICAL MODELS
OF THE DIFFUSION OF INNOVATION AND THE
DEVELOPMENT AND DIFFUSION OF THE PUBLIC
LIBRARY ASSOCIATION'S PLANNING PROCESS
  Verna L. Pungitore   39

LIBRARIES, ACCESSIBILITY AND THE
AMERICAN WITH DISABILITIES ACT
  Willie Mae O'Neal   75

SOME THOUGHTS ON THE FUTURE
ACADEMIC LIBRARY
  Murray S. Martin   85

LIBRARY STORAGE:
ACHIEVING SYSTEMATIC CONSIGNMENTS
  Cordelia W. Swinton   109

SLAVIC AND EAST EUROPEAN LIBRARIANSHIP:
PROBLEMS, ISSUES, AND OPPORTUNITIES IN THE
POST-SOVIET ERA
  Mark J. Bandera   125

FOURTH I. T. LITTLETON SEMINAR

VIRTUAL COLLECTIONS: ONLY KEYSTROKES AWAY
  Tracey M. Casorso   145

VIRTUAL COLLECTIONS: THE IMPLICATIONS
FOR LIBRARY PROFESSIONALS AND THE ORGANIZATION
  Sheila D. Creth   149

NEW TECHNOLOGIES, INTERLIBRARY LOAN,
AND COMMERCIAL SERVICES: A SYMPOSIUM
ON THE DESIGN AND FEATURES OF
ELECTRONIC DOCUMENT DELIVERY SYSTEMS
   John E. Ulmschneider   161

IMAGE-IN THAT! GREAT IMAGES
SENT 'OR ERE YOUR PULSE BEAT TWICE
   Marilyn Roche   167

THE OHIO STATE/CICNET NETWORK FAX
PROJECT: COOPERATIVE LIBRARY PROJECT
   Robert J. Kalal   175

NCSU DIGITIZED DOCUMENT TRANSMISSION
PROJECT: A SUMMARY
   Tracy M. Casorso   189

PETABYTES OF INFORMATION:
FROM AUTHORS TO LIBRARIES TO READERS
   Malcolm Getz   203

A MODEL AUTOMATED DOCUMENT
DELIVERY SYSTEM FOR RESEARCH LIBRARIES
   John E. Ulmschneider   239

SHOWCASE PRESENTERS   253

ABOUT THE EXHIBITORS   265

ABOUT THE SPEAKERS   271

ABOUT THE CONTRIBUTORS   275

INDEX   277

INTRODUCTION

With this volume the original editors close our responsibilities for *Advances in Library Administration and Organization*. Both of us have divided sentiments about our decision to resign: happy that ALAO is now an established major voice in the profession, sad that we will no longer be working with the great contributors who have lifted ALAO to its current position; happy that ALAO will continue, sad that we will not be the directing force. However, we both have important commitments: Jerry with another addition to his list of publications, *Academic Libraries: Their Rationale and Role in American Higher Education*, Bern with the growth of his new publishing house, Bear Klaw Press. We are particularly happy, however, that Doctors Edward Garten and Delmus Williams have agree to edit ALAO. We wish them enjoyment and success in their new venture.

ALAO was the concept of the late W. Carl Jackson, tragically lost at sea in 1981, who conceived of an annual that would publish long research papers on the many changes and challenges that libraries face. In this introduction to volume 1, which he never saw, he wrote: "Realizing that change begets change, we hope and intend that *Advance[s] in Library Administration and Organization* will be a source of help in anticipating and adapting to these changes that face the profession, to the ultimate benefit of librarians as well as libraries and the publics they serve." We tried to adhere to this ideal and we are certain our successors will as well.

For the second time we open a volume with a paper by Sheila Intner. Only Allen B. Veaner has had that distinction prior to this point. Her insightful paper on decision making in collection development is pertinent to both academic and public libraries. Following that article, Verna L. Pungitore studies the Public Library Association's Planning Process. Her research was supported by the U.S. Department of Education through the Higher Education Act. Following these two library education leaders, Willie Mae O'Neal adds further to the literature on the Americans with Disabilities Act.

The following two papers relate to library building planning: the first considers the future academic library, and the second storage of library materials. The two authors, Murray S. Martin and Cordelia W. Swinton, are recognized authorities in these branches of library planning. While these two papers related to academic libraries, public librarians and library planners will find them useful and apt, and will do well to read them.

Mark J. Bandera enlightens readers with his review of Slavic and East European Librarianship. He points out the differences between imposed Soviet ideology for libraries and the realities of other Slavic library practice and philosophy. There is much for western librarians to learn about their counterparts in the newly emerging countries as the libraries withdraw from decades of tyranny, oppression, and suppression in their former soviet states. Bandera points out that democracy should and will provide the opportunity for self expression among the now free Slavic librarians and it will allow them to open their collections to free access by the people they want to serve. The problems though are numerous and Bandera does not shirk from identifying them.

Finally we conclude with six excellent papers from the I.T. Littleton seminar. This major series is capably edited by Traci Casorso of North Carolina State University Library.

Gerard B. McCabe
Bernard Kreissman
Series Editors

OWNERSHIP OR ACCESS?
A STUDY OF COLLECTION DEVELOPMENT
DECISION MAKING IN LIBRARIES

Sheila S. Intner

BACKGROUND OF THE STUDY

Collection development in libraries traditionally has consisted of buying whatever materials librarians identified as being needed by the public being served.[1] This might have succeeded when collection developers had the resources—staff, time, and money—to identify all available materials, select the titles they believed would be needed by patrons of their libraries, and buy all selected materials. The purchases of good collection builders might include some titles that were not used, but not many of them, and they would certainly include virtually all of the titles that were needed, requested, and used. For collection builders in research libraries, buying something that was not used immediately could be justified on the basis of its potential use in the future. This collecting scenario could be called "just in case," that is, buying titles because they *might* be needed.[2]

No matter how excellent the purchasing, however, members of the public could be depended upon to request titles that the library did not have, either

Advances in Library Administration and Organization, Volume 12, pages 1-38.
Copyright © 1994 by JAI Press Inc.
All rights of reproduction in any form reserved.
ISBN: 1-55938-846-3

1

because they were not identified as being available, or because they were not selected, or if selected and ordered, because they were not received. Libraries never have been able to anticipate all the materials they might be called upon to provide to satisfy every need of every library client, and alternatives such as interlibrary lending have long been used to supplement local holdings. (Library historians suggest resource sharing arrangements similar to interlibrary loans go back to the monastery libraries of medieval times.) Before the rise of computerized bibliographic networks, however, *needed* materials—materials for which requests could reasonably be anticipated—had to be purchased, because librarians had few resources giving bibliographic information for titles they did not own. Even when catalogs of the holdings of other libraries were available, the interlibrary lending process was complex and time consuming, and sometimes costly, which discouraged members of the public from using it. Interlibrary loan procedures required searching, verifying, and handling materials by both the borrowing and the lending libraries, which discouraged them from promoting too much dependence on it. Thus, interlibrary loan was a special service reserved for materials considered out of scope or marginally useful in the local library, for which a need could not easily be anticipated.[3]

During the last 15 to 20 years, three trends converged that created problems for the "just in case" method of building collections: (1) titles in all media were being produced in increasing numbers; (2) materials prices were rising steeply; and (3) library materials budgets were being cut or frozen, or simply were failing to increase fast enough to keep pace with inflation. In addition, funding authorities, anxious to justify their allocations, began holding collection developers accountable for their decisions. The tighter money became, the more important it was to buy only needed titles. In this darkening scenario, collection builders could consider themselves lucky if they purchased needed titles in time to fulfill the requests for them. This "just in time" scenario became a hallmark of a more difficult collecting environment.

Throughout this period, computer-based library networks for shared cataloging and resource-sharing, such as the Research Libraries Information Network (RLIN) and Online Computer Library Center (OCLC), flourished, furnishing each library that joined with instant access to bibliographic data for millions of titles owned by network partners. As networks grew and developed, it became clear that titles could be identified and borrowed through computerized interlibrary loan very quickly—in some instances within 24 to 48 hours. Given the increasing difficulty of buying everything one's patrons might need, access to information about materials began to be perceived as nearly as good as having the materials themselves. If one could identify an owning library in the state or region, and if a message could be sent electronically for desired titles, the partner could comply with the request within hours. Added to the library-based networks were commercial suppliers of bibliographic data such as DIALOG, which indexed millions of articles appearing in journals, reports, proceedings, etc.—far more publications than any individual library would collect, regardless of the status of its budget. Patron searches in DIALOG produced bibliographies that could never be satisfied by local collections alone, and document delivery services were offered by the company to consumers who chose to pay for them.

Before long, two fundamentally different collection development alternatives began to emerge: (1) purchasing materials so these holdings were available for use within the library; or, (2) providing access to bibliographic data for materials that were not part of the library's holdings, but which might be obtained from other libraries, from producers, or from a variety of commercial suppliers. The second option was not entirely new; reference sources always have supplied bibliographic citations likely to be outside a library's holdings. But the enormous number of titles, measured in the millions, and their rapid dissemination to searchers via computerized databases such as DIALOG, OCLC, and so forth, as well as the potential to receive the full text of documents—a still more recent development—changed the nature of the option and made it more nearly equivalent to the option to purchase materials.

To sum up, the exponential production of informational materials and concomitant restriction of library materials budgets, staffing, and physical resources have required libraries to consider alternatives to purchasing everything they need,[4] and the simple, easy, and virtually instantaneous electronic transmission of computerized data (bibliographic and/or full text of documents) has changed temporary access into a viable alternative to purchasing and owning materials.

Temporary access is the sole method by which some materials can be obtained, because their publishers prefer leasing or licensing to selling them outright. Computer software packages, for example, often are licensed, not sold, and their contracts have limitations that do not apply to ordinary purchases. For other materials, the costs of outright ownership are beyond the purchasing power of individual libraries, making temporary access such as rental or lease the only realistic possibility. Entertainment feature films are one example of the kinds of materials that fall into this category, and often they are shared by a large cooperative organization that purchases one copy for the benefit of all its members.

In all instances, however, the assumption on which this study was based was that collection developers now are faced with more complex decision making and the range of alternatives has expanded to include various forms of temporary access to materials.

THE PROBLEM

Despite its potential, access has lacked the kind of systematic, proactive planning librarians have come to expect from an acquisition process appropriate to deem part of "collection development." It seemed to be a hit-or-miss method of obtaining materials. Access was a reactive technique, called into play only after a desired item was found to be unavailable in a library's holdings. It was not used as a method of developing collections, but solely as an *ad hoc* way of supplementing them.

Access may have been used more often in the last decade, but the idea that it could be used systematically and proactively was not much pursued, even as the number of desirable materials continued to increase in number and in price, while the real market value of materials budgets continued to fall. Yet, opportunities for obtaining materials temporarily were increasing in number and diversity and becoming more efficient thanks to technological progress, particularly in telecommunications. The question contemplated here was *how could access be incorporated more effectively and systematically into the collection developer's arsenal of methods?*

One way to address this question was to examine an immediate problem facing collection development officers in large libraries today: *identifying categories of materials which can be provided to users solely on a temporary basis,* even though librarians recognize and acknowledge that the materials probably will continue to be needed.

Clearly, one factor in the choice between purchase and access is the extent to which decision makers believe forfeiting ownership of the materials will have a negative effect on future collections. Applying this criterion, for example, public libraries might be willing to lease multiple copies of best selling novels thought to have little future value, while academic libraries might be willing to lease multiple copies of basic texts likely to be revised regularly. Another factor is the difference in cost between temporary access and ownership. Applying this criterion, research libraries might decide to share the ownership of long-lived microform masters with partners because they are extremely costly to obtain, and use them to generate relatively inexpensive but short-lived copies for actual use. A third factor to be considered is the waiting time involved in providing temporary access to materials in place of purchasing and maintaining them on library shelves. Applying this criterion, research libraries might opt to borrow dissertations from other institutions through interlibrary loan even if it takes several days or weeks, because users of dissertations typically are able to wait for them, but they might not do so for reference works or popular treatises, which typically are needed on the spot or within a day or two at most.

A conscious decision not to purchase needed materials is never made lightly. Despite the popularity of online and/or optical disk indexing and abstracting services, librarians who lease them resist substituting them for subscriptions to the printed book counterparts. The investigator has been told the reason is that they are required to return any electronic materials left in the library's possession when leases end, whereas they own and may keep all the printed books purchased by subscription. This can be perceived as an ownership versus access dilemma, since electronic indexes have a number of distinct advantages, including being more up-to-date, accessible anywhere in an institution's computer network, and possessing far more versatile search options. In contrast, print indexes are not only less timely and available only in reference areas of the library, but they consume inordinate amounts of shelf space and offer little flexibility for retrieval.

As finances become tighter, however, librarians have begun to turn more often to alternatives to ownership. Methods of selecting which materials not to buy or to stop buying have become as important or, in some instances, more important than selecting those that will be purchased.[5] This study sought to discover a more systematic process by which access might be selected over ownership as well as to identify the kinds of materials to which these decisions most fruitfully be applied.

DEFINITIONS

Collection development was defined as that combination of predetermined policies and procedures whereby materials are added to or removed from the holdings of a library.

For the purposes of the study, *access* was defined as the temporary availability of materials without permanent ownership. Thus, it includes but is not limited to purchases made cooperatively with other libraries; leases and licenses for books, films, and so forth, and electronically transmitted materials; document delivery services in which the library acts as a purchasing agent for the user without retaining any ownership rights over documents thus obtained; and interlibrary loans.

In contrast, *ownership* was defined as the permanent addition of materials to a library's collections with the full rights of ownership, including the right to display and sell the purchased item as well as to use it in any way the library deemed appropriate.

PURPOSE OF THE STUDY

This research sought *to identify specific categories of library materials for which access was perceived by collection development librarians to be an acceptable alternative to purchase.* The materials in question had to be within the library's collecting scope—materials for which users' needs were consciously anticipated—but for reasons such as lack of funds or lack of storage space to house them, a decision was made not to purchase. Instead, the choice was to lease or borrow these materials temporarily, or alternatively, to facilitate their purchase by an end user, that is, a member of the public being served by the library, with the library acting as an intermediary in the transaction. The study sought to identify the rationale offered for such decisions, the relative balance of priorities among the identified material categories in six libraries, and the presence, if any, of institutional polices that supported decisions to access the materials, not to buy them.

The study was intended to help librarians recognize and evaluate alternatives to purchase and ownership of materials, and offer models for making the increasingly difficult choices they face about what to buy.

METHODOLOGY

The study was conducted in four phases: (a) *preparation:* identifying and contacting a selected group of institutions that constituted the study population, and developing research instruments for collecting appropriate data, that is, interview schedules and questionnaires; (b) *testing:* administration of pilot tests of the research instruments to administrators and collection development librarians in one institution and the investigator's collection development classes, and subsequent evaluation and adjustment of the instruments; (c) *data collection and analysis:* administering the instruments in the libraries selected for the study population, analyzing the collected data and interpreting the results; and (d) *reporting:* submitting a research report to the Council on Library Resources and disseminating it to the field through publication in the professional literature.

Preparation

Population: Five libraries falling into three categories were studied and as well as a sixth pilot test site: three academic research libraries (University Library, 1, 2, and 3); two college libraries (College Library 1 and 2) which, although serving academic institutions, did not have primary emphasis on the research mission, and one public library (Public Library 1), a county-wide system consisting of a large number of independent local agencies serving the informational and recreational needs of their communities.

Libraries selected for the study were located in the northeastern United States in order to minimize the need for the investigator to travel to distant sites. In most instances, the directors and/or chief collection development officers were known to the researcher and promised their full cooperation upon being approached to participate. In two instances, the directors did not know the researcher before the study commenced, but agreed to participate after consulting with members of their staff.

Libraries serving both large and small constituencies were included in the study population to overcome the possibility of encountering biases related to size; however, to be selected, participating libraries had to be sufficiently large to have at least one administrator with responsibility for collection development, or a designated collection development librarian. (Practically speaking, this was not a problem. Even at the test site, a small college serving a population of only about 3,000 students and faculty with relatively small collections, one staff member was designated collection development librarian.)

The selected libraries constituted case study settings in which the collection development decision process was explored and analyzed in terms of ownership versus access decisions.

Instruments: Two data gathering methods were implemented: (1) on-site focus interviews, in which open ended questions were discussed informally among small groups of policy makers including but not limited to library directors and chief collection development officers;[6] and (2) mailed questionnaires administered to all collection development staff members, for example, acquisition librarians, bibliographers, and selectors, who did not necessarily perform these tasks on a full-time basis, but served their libraries in other capacities as well.

The interview schedule consisted of five questions:

1.   Did an "increasing pressure scenario" in which collecting decisions were becoming vastly more difficult reflect the reality of your library's situation? [The point of this question was to establish that the participants did not perceive their library could buy all needed material, and obviate a reply to question 4, below, that only out-of-scope materials were appropriate to access.]
2.   What methods for obtaining temporary access to materials were considered viable?
3.   How did members of the public perceive access?
4.   What categories of material can be accessed successfully?
5.   What do they expect will happen in the future?

The focus interviews were audiotaped and the tapes transcribed so the investigator could review the conversations in a convenient format. For each group, answers to the five questions were summarized by the investigator and sent to each interview participant. Participants were asked to examine the summaries to be sure the general gist of the conversations and specific remarks were reported accurately, and to respond with approval and/or corrections as well as any additional comments they chose to make.

The investigator then used the approved interview data as the basis for designing the second instrument used to survey all collection development staff in the participating institutions. By developing the survey instrument after conducting the focus interviews, questions were formulated and acknowledged and took account of the libraries' "policy environment"—that is, the expressed visions, goals, and intentions of top-level decision makers.

Questions on the survey instrument were grouped into five general categories similar to the focus interview schedule, following an added category for demographic data. Under each of the general headings, a series of closed questions were presented, each having a limited number of potential responses, plus a space for other answers or comments proposed by the respondents. (See a copy of the instrument in Appendix A.)

The survey instruments were mailed to the library directors or chief collection development officers at three institutions, who distributed them to all potential respondents in their libraries. The investigator was provided with a list of individual respondents at the other two institutions, and sent the questionnaires directly to each person, accompanied by a cover letter explaining that the library's administrators had agreed to institutional participation, provided their names, and requested that they respond.

Testing

Focus interview schedule: Before it was used, the focus group interview schedule was sent to Peggy Johnson, Assistant Director of Libraries at the University of Minnesota, St. Paul Campus, who evaluated it and offered suggestions for improvement.

The investigator conducted pilot tests of both instruments with members of the staff of one of the college libraries. The focus interview pilot test had seven participants, including the library director and head of collection development. It took place at a breakfast meeting and was audiotaped exactly as were the interviews conducted for the study. The researcher gained much valuable experience encouraging people to speak up and discuss their opinions and ideas during the test as well as ways of handling the distractions of taping (tapes tend to come to the end at inopportune moments). Since the questions on the interview schedule were brief and open-ended, they did not require much revision; but the researcher had to refrain from saying too much in her introduction, or conveying the idea that some replies were better than others.

Survey questionnaire: An early draft version of the survey questionnaire was used with selected students from the investigator's fall 1991 Collection Development class at Simmons College's Graduate School of Library and Information Science, and comprised the basis of a simulation exercise during a class session in which students assumed the roles of library directors at a meeting exploring resource sharing in their locality. After some revision, a second draft version was submitted to Ms. Johnson for review and critique.

Draft survey instruments for the pilot test library were distributed by the library director. Five replies were received and because, in all but the most minor respects, the questions were identical to those in the final survey instrument, they were counted along with those of study participants.

Data Collection

Focus interviews: The focus interview groups consisted in every instance of the library director or university librarian, the chief collection development officer (with one exception—a library that was conducting a search for a collection development officer), and additional members of the library's administrative decision making team, for example, assistant, associate, or deputy directors or university librarians; assistant, associate, or deputy collection development officers; and department heads, special collection librarians, and/or branch librarians. Focus interview groups are best limited to a small number of people, more than one or two, but fewer than 10 participants. In this study, two groups had two participants each; one had four participants; one had five participants; and one, the largest group, had eight participants.

Focus interviews are best conducted in a relaxed, informal atmosphere in which people feel encouraged to speak their minds fully and frankly. To achieve this kind of environment, the investigator arranged for interviews to be held in two-hour sessions, from 12:00 noon to 2:00 PM, at sites where the conversations took place over lunch. Not only did this promote relaxation and informality, but two additional advantages of the arrangement were that library administrators, taken out of their offices, were not subject to the usual interruptions that might be expected to occur in their busy libraries, and less time was taken away from participants' working day, because interview sessions included the lunch hour.

Survey of collection development librarians: At the directors' requests, a total of 200 survey instruments were sent, some to individuals they had identified and the rest in group mailings to the directors, for staff members having any type of collection development responsibilities. The mailings were timed to arrive at the libraries approximately 10 working days before the deadline set for their return. It has been the investigator's experience that respondents either fill out a questionnaire within days of receiving it or put it aside for some future time, which usually results in failure to respond at all. The investigator assumed correctly that the response rate was likely to meet or exceed a target minimum of 50 percent because of the library administrators' commitment to participate in the study.

No effort was made to follow up with staff members who did not respond. Not only was the time frame too short to allow for such follow ups, but, in those institutions where the library directors had distributed the questionnaires, no contact was possible directly with individual respondents. Contacting the other potential respondents a second time to prompt additional replies would have constituted a difference in data collection that the investigator did not believe was warranted by the circumstances. Requests for additional questionnaires were received shortly after the initial mailing. Cover letters accompanying the second mailing of instruments indicated a new return date two weeks later than the end date printed in the questionnaire, and many of these instruments subsequently were received and analyzed.

In all, 107 responses were received, of which 103 were included in the analysis. Four responses were not counted, either because they contained solely the demographic data and explanations that the respondents believed themselves to be unable to answer the questions, or, in one case, because the returned instrument was entirely blank.

Data Analysis

Focus interviews: For each of the five questions, conversations first were divided into a series of remarks, then the remarks were categorized according to content (i.e., topic or sub-topic) and tone (i.e., the attitude expressed—positive, negative, neutral). Then the remarks were regrouped and summarized. Interviewees were asked to confirm that the investigator's summaries were accurate reflections of their group's conversation, and in all but two instances they were approved as given or with some additional elaboration. In two instances, participants had different perceptions of one of the details in the summary, and the investigator corrected both the wording of the summary and her understanding of the conversation to address the criticisms. Individual remarks that captured specific ideas or sentiments particularly well were retained intact, and some of those appear in the findings section, below.

It became apparent to the investigator that the focus interviews were valuable in and of themselves, not only to provide a basis for the survey instrument, but as reflections of the ideas, sentiments, and visions of this small but powerful group of professional leaders—even though they were just a few people from only five institutions. The five directors included persons noteworthy because of their writings and/or high positions in national bodies and/or innovative projects. Therefore, the findings section below includes detailed summaries of the focus interviews.

Survey of collection development staff members: Replies to the questions on the survey were coded and entered into a *StatPac Gold*™ codebook database, a program package for statistical analysis. Questions that had yes-or-no replies were coded "1" for yes, "O" for no, and ".5" for a qualified reply. Questions that had acceptable-or-unacceptable replies were coded "1" for acceptable, "O" for unacceptable, and ".5" for a qualified reply. Replies which indicated various shades of interpretation were interesting and worthy of note, however, the investigator aimed toward obtaining the most specific decision climate possible, which, by definition, cannot be equivocal. Equivocal replies indicated that a decision might be made differently according to circumstances for which this study did not control, and which would not help clarify the elements in the investigator's potential decision making model. Thus, qualified replies (i.e., replies with the value ".5") were noted and reported, but they were discounted in interpreting the data.

Descriptive statistics were tabulated, both for the replies as a whole and for each of the five cohorts. Since the five libraries participating in this study were considered five case studies, no attempt was made to compare replies among institutions or generalize the replies to peer institutions in the library community. Nevertheless, the investigator could not help but observe certain obvious differences, which are noted in the findings, below. The meaning of inter-institutional variation is interpreted very cautiously and with much hesitancy, for three reasons: (1) the population of this study is very small and unsuitable to generalize; (2) factors such as geographic location, the status of automation in the individual library, its locality, or its region, new vendor offerings, new programs, and so forth, can have important impacts that might elicit very different responses to the study's questions; and (3) the situation is dynamic everywhere, even in the five participating libraries.

FINDINGS

Focus Interviews

Research University 1: Librarians agreed that the "increased pressure scenario" was true of the current situation at RU1. Serials and nonprint media were two areas under particular pressure at this time. While budgets were still increasing modestly, the increases were not keeping up with inflation.

Viable routes for temporary access to materials included interlibrary loans (ILL); other cooperative agreements with facsimile partners and mutual acceptance of patrons, especially among the outstanding academic and research libraries in the city's metropolitan area; formal and informal networking, for example, use of the Internet; and commercial vendors supplying tear sheets, etc. Access is perceived as getting better all the time, but not as good as having the item on the shelf. Every success in lowering ILL turnaround time results in increased requests—more than current staffing and funding levels can support. This was seen as approaching crisis proportions, especially in view of RU1's emphasis on scholarly research.

Categories of materials that can be accessed included materials used by fewer rather than large numbers of users, for example, faculty research materials; retrospective materials; foreign language materials except for those supporting language and literature curricula and research; primary research materials; recreational items; documents in multiple formats; documents in multiple editions, particularly costly reference annuals; prefer to access materials that address current collection weaknesses and continue buying those that add to traditional areas of strength. People come to RU1 because of certain strengths and they expect to find large, comprehensive collections in those subjects. Failing to continue building those areas could conceivably jeopardize the institution's strength and appeal to scholars.

In the future, pressures will increase, especially budget pressures. All libraries will have to access larger proportions of needed materials. Interactive multimedia materials which offer users opportunities to create their own individualized "editions," will become a critical need that could consume large amounts of materials budgets if the library invests in hardware, telecommunications links, and the growing body of software, but one that some of the interviewees believe must be met somehow. The need for greater cooperative spirit among libraries will intensify.

Research University 2: Until the present, library materials budgets have always been extremely generous and they remain so; however, the rate of annual increases is beginning to decrease. The handwriting seems to be on the wall. The probability of increased financial pressure in the foreseeable future is high, but the libraries have other problems. At the moment, severe limitations on storage space are reaching critical proportions in some units. A policy has been established that no one can buy documents they cannot shelve upon arrival, which is creating pressure as great as if budgets were limiting purchases.

Access routes considered viable include ILL; other cooperative arrangements, especially with area research libraries; formal and informal networking, such as that conducted with RLIN partners outside the region, via use of the Internet, and so forth; services such as CARL-UnCover and commercial vendors who supply tear sheets, and so forth. Access is perceived as getting better all the time thanks to technological progress, but not as good as having a document waiting on the shelf. There is one exception to this rule of thumb: online data that end users can obtain directly through their personal computers is perceived as better than documents on library shelves, because it enables them to avoid trips to the library and time taken to locate and retrieve materials from the shelves.

Categories of materials that can be accessed include materials used by fewer rather than large numbers of users, for example, primary research materials wanted by students doing these in areas in which RU2 doesn't have programs or interests. [Note: this category was interpreted specifically *not to include* materials for faculty research or primary research materials in areas in which the university does have programs or interests.] Librarians prefer to access materials that redress weaknesses in the collection and continue to buy those that maintain traditional strengths.

In the future, budget pressures will increase. If the information explosion continues indefinitely—and it is by no means clear that it will—all libraries will have to access larger proportions of needed materials and be highly motivated to cooperate and pursue technologies that improve access. This scenario may change if conditions change, for example, if the information explosion begins to slow, end, or retreat, or if new technologies furnish different and more effective means of access.

Research University 3: Librarians agreed that the "increased pressure scenario" definitely described the current situation at RU3. Budget cuts have been severe and there was no guarantee they were over even at the time of the focus interview. Some years ago, RU3's libraries endured a relatively long period of budgetary neglect, making today's cuts particularly distressing. The collections have large gaps as a result of previous problems, and in the future, the librarians feared, there could be a second gap resulting from the current budget cuts.

One of the most important access routes is *intra*library loan. Loans of materials to patrons from RU3 units other than the owning unit now are given high priority, and a new systemwide policy mandates that staff serve patrons from other RU3 units as if they were patrons from their home units. In addition, RU3 librarians use ILL; other cooperative arrangements; formal and informal networking such as OCLC, RLIN, the Internet, and so forth; services such as CARL-UnCover; and, finally, commercial suppliers such as tear sheet services. Access was perceived as good and getting better, but not as good as having documents waiting on the shelf.

Primary research materials and journals with few readers were identified as materials that can be accessed, along with materials used by smaller numbers of users. Many decisions must be made on a case-by-case basis, and collection developers always have to strike balances between access and ownership.

In the future, budget pressures will continue to build and all libraries will access larger proportions of needed materials. Librarians will be highly motivated to cooperate and pursue technologies that improve access. There is a great need for a national information policy to aid libraries in the support of scholarly research and teaching.

College Library 1: The "increased pressure scenario" definitely applied to the situation at CL1. Budget cuts have been severe—on the order of 20 percent of the total materials budget—and there was no guarantee they have ended. The libraries knew cuts were coming and librarians were well prepared for it, but no matter how one prepares, it is a shock when it happens and plans for retrenchment begin to be implemented. In particular, faculty have been kept apprised of developments and have been supportive in every way possible, but the financial situation is serious and goes beyond materials budgets to staff budgets, and so forth. [The day before the focus interview, the college's president suddenly died; the day of the interview a water main serving the library burst, adding new and different problems to their list of woes.]

ILL, particularly practiced with certain other members of the university system to which CL1 belongs, and selected area libraries, was named as the best access route. Other cooperative arrangements, formal networking through OCLC, informal networking via the Internet, and commercial services were also viable access routes.

Access was perceived as not bad and improving, but not the same as having documents waiting on the shelf. CL1 patrons are aware of the library's desire to help them and the efforts made to obtain documents quickly. Thus, patrons have been understanding about the library's problems and supportive of its positions.

Materials that can be accessed include materials used by small numbers of users such as primary research materials, journals with few readers, and nonbook entertainment items. Balances between ownership and access must be struck in different ways for different materials and many decisions must be made on a case-by-case basis.

The future is likely to witness increased budget pressures. All libraries will have to access larger proportions of needed materials. Librarians at CL1 and elsewhere will be highly motivated to cooperate with partners they trust and who trust them, and to develop more such partnerships with peer institutions.

Public Library 1: The "increased pressure scenario" was seen to be an accurate depiction of the situation at PL1. Budget cuts had been sustained and it was possible though not certain that more could occur.

Access routes perceived as viable included ILL, patron exchanges among various units within the county; formal and informal networking via OCLC and area libraries; services such as CARL-UnCover, which had been inaugurated just a few weeks before the focus interview; and other commercial suppliers of materials. Access wasn't too bad, but patrons don't understand the ILL process and why it takes so long. The advent of CARL-UnCover may change that for the better. Many people don't know the library can get materials for them from other sources and it hasn't been highly publicized, but once they learn about the service, they like it and the library might be faced with more business than they can handle.

Categories of materials that can be assessed include materials in multiple formats (the library might buy one format and access the others; materials in multiple editions, especially reference materials issued annually that vary in minor ways from year to year; nonbook materials in formats where the budget allocations can't be changed quickly enough to accommodate demand, such as videos and sound compact disks; materials with fewer potential users; and foreign language materials, except in libraries where the language was needed by a target group in the community.

Librarians said they believed budget pressure would continue to increase and all libraries will have to access larger proportions of needed materials. Librarians at PL1 expect to reply on services such as CARL-UnCover more, and to educate the public to use them.

Summary: The combined answers to the five interview questions revealed the following opinions and ideas:

1. Does the increased pressure scenario apply to your library? All participants said yes, but two institutions qualified their positive replies. Four of the institutions had recently sustained large cuts in materials budgets. Two of those said it was realistic for them to expect more cuts in the near future. One institution said annual increases were not keeping up with inflation and their serials and nonprint media budgets were under pressure because of the large sums of money involved. One institution said budgets still were generous but annual increases were falling and space problems were intensifying to the point that library policies now did not permit buying any materials that could not be shelved.

2. What access routes are viable alternatives to ownership of materials? All five institutions currently used the following: intralibrary loan; interlibrary loan; local cooperative agreements without regard to library type; formal networking through bibliographic utilities; and other information networking through Bitnet, the Internet, or other non-utility networks. Three institutions used the CARL-UnCover document delivery service. Two institutions had informal agreements with one or more facsimile partners, without contracts or other codification. Two institutions used commercial tear sheet services to obtain some materials. One institution used the Center for Research Libraries as a source for obtaining some materials. Because end users (recipients of the documents obtained) could download or print copies of materials obtained through commercial full-text CD-ROM or online services for their permanent use, none of the five groups considered such services as modes of temporary access. Instead, they were considered the full equivalent of purchasing materials for collections, despite the fact that the documents did not remain in the collection for use by other library users.

3. How do patrons perceive access? In general, all five groups agreed that patrons found access as good and getting better all the time, but not as good as having an item waiting on the shelf to answer a request immediately. Administrators also agreed that when patrons can obtain online data directly through their personal computers, *access was better* than having the documents in print form on library shelves. One group emphasized, but several more concurred, that success with interlibrary loan results in more requests than the library had staff to handle, and another group said that patrons don't always know the library can get materials for them, but when they find out, they like the service and use it. Several academic librarians said that, despite improvements in access and ready availability of documents, faculty still want the library to purchase, store, and maintain their "pet" journals.

4. Which categories of materials may be accessed successfully? The following ten types of materials were suggested to be appropriate to access

by several, though not necessarily all, of the groups (the order of listing is not significant):

- primary research materials
- materials that redress weaknesses in the collections
- foreign language materials
- materials in multiple formats
- nonbook materials

- faculty research materials
- multiple editions, especially annuals
- retrospective materials
- recreational materials (in academic libraries)
- journals with small audiences

One problem that emerged during this part of the discussions was that collectors' might wish to shift purchasing from one subject or format to another, but be unable to change line item allocations for at least one and sometimes more than one budget cycle. In such cases, access could solve the problem in the near term, even if new purchasing patterns eventually provide solutions in the long run. In nearly every group, one or more librarians commented that decisions to buy or access materials often must be made on a title-by-title basis.

5.   What will happen in the future? Nearly all interviewees made the following forecasts about the future of collection development in their libraries as well as in the library world at large:

- purchasing power will continue to decline
- willingness to cooperate will become more important
- successful libraries will build partnerships among their neighbors and peers to increase opportunities for access
- libraries will have to access larger proportions of their materials unless the information explosion unexpectedly slows or changes
- new media may provide opportunities for users to have individualized "editions" of documents and libraries must make this a top priority for development
- a national information policy to provide national access and resource sharing beyond interlibrary loan is imperative
- decisions will not involve ownership *or* access, but ownership *and* access
- librarians will pursue technology aggressively to improve access.

Survey of Collection Development Staff Members

Demographic Data: Total numbers of respondents from the various institutions were as follows: RU1—19; RU2—33; RU3—32; CL1—6; PL1—13; and CL2 (the pilot test library)—5. Respondents were primarily highly educated senior staff members. Slightly more than four-fifths of the group had been in collection development work for five years or more, and approximately 60 percent had spent more than ten years in the specialty. Half the respondents possessed one master's degree; all but one of the rest had additional education, with one-fifth having received a Ph.D. An interesting contrast was in evidence regarding the number of years respondents had spent in collection development and the number of years they were in their current jobs. The curve representing the number of years in collection development had two peaks at 12 years and 21 years, while the number of years in the current job peaked at 2 years and 12 years (see Figure 1). These data seem to indicate that "collection development work" covers a variety of specific jobs and offers librarians both the flexibility and the opportunities to move from one job to another as they gain experience and seniority.

The "Increased Pressure" Scenario: Three-quarters of those responding believed they had to buy more materials with fewer "real" dollars than in previous years, and nearly 90 percent believed library materials budgets were

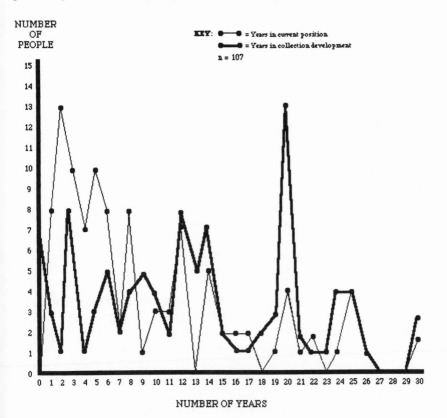

Figure 1.   Respondents' Service

shrinking or slowing in growth. More than three-quarters claimed that users currently required more materials to fill their needs and more than 85 percent said that more materials were being produced in their interest areas. Slightly more than three-quarters replied that they now buy less of what is available in their users' interest areas. More than 95 percent said they thought about money matters when they performed their job.

The proportion of respondents who said it was now more difficult to do their jobs than in the previous four or five years was slightly more than 70 percent, which is consistent with replies documenting an "increased pressure scenario." Many of the respondents' added comments cited money (or lack of it) as the chief reason for their predicament. Others made reference to time pressures, the need to select from among competing formats, and growth of the literature and patron expectations. The following quotations are illustrative:

> Electronic formats have been added without equipment funds.

> More users means less time to spend on collection development—also less money and no staff growth.

> ...more demands for services, increasing subject parameters.

> In the past 5 years, the cost of psychology materials has risen so sharply that I have had to be extremely selective. Having to be more selective takes a great deal of time and thought.

> More publications, less money, no space.

> More choices, more needs, less $, and limited window of availability.

> Juggling becomes a required attribute. Expansion in various subject areas rarely equals expansion in budget...

> ...the difficulty of balancing immediate, known user needs with those that are potential, unrealized or undeveloped as yet in a limited (by budget) collection.

And a media librarian at an academic research library added:

> Copyright issues are much more complex with 'home use video' and off air taping so popular with faculty.

Methods of Access Constituting Alternatives to Access: Five options were offered as methods of access—interlibrary loans, rental collections and/or subscriptions to full-text data-bases (the latter are leased, not owned), document purchases on behalf of a patron who paid for them, shared purchases with other libraries, and electronic network services, including CARL-UnCover—and respondents were asked to rate them as acceptable or unacceptable alternatives to purchase.

Only ILL and electronic networks were perceived as acceptable by large numbers of those responding, although all the options but one were deemed acceptable by a larger proportion of people than found them unacceptable. The exception was purchasing documents and charging patrons for them, that is, acting as information brokers. ILL received the highest proportion of positive replies, more than 90 percent; electronic networks ranked second, more than 80 percent; shared purchases ranked third, more than 60 percent; rental collections ranked fourth, more than 50 percent. However, only 43.6 percent of those responding believed information brokering (i.e., buying documents on behalf of a patron who then pays for the purchase) was an acceptable alternative to purchasing materials for the library collection.

Individual respondents added the following options to the printed list provided by the investigator:

- refer to depository libraries in the local area
- advice to travel to sources
- journal exchange agreements
- electronic journals (omitted because it relates closely to database subscriptions)
- *intra*library loan (omitted because the library does purchase items, although not multiple copies)
- donated items.

In certain situations, gifts, exchanges, and recommendations to travel to other libraries are appropriate sources for materials, though not necessarily as substitutes for purchases. *Gifts* are essential sources of materials for rare book and historical collections; *exchanges* may be the only sources for foreign university publications; and *travel to other sources* may be required for materials that cannot be removed, photocopied, or otherwise transmitted by a holding library to other institutions. All are viable methods of obtaining materials under these and other specific circumstances; however, buying copies of these materials may not be an alternative, because they are not available for sale.

Patron Perceptions of Access: Respondents were asked how they believed their patrons would view the same list of options, that is, as acceptable or unacceptable alternatives to purchases. Once again, more than 90 percent of those responding thought patrons found ILL acceptable and more than 80 percent believed patrons found information accessed via electronic networks acceptable. The third ranking alternative, however, was information brokering—having the library buy the desired materials on behalf of the patron and charge the patron for them. More than 70 percent of the responding librarians said patrons would find this an acceptable method of access. Both of the remaining alternatives, that is, rentals/leases and shared purchases, received positive replies from more than 50 percent of those surveyed. Thus, a majority of the respondents said patrons would find all of the access methods acceptable alternatives to ownership of materials.

Staff Perceptions of the Speed and Cost of Access: In this set of questions, librarians were asked to evaluate the access methods in terms of their speed (fast or slow) and cost (high or low). ILL, the most popular access alternative, was perceived as slow by more than half the respondents, but low in cost by two-thirds. Nearly one-third of those surveyed found ILL to be both fast and low cost, while slightly more than one-fifth believed it to be both slow and high in cost. (See Table 1).

Electronic network databases, the second most popular alternative, was perceived as fast by nearly everyone (only 2.2% of the those responding thought it was slow), but more than 90 percent believed it also was high in cost.

Information brokering was thought to be both fast and high in cost by more than 40 percent of the respondents. More than a third believed it to be slow despite its high cost. A small group thought information brokering was low in cost (18.6%), but more than twice as many people in the group also believed it was a slow method of procurement rather than a rapid one.

More than three-quarters of those responding believed access via rentals or leases was a speedy way to obtain materials (76.2%). Nevertheless, nearly as large a group found it high in cost (74.5%).

Shared purchases, the final access option, was generally perceived as low in cost (65%), but fewer than one-fifth thought it would be speedy (18%). Fewer than 10 percent of the respondents believed shared purchases were both fast and low in cost.

Arranging the responses by attribute instead of by option, the best possible combination of attributes was fast for obtaining material and low in cost. ILL was thus ranked by the largest group of respondents, followed by rentals/leases, electronic network databases, shared purchases, and information brokering, in descending order. Looking solely at speedy procurement, electronic network databases were ranked first, followed by rentals/leases, information brokering, ILL, and shared purchases, in that order. Looking solely at low cost, ILL ranked first, followed by shared purchases, rentals/leases, information brokering, and electronic network databases. (These results were calculated by combining, for the attribute of cost, the numbers of persons replying that ILL was both low cost and slow with those who said it was both low cost and fast; and for the attribute of speed, combining the numbers of persons replying that ILL was both fast and low cost with those who said it was both

Table 1.   Evaluation of Access Options

ILL		Elec. DB		Shar. Purchase		Rental/Lease		Info. Broker	
Slow/low	35.0%	Fast/high	88.8%	Slow/low	56.6%	Fast/high	54.2%	Fast/high	45.3%
Fast/low	32.0%	Fast/low	9.0%	Slow/high	25.3%	Fast/low	22.0%	Slow/high	36.06%
Slow/high	20.4%	Slow/high	2.2%	Fast/high	9.6%	Slow/high	20.3%	Slow/low	13.3%
Fast/high	12.6%	Slow/low	—	Fast/low	8.4%	Slow/low	3.4%	Fast/low	5.3%

Table 2. Rankings by Attribute

Fast + Low Cost	Fast	Low Cost
Interlibrary loan	Electronic databases	Interlibrary loan
Rentals and leases	Rentals and leases	Shared purchases
Electronic databases	Information brokering	Rentals and leases
Shared purchases	Interlibrary loan	Information brokering
Information brokering	Shared purchases	Electronic databases

fast and high cost.) (See Table 2). If, however, numeric values were assigned to each option in columns two and three in descending order from 5 to 1, the combined rankings that result would differ slightly from those in column one— that is, ILL and rentals/leases would actually tie for first place with combined totals of 7 points each; electronic databases would be second with a combined total of 6; and information brokering and shared purchases would tie for last place with totals of 5 points each. While the difference may appear negligible, decisions to rent or lease materials might be more attractive if this "secondbest" option were thought to be "as good as" ILL. Of course, when cost is weighted more important than speed, as often is true in libraries, the equality would not hold.

Material Types Appropriate to Purchase and Access: This was the "nitty-gritty" of the study—identifying categories of materials for which respondents said access could take the place of ownership. Eighteen types of materials, combining various aspects of medium, average use, subject, and so forth, were listed as well as a blank space for additional types. Two alternatives were provided for each type: "must buy" and "access OK." Responses are indicated in Table 3.

Academic library respondents were asked to make similar choices for four additional types of materials, which would not be at issue in public libraries: dissertations, popular recreational books, popular recreational magazines, and popular recreational audiovisual or computer materials. Table 4 shows the results:

Examining this set of replies by institution, there was a sharp distinction between the academic and public librarians in the replies about periodicals. Only the public library had a large proportion of respondents (69.2%) who said periodicals used once a month should be accessed. In contrast, 100 percent of the college library respondents and large majorities of the university librarians (more than 60% in each institution) said periodicals used once a month should be purchased. On the other hand, the public librarians agreed unanimously that periodicals should be accessed if their importance was due to a staff member publishing in them or serving on their editorial boards. Many academic librarians (groups between 39.2% and 66.2% of all respondents from the academic libraries) replied that such titles required purchase. Academic

Table 3. Acquisition Choice by Type of Material

Type of Material	% Must Buy	% Access Ok
● Periodicals		
- used once a month	66.3	33.7
- used twice a month	89.3	10.7
- faculty/staff on editorial board	40.8	59.2
- faculty/staff/patrons publish in it	46.1	53.9
- faculty/staff use for personal use	13.9	86.1
- faculty staff use for library work	61.6	38.4
● Books:		
- used four times a year	86.8	13.2
- used eight times a year	99.1	0.9
- used twelve times a year	99.1	0.9
- book/serial needed to complete a set	73.0	27.0
● Other materials:		
- sound recording in important subject	50.5	49.5
- online database in important subject	49.5	50.5
- CD-ROM in important subject	70.8	29.2
- video in important subject	43.3	56.7
- encyclopedia in important subject	85.7	14.3
- index in important subject (library owns 50% of periodicals indexed)	85.3	14.7
- almanac or directory in important subject	88.3	11.7
- material for small but vocal user group	58.6	41.4

Table 4. Acquisition Choices of Academic Librarians
for Other Types of Materials

Type of Material	% Must Buy	% Access Ok
- dissertation in important subject	22.8	77.2
- popular recreational book	6.8	93.2
- popular recreational magazine	5.7	94.3
- popular recreational AV or computer item	1.1	98.9

librarians were slightly more favorable toward purchasing titles in which faculty or staff published, rather than those in which they were members of the editorial boards.

Similarly, there were sharp differences in replies about audiovisual materials. If a non-recreational sound recording was in an important subject area, 80 percent or more of the college library respondents and nearly 70 percent of the public library respondents considered it a must buy item, but far fewer university librarians agreed (32.1%; 40.7%; 64.3%). Online databases in important subject areas were must buy items for large proportions of public library and one university library's respondents as well as half of those from one of the colleges, but majorities from the rest of the institutions thought they were satisfactory to access. Videos in important subject areas were must buy items for most of the public librarians (84.6%) and fully two-thirds of one college's respondents; but much smaller proportions of respondents from the other institutions agreed (22.2%; 32.0%; 40.0%; 57.1%).

Comments in this set of questions suggested use was paramount, and when wording did not make clear how much use materials would receive respondents were uncomfortable about their replies, for example, people wrote: "it would depend on the title, its anticipated use, whether other materials are already owned [etc.]" and, regarding an item used for library work, "if used frequently, more than once a month."

Opinions about the Future: The final section of the questionnaire explored respondents' opinions about what might happen in the future. Asked whether choosing to access materials might, as an unwanted side effect, cause libraries to jeopardize their future collections, more than 60 percent said it would. While those who disagreed were a large group, they were, nevertheless, a minority. One thoughtful comment added here said, "Need to target specific areas for buying and specific areas OK for access."

More than 75 percent of the respondents said an item's value to patrons was more important than its cost, indicating that they had a strong identification with patron needs. On the other hand, one librarian commented, "As long as [the Library] can access, ownership does not matter." Nonetheless, most were realistic about developments in the near term and more than 90 percent replied they believed more materials would have to be accessed in the next three to five years than is happening now. One librarian commented: "So much of 'access' has to do with the computer industry, where high profits are the norm, one has to worry about what will remain retrospectively 'accessible'— back issues, and so forth. Who will be the owner? How ephemeral is this world?"

The last question asked whether new ways to obtain materials must be found, and more than 95 percent replied in the affirmative. One optimist edited the printed question to read "Libraries *will* find new ways to access materials..." rather than "Libraries *must* find new ways to access materials..." Several comments added to this last question referred to full-text databases as warranting further development. Examples include the following:

> Full-text retrieval of materials in electronic format is most significant.
> I am watching the development of full-text databases in commercial as well as networks owned by not-for-profit organizations. Where will printed materials be given a life expectancy of 50 years or more?

[This respondent added a chart indicating that a humanities monograph might remain in printed form for about 30 years and beyond this, if its value continued, it would be converted to an electronic database for usage and/or to a microform copy for archival purposes.]

Clearly having electronic access to all sorts of things vastly increases all kinds of options. Patrons may access directly—bypass library.

... for us, 'access' is a much more labor-intensive project for staff than ownership. We need to find ways to provide access that don't require staff to interrupt other activities, or learn many new systems...

Improving quick reliable, cheap access is the most important factor in deciding to drastically reduce acquisitions.

How about selective thefts?

[The last comment was undoubtedly a tongue-in-cheek remark; it came from a Special Collections librarian concerned primarily with old, rare, and valuable materials.]

Respondents also added comments in a blank space left for that purpose below the last question. Many described their collections, users, and the frustrations of wanting to do more than current library budgets permitted. Illustrative examples are:

The *** is a course-support library whose clientele are extremely busy and under intense pressure. Immediate or quick, easy access to the materials they need is a high priority. Library budgets take the element of 'choice' out of most of these decisions. If something is in 'an important subject area' but you cannot afford it—then there is no *choice*—you access.

A small number of others expressed dissatisfaction with the survey and its questions, for example:

Items about recreational books, magazines, AV & sound recordings don't really apply here. We're a special research library.

As always, questionnaires are very difficult to respond to... We are an undergraduate library with not much faculty interaction.

I feel like these questions are loaded. Too general to get any but the answers I gave in most cases.

This questionnaire is too simplistic. Very few of the questions can be answered in an *either/ or* fashion. Good luck!

[This respondent qualified many of the questions by adding 'in some cases" and wrote "depends" for others. Emphasis was in the original]

Other general comments of interest included the following:

My budget is always adequate for monographs and serials meeting my collection development policy. What fluctuates wildly is money left over for microforms/CD's/ databases. We do *not* get A/V materials...

[The balance of the statement indicated that "CD" referred to CD-ROM bibliographic, not full-text, databases, not to sound recordings on compact disc. Emphasis was in the original.]

The role of the written collection development policy is crucial to the question of ownership vs. access. The higher the level of collecting in a particular subject area, the greater is the need to acquire rather than borrow. If the costs... become prohibitive, then a review of the collection development policy becomes necessary.

As budgets get tighter selectors tend to focus more narrowly on their fields. As a result material that is interdisciplinary frequently does not get purchased.... Overall, this leads to less well balanced and more specialized collections.

Access over ownership must remain the only viable way of addressing the information needs of a complex and sophisticated patronage. However, priority needs to be given to ownership or some other form of *immediate* access for critical daily needs. For an academic institution, this means journals must be purchased or the full-text accessed upon demand on the spot in many areas.

[Emphasis was in the original.]

In our zeal to reduce costs, libraries must also consider who will preserve back runs of periodicals and older materials. Programs such as the [Center for Research Libraries] or a 'last copy' depository would help insure that the info is available even if every library stopped subscribing.

Summary of Survey Findings

Respondents agreed overwhelmingly that the increased pressure scenario accurately described their situations. Comments emphasized that budget pressures were, indeed, critical, but that heightened patron expectations, increased demand for materials, and continuing expansion in the numbers and types of materials perceived as needed also impacted importantly on the scenario.

Interlibrary loan still is considered the cornerstone of access for most librarians, perceived as the lowest cost and not necessarily the slowest option, although the majority of respondents thought it was slow. Electronic databases, perceived as the most rapid method of obtaining information temporarily, also was found to be the most costly. Information brokering, or performing the task of a purchasing agent for patrons, was not much welcomed. Remarks and grimaces during the focus interviews indicated that administrators held this opinion in agreement with many of their staffs. Brief notes written on the questionnaire by some academic librarians indicated they did not use methods of access such as shared purchasing or library rentals and leases, or they were not familiar with them. A very small number of comments indicated similar lack of knowledge about electronic databases.

Patron perceptions of access were visualized as generally positive and flexible, with more than half the survey group finding all of the options satisfactory to patrons. Interestingly, respondents said patrons would find information brokering more acceptable than it was to the respondents themselves. More than 70 percent of the respondents said information brokering was acceptable to patrons, while fewer than 50 percent said it was acceptable to them.

Material types most amenable to access were those perceived as peripheral to the respondents' library collections: for the academic librarians, dissertations and recreational items headed the list (public librarians were not asked to evaluate these material types); and for all respondents, the list included non-recreational audiovisual materials with the exception of CD-ROMs, serials whose importance was related to personal involvement (persons served on editorial board, persons published in the serial), and materials intended for person use. Close behind these were materials demanded by small but vocal user groups or intended solely for library work. Books were considered must buy materials by most respondents even if they were used only four times a year.

Most respondents had a gloomy view of the future in which library collections were in jeopardy and more materials would have to be accessed temporarily despite their value to patrons, but some were optimistic about the ability of new technologies to extend and improve access. Summing up the frustrations and concerns held by many colleagues, one university librarian wrote: "My opinion is that libraries have a valid, legitimate, and necessary role as warehouses of recorded human knowledge. Whereas for some libraries the function of providing access to some materials may grow, someone somewhere must continue to collect, organize, make accessible, and maintain all the bits and pieces of recorded knowledge."

CONCLUSIONS AND RECOMMENDATIONS

Case studies in five libraries (plus the sixth institution that served as a test site), do not constitute a sample of sufficient size to draw conclusions that can be generalized to the whole population of academic and public libraries; but they do furnish sufficient data to suggest patterns of behavior within the institutions studied, which also might be occurring among peer libraries in the larger community. The conclusions that follow are drawn with some hesitancy, recognizing the inevitable desire to accept them as demonstrated by the data described above, yet knowing that conditions are never static, but change to reflect an extraordinarily dynamic situation with regard to information production, pricing, telecommunications, and so forth, as well as institutional budgets, staffing, user needs, computing potential, and other institution-specific factors in the libraries studied. These conclusions apply solely to the libraries and librarians who participated in the study, not to the library community in general.

Conclusions

• *Collection development librarians are, for the most part, still deeply committed to perceiving needed materials primarily in terms of printed books and journals, and attempting, to the best of their abilities, to buy them all.*

Two equally disturbing elements are embodied in this conclusion: (1) library collecting still appears to be highly bibliocentric and (2) librarians still aim to buy everything they consider truly needed material.

A scan of the figures in Table 3 indicate that the medium of the material is an essential attribute—possibly even more important than expected use—for librarians in deciding whether access was "okay" or purchase was imperative. The most obvious figures are those for books, which was almost always considered must-buy materials, even if they were being purchased solely to complete a set and no use at all was guaranteed. A book used eight times a year was a must-buy item for virtually all respondents, while a periodical used 12 times a year was a must-buy selection for a considerably smaller group. In fact, a book used only four times a year would be selected for purchase by nearly as large a group of respondents as a periodical used three times more often.

The only type of nonprint material selected as must-buy by large groups of respondents were CD-ROMs; but new encyclopedias, almanacs and directories, and indexes (which usually are assumed to be in book form, but *could* be in any nonbook format) all were selected as must-buy by more than 85 percent of those responding. The ambiguous wording of the instrument, unfortunately, does not reveal whether this assumption was operating or genre was genuinely considered more important than the format in which items might be manifested.

Access was perceived as okay for non-core materials only. Even when pressed, and even as they admitted to facing shrinking budgets, burgeoning demand, and larger amounts of materials to be acquired, focus interview participants did not wish to identify core (which this investigator called "needed") items to be accessed. One university science librarian replied in all seriousness, on being pressed to give an example of a title she would be willing to access, "the *Siberian Journal of Epidemiology*." It may be that this is an important title not only for epidemiologists, but for other medical and scientific researchers, but this investigator interpreted her answer to mean *peripheral materials, titles with very few readers.*

Given that access to nonprint materials typically is more difficult than to journal articles and books because fewer libraries are willing to lend these outside their own user base, this investigator believes the data indicate nonprint materials such as sound and videorecordings still are thought to be peripheral to the core of most subjects and less important than printed materials in answering the research needs of library users. Such bibliocentricity is consistent with published collections budgets the investigator sees as part of student collection development term projects, which tend to be divided into books, serials, microforms, and audiovisual materials, in that order, with the book and serial lines consuming anywhere from 75 percent to 99 percent of the total. However, since these observations are not part of a systematic survey of any kind, they are included here strictly for illustrative purposes, not as corroborating data.

• *Very few study participants believed it was imperative to buy primary research materials. As several people commented, if no one collects it, organizes*

it, and preserves it, primary research material might become inaccessible to
libraries and the researchers they claim to support.

It is not difficult to imagine a scenario in which primary research materials
are either lost entirely to posterity or pass into the hands of private collectors
who have no mechanisms in place to share them with interested scholars,
because libraries—the institutions that normally collect them—are unable to
do so. The nearly universal willingness to give up collecting primary research
materials (which this investigator interprets broadly as including journals that
publish original articles and literary pieces) and to access them from outside
sources could have such a result if policies of the sort became standard practice
in all research libraries. Nor are research libraries the only collectors of such
materials. Non-research institutions also collect primary research materials in
some areas in which they have special strengths to support or where they have
had to endure the determined prodding of a leading local scholar. Even public
libraries may collect and maintain primary research materials in the areas of
local history and genealogy. If all of these efforts were suddenly to cease, future
scholars might face a very difficult and gloomy research environment, indeed.

• *Bibliographic databases on CD-ROM—in contrast to the same databases*
received on local library terminals as online files accessed from a remotely based
host system—are perceived as being purchased and owned in much the same
way as printed serials, even though they are, in fact, leased or licensed
temporarily.

Conversations during the focus interviews as well as informal discussions
with many librarians outside of this research study suggest that CD-ROMs
have not only gained acceptance in libraries, but are perceived as materials
the library owns as much as they own the copies of printed indexes to which
they subscribe. At one of the focus interviews, an administrator said, "Don't
count CD-ROMs as access—for all intents and purposes, we own them."

Policies of producers and distributors of these databases are changing rapidly
and some CD-ROM services allow subscribing libraries to retain older disks
if they wish to do so when new disks arrive or when subscriptions end. To
some degree, this is not so much a matter of generosity on the part of the vendor,
but of the added costs of handling returned disks, which, in any event, cannot
be recycled for additional use. More likely, these policies make sense when
one considers that vendors are constantly revising their retrieval software and
associated hardware, so that older disks will not be able to operate with the
newer systems, and newer systems quickly replace the older ones.

Focus interview participants were more concerned about the pricing
structures in current practice by CD-ROM producers, which make the optical
disk product much more costly than its printed counterpart, and buying the
combination of disk and printed versions most attractive. As a result, they find
it more advantageous to continue using both formats than converting solely
to CD-ROM. Several administrators said that if both formats were priced

similarly (not identically, which would not be logical to expect), they would have no difficulty selecting to buy one and drop the other; however, there was no incentive to do so under the current pricing structures.

• *Collection development librarians still find interlibrary loan the most attractive way to obtain needed materials temporarily despite its perceived lack of speed, and they believe interlibrary loan is low in cost, even though some cost studies suggest that may be a false assumption.*

Not only was interlibrary loan the clear favorite of responding librarians and librarians' estimates of patron preferences, but access was synonymous with interlibrary loan for many of the administrators participating in the focus interviews. When I introduced the study to them by its title in my opening gambit, some immediately echoed "Oh, you mean interlibrary loan?" When I reached the question about viable access routes, interlibrary loan always was the first method named. A few people went so far as to add, "That's it. What else is there?"

Most surprising to this investigator, given the financial austerity of the times, was the low esteem in which purchasing materials for patrons and charging for them (also termed information brokering) was held by librarians, even though most of those surveyed believed patrons would find it more acceptable than two other methods of access. Focus interview participants literally, physically, turned their noses up at the idea when it was presented by the investigator, and some exclaimed, "We would never do that!" Yet they were quick to point out that their libraries could not handle growing demands for interlibrary loans because they did not have the money to hire needed staff, which might result in leaving patrons to their own devices regarding requested materials the library did not own and could not buy.

In their book *Access versus Assets,* Barbra Higginbotham and Sally Bowdoin, discussing the use by libraries of fee-based services for obtaining materials a library does not own, said: "What factors have contributed to the growth of the commercial document delivery industry? For libraries, the sheer number and escalating costs of journal and document titles, *the perceived inadequacies of interlibrary loan, and a growing realization of the true costs of interlending* have had a major impact."[7] Barbara Quint also highlights librarians' anxiety over finding free information, claiming, "In the search for 'free' interlibrary loan, staff often overlook the internal costs. Since many ILL departments have not undertaken cost studies to determine their borrowing costs, it is easy to assert that it costs less to order from another library than from a document supplier. This may well be false economy."[8] Libraries need not charge their users fees even when the use of a commercial document supplier means the library must pay to obtain requested information, but the presumption that they will is clear. Higginbotham and Bowdoin rightly claim, in this investigator's opinion, that charging fees for obtaining information for a library user is an ethical issue that must be decided individually within each library and each institution.[9]

- *Despite growing dependence upon temporary access to obtain needed materials, it is perceived by many as difficult to systematize, thus limiting its potential role in collection development processes.*

Comments written on the instruments by respondents (such as "it depends," "sometimes," and "hard to answer") demonstrated they were not comfortable with making categorical decisions about access. Focus interview participants—few of whom actually made individual selection decisions themselves—remarked over and over that decisions to access materials are and should be made on case-by-case bases. These top-level decision makers were unable to articulate a more specific and identifiable role in collection development for access, except that it was becoming a more frequently used pathway to materials, while purchases were responsible for smaller proportions of the total amount of materials needed to satisfy their users. Collection development staff members, in contrast, were able to identify some categories of materials for which they deemed access was appropriate, although the categories were few in number and seemed to emphasize nontraditional or noncore sources.

- *Although many in the study population agree new technologies have the potential to improve access and provide new ways to educate, they do not believe libraries have either the resources or the will to implement them at this moment in time.*

A small number of administrators who participated in the focus interviews—and not only the nonprint materials specialists—were vocal about creating an environment in the library for different types of materials, primarily to tap the growing bounty of electronic publishing, full-text databases, interactive multimedia, and other computer-based documents. These people believed the main obstacle to better access was an inadequate supportive infrastructure in libraries and their parent institutions (for public libraries, the community), or the ability and willingness to commit budget dollars to build a state-of-the-art electronic infrastructure. They described an adequate infrastructure as sufficient numbers of computer terminals and telecommunications equipment adequately deployed throughout the library and the parent institution, adequate wiring and other physical interconnections both within and outside the library and the parent institution, state of the art software, and enough well-trained staff with advanced electronic systems.

This investigator was disheartened to find so many administrators and collection development staff alike pessimistic about library implementation of new technologies that could speed access to materials held at remote sites as well as support new materials requiring sophisticated technical environments. Even as they deemed new technologies the wave of the future and the key to solutions for the problems of trying to buy more materials with less money each year, study participants evidenced lack of conviction that the necessary decisions could be made in their libraries. Decisions to adopt and experiment with electronic media and other new systems were not thought to be controlled solely by the libraries, but in some places by their parent institutions; however, even where the library was in control, the likelihood that those decisions could and would be made were thought to be minimal. They said they believed their libraries were unable to make such investments now and would be hard-pressed even to complete projects already begun in the foreseeable future.

Recommendations for an Access or Ownership Decision Making Model

The investigator intended to build a model for collection development decision making that identified particular types of materials appropriate to consider for access beyond the amorphous and very general "least needed" category of material. In this endeavor, she has been partially successful. The recommendations that follow, taken together, comprise a first-step toward collection development decision making that acknowledges the role of temporary access to needed materials and attempts to systematize it as far as possible.

1. *Collection weaknesses uncovered by carefully conducted evaluations should be used by libraries as a pool of subject, medium, or audience-level acquisitions to be obtained through access, not purchase.*

Giving up the obligation to buy materials that address weaknesses in the collections—not merely areas for which there are no titles or few titles among the holdings, but areas in which the library's users need materials *and* the library owns no titles or few titles—would relieve library budgets considerably, and enable libraries to focus on spending their precious budget dollars to continue building areas of strength. Not only could current collecting be avoided in the weak subject or medium, or at the particular audience-level, but retrospective collecting to bring historic holdings up to standard also could be avoided. It would not be necessary to hire staff with the missing expertise, but it would be important to spend the time and money to educate current staff to identify and locate materials in the area of weakness, so they could be accessed upon request.

2. *Retrospective collecting should be avoided and documents required to complete serial runs or fill in missing or deteriorated retrospective holdings should be accessed when it is possible to do so.*

This recommendation, which should not be interpreted as applying to historical, rare, or valuable materials or special collections, has far-reaching implications for preservation decision making. If a library follows the suggestion rather strictly, replacement of deteriorated items might be virtually eliminated from the array of preservation choices, and reformatting and repair might be selected less often. The preferred decision would be to access the material from another source, unless the likelihood was that no other source could provide it. Distinguishing between documents accessible from other sources and unique items held locally (which would have to be reformatted, repaired, or lost forever) would be done first, before turning to the remaining preservation actions.

3. *Budget dollars available for obtaining materials should be regarded and reconciled with costs in defining the core literatures for the subject areas the library supports.*

The data from this study—both from the survey questionnaire and the focus interview discussions—suggest that selectors hesitate to believe they do not buy all "needed" (they called it "core") material in the subject areas they support. There are no absolute boundaries defining core material. It may be viewed in two ways: a nucleus of materials central to a subject; or, materials in a subject area that receive the heaviest use. In the first view, titles to be included within the boundaries of the core are selected subjectively before acquisition. In the second view, core literature can be defined absolutely once "heavy use" is defined; however, it can only be done after materials have been acquired and used. Selectors, in choosing titles to buy, must predict which will meet the test of "heavy use.' Neither view takes account of how much money it costs to obtain core material. In the first view cost is not a factor; in the second, the money must be spent before the core can be determined.

In order to utilize access effectively as a collection development tool for obtaining needed materials, core literature cannot be defined without regard to purchasing power. Core titles may be selected as a first step and the cost of buying them outright compared with target budget figures second, but the second step cannot be ignored. Otherwise, the librarians who claimed to buy all core materials in their fields either (1) have generous budgets, (2) are defining core as what they buy, or (3) could be committing their libraries to deliberately overspend their budgets to obtain it all.

There are many opportunities for gaps to exist in the operations that occur between perceived need and selection, acquisition, and budget management. The same people probably will not handle all these operations in most libraries, and each will focus only on his or her part of the process; materials may be ordered weeks or months before payments are issued; ordering must exceed budgeted amounts by some margin, because a proportion of orders will not be filled but the dollars earmarked for them still need to be spent; final reconciliation of an annual budget occurs some time after the fiscal year is ended and a new one begun. As a result, it is not difficult to imagine why selectors and bibliographers are justified in claiming they buy everything they need, or, though they claim they cannot buy everything they need, that they are unable to identify any category of needed material they will not buy. This situation makes systematic planning for access very difficult.

It may be that the investigator's study was too far in the realm of theory to obtain more specific results. Putting things into concrete terms may improve the potential for systematic access, for example, if the same selectors, bibliographers, and so forth, were faced with a set of titles and a budget insufficient to buy them all, they might find it easier to identify materials they would choose to access and those they could choose to buy. Being asked to identify, hypothetically, types of titles they would choose to access or buy without reference to any specific body of literature caused them great difficulty in replying. Therefore, the suggestion is that decisions about the use of access be made for a collecting cycle in concrete terms, with specific groups of titles and a target budget in mind.

4. *Special efforts should be made by library leaders and leading libraries to encourage both the purchase and interlending of those nonprint materials (sound recordings, videorecordings, computer software, etc.), that are appropriate to each library's particular mission and strengths.*

The data gathered for this study seemed to indicate a traditional view, particularly among academic librarians, that nonprint materials are less critical to library core collections and, therefore, more appropriate to obtain temporarily from sources outside the library. It is this investigator's opinion that, if they thought about it, the same librarians might admit that nonprint materials often are excluded from library interlending agreements, making them considerably more difficult to obtain that way. One of the unusual aspects of Illinois' statewide networking program, aside from its size and multitype character, is its gentle pressure to include nonprint materials in the array of borrowable materials. Reports claimed this aspect of borrowing and lending had no observable problems other than the usual ones of unfilled requests, slow delivery, and occasional errors.[10]

In view of the likelihood the increased pressure scenario will grow and limit what libraries can purchase annually, it seems important—even critical—that academic libraries continue buying nonprint materials that are valuable to them as well as loosening ILL regulations that prevent lending them to other libraries. If action is not taken, there may be an attitudinal return, if not an actual return, to the days when academic libraries lagged in the collection of nonprint titles.[11] Leaving the worries about buying and accessing nonprint titles until after the problems of obtaining book and journal titles are solved could doom them to failure.

5. *Special efforts should be made throughout the profession to encourage both the purchase and interlending of those primary research materials that are appropriate to each library's particular mission and strengths.*

When an institution chooses to access larger proportions of materials, its collection development staff members have a special obligation to choose wisely what to buy with its precious budget dollars. Use is but one indicator of importance in a collection and it may not always be the most critical. The goals and objectives a collection is intended to serve ought to help guide the choices of what to purchase and what to access. It is a very difficult task to balance competing demands and limited resources—one with which selectors wrestle mightily. All the investigator wishes to suggest here is that primary research materials that will find users both within the local institution and, through interlending, in the world outside the institution, should not automatically be excluded from the library's purchases because they are used for research instead of class readings. And once purchased, cataloged, and integrated into the library's collection, primary research materials should not be excluded from interlending. Instead, uses outside the library should be recognized as a local institution's contribution to education in the larger community, ultimately enhancing its status and reputation everywhere.

   6. *Libraries should develop and maintain up-to-date local cost figures and average turn around times for several access options and allow users to choose the one most appropriate to their needs.*

   If access is to be used successfully in obtaining larger proportions of needed materials, libraries should not make unilateral decisions about which access methods will be used to obtain them. Library users deserve to have the opportunity to influence access policies and practices. User needs vary considerably and all of them may not be satisfied equally well with the use of one method of access. In particular, if ILL is the method of choice and it is slower than other options, libraries should provide speedier methods in addition to ILL, even if using them means charging users a fee.

   Local libraries should determine whether it truly is less costly to use ILL than to buy materials from commercial suppliers, whether or not fees are involved. It is certain that ILL is not free. In figuring its real costs, libraries may find that ILL is more costly than other choices and switch some or all of their business to those access sources, or they may find they can speed the process and save money by streamlining their ILL procedures. Libraries must remember that the cost of borrowing materials from other libraries includes the obligation and the costs of lending materials to ILL partners in return— an added cost factor that may be overlooked.

   If, as is likely to the case in many localities, there are great variations in cost, speed, and the quality and utility of supplied materials among different access sources, library clients might wish to defray the added costs of having their materials faxed, transferred to email mailboxes, or delivered to their offices by an overnight courier. Why should the library decide for all clients that they should not have these opportunities? Academic librarians, consulting with grant seekers, might recommend that they include funds for deposit accounts with one or two major suppliers of any specialized research materials needed for a particular project, instead of finding out by surprise one day that Dr. N. and her team of AIDS researchers need a dozen articles from the *Siberian Journal of Epidemiology* and a large number of other medical and scientific journals the library does not own. Librarians need to take the initiative in becoming information consultants to researchers; to this investigator's knowledge, it is not standard operating procedure.

7. *Libraries should redouble their efforts to build the technological infrastructure necessary to improve access via electronic networks and utilize new media.*

Clearly, most librarians would like to adopt this suggestion. The inevitable issue is finding the money to pay for it. For some institutions, buying any new equipment, software, network access, and so forth, might have to take the place of buying materials, and in some cases, buying technology might be worth that extraordinary sacrifice, although the decision cannot be made lightly. But for others, including the participating institutions, the process of acquiring a technologically advanced infrastructure is likely to take time and be accomplished incrementally. This suggestion is a reminder that work toward the goal ought not stop because libraries have had to cut back in other areas. As needed systems are put in place libraries can begin to take advantage of *both* more materials and more access options than they currently do.

Startup costs are the biggest hurdle that must be overcome in utilizing computer-based systems—and a technological infrastructure is built on computers and computer linkages although they are not the only machines involved—but once in place, ongoing operating costs can be expected to assume bearable levels while service potential rises dramatically. Librarians responsible for collections should not be persuaded by current exigencies into believing that buying books and printed journals is their sole concern. An electronic world of opportunity is developing, with benefits that will be valued by the people who use libraries. As one participant wrote, the future will include ownership and access, not ownership *or* access.

ACKNOWLEDGMENTS

This study was supported by a grant from the Council on Library Resources for which the author is grateful. She also wishes to acknowledge the contributions of Peggy Johnson, collection development officer at the University of Minnesota's St. Paul Campus, whose evaluations and advice about the research instruments were essential to the conduct of the study, Linda Watkins, library science librarian at Simmons College, whose assistance in obtaining materials for the study was unfailing, and Linda Wiley, faculty assistant at the Graduate School of Library and Information Science during the conduct of the study, and thank them for all they did.

NOTES

1. This traditional perception is not inconsistent with a 1979 textbook definition by author G. Edward Evans in which collection development was equated with "information acquisition." Evans has since broadened his definition by dropping the part about acquisition and recasting it in terms of meeting users' information needs. *Developing Library and Information Center Collections,* 2nd ed. (Littleton, Colo.: Libraries Unlimited, 1987), p. 13.

2. "Just in case" versus "just in time" is a code phrase among collection development librarians for two different styles of collecting one relaxed and expansive (assuming generous budget support) and the other pressured and limited (assuming meager materials allocations). Peggy Johnson alludes to these matters in "Dollars and Sense: When Pigs Fly, or, When Access Equals Ownership," *Technicalities* 12 (Feb. 1992):4-7.

3. Model interlibrary codes for groups of cooperating libraries and for libraries operating individually, outside of a group, developed by committees of the American Library Association, which authorized them for use within the U.S., include provisions that preclude asking to borrow material falling within the requesting library's collecting scope. These codes and similar ones for international lending and borrowing, continue to make this a guiding assumption, despite the fact that the profession's commentators argue persuasively that libraries can no longer buy everything they need.

4. Maurice B. Line explained the situation eloquently, speaking at the first International Conference on Interlending and Document Supply in 1988, saying: "Before World War II interlending was regarded as an optional extra, a grace and favour activity, to be indulged in sparingly; any research library considered it an admission of failure to have to obtain any item from elsewhere. Now every library, however large, accepts that it cannot be self-sufficient, and some of the largest obtain the most from elsewhere." From "Interlending and Document Supply in a Changing World," in *Interlending and Document Supply: Proceedings of the First International Conference Held in London, November, 1988,* Graham P. Cornish and Alison Gallico, eds. (Ballston Spa, England: IFLA Office for International Lending, 1989), p. 1.

5. In the last few years, more articles in the literature about serials discuss journal *deselection* than selection. Jana Lonsberger reports, in "The Rise in Consumerism: The Year's Work in Serials, 1990," *Library Resources & Technical Services,* 35 (July 1991):321-322, "The pricing crisis has also contributed to the growing body of literature focusing on de-selection, or (to invoke the more negative but widely used phrase) cancellation projects. There are an increasing number of tales of painful lessons learned through frequent practice, as large rounds of cancellations have become more common." She goes on to cite nine studies worthy of notice. The overarching theme of Lonsberger's literature review was the serials pricing crisis, to which cancellations were just one in an alarming array of desperate, angry reactions.

6. Information on the uses, design, and conduct of focus interviews was found in the following sources: Richard A. Krueger, *Focus Groups: A Practical Guide for Applied Research,* (Newbury Park, Calif.: Sage Publications, 1988); David L. Morgan, *Focus Groups as Qualitative Research,* (Beverly Hills, Calif.: Sage Publications, 1988); and David W. Stewart and Prem N. Shamdasani, *Focus Groups: Theory and Practice,* (Newbury Park, Calif.: Sage Publications, 1990).

7. Barbra B. Higginbotham and Sally Bowdoin, *Access versus Assets: A Resource-Sharing Manual for Academic Librarians,* (Chicago: American Library Association, 1993), chapter 6. Emphasis added. Later in this chapter, in a section devoted to library fee-based document delivery services, they state: "As illustrated by the number of institutions listed in the 1990 FISCAL Directory of Fee-Based Information Services in Libraries (214 fee-based services from 145 academic libraries ...) and the existence of an Association of College and Research Libraries (ACRL) discussion group for fee-based information service centers, a number of libraries do not find selling information objectionable.

8. Barbara Quint, "Connect Time: Where's Your Parachute?" *Wilson Library Bulletin,* 66 (April 1982):85.

9. *Access versus Assets,* chap. 1.

10. ILLINET is changing the language of its statewide ill code to reflect this stance. A draft version expected to be approved in fall 1992 now reads: "Any type of library material needed for the purposes of study, instruction, information, recreation, or research may be requested from another library." Conversation with Kathleen Bloomberg, Associate Director for Library Development, Illinois State Library, 23 July 1992.

11.　A 1975 study for the National Commission on Libraries and Information Science conducted by Boyd Ladd to count library nonprint materials holdings and compare them with standards established by professional organizations, measured academic library holdings in terms of "volumes" without specifying what constituted a nonprint "volume." The aggregate holdings of academic libraries lagged behind those of public school and community libraries. A detailed discussion of the rise of nonprint collections in U.S. libraries is given in Sheila S. Intner's "Components of Media Librarianship," in *Access to Media: A Guide to Integrating and Computerizing Catalogs,* (New York: Neal-Schuman Publishers, 1984), pp. 23-58.

REFERENCES

"ARL Statistics Show Shift from Ownership to Access." Washington, D.C.: Association of Research Libraries, April 17, 1992. [Press release showing graph of supply and demand in ARL Libraries, 1985-86—1990-91.]

Butler, John, "Collection Building vs. Document Delivery: An Evaluation of Methods to Provide NTIS Documents in an Academic Engineering Library." Rockville, MD: ERIC, 1987. ED 286 510

Cornish, Graham P. and Alison Gallico, eds. *Interlending and Document Supply: Proceedings of the First International Conference Held in London, November 1988,* Ballston Spa, England: IFLA Office for International Lending, 1989.

Dougherty, Richard M. "A Conceptual Framework for Organizing Resource Sharing and Shared Collection Development Programs." *The Journal of Academic Librarianship,* 14 (Nov. 1988):287-291.

Downes, Robin. "Resource Sharing and New Information Technology—An Idea Whose Time Has Come." *Journal of Library Administration,* 10 (1989):115-125.

Evans, G. Edward. *Developing Library and Information Center Collections,* 2nd ed. Littleton, CO: Libraries Unlimited, 1987.

Halsey, Kathleen F. "An Evaluation of Document Delivery Service to Interlibrary Loan: A Commercial Firm and a Traditional Library Source." Rockville, MD: ERIC, 1988. ED 302 261

Higginbotham, Barbra Buckner and Sally Bowdoin. *Access versus Assets: A Practical and Philosophical Manual for Academic Librarians,* Chicago: American Library Association, 1993.

Holicky, Bernard H. "Collection Development vs. Resource Sharing: The View from the Small Academic Library." *The Journal of Academic Librarianship,* 10 (July 1984):146-147.

Interlibrary Loan Committee, Reference and Adult Services Division, American Library Association. *Interlibrary Loan Codes, 1980,* Chicago: American Library Association, 1980.

International Federation of Library Associations and Institutions, Section on Interlending. *International Lending Principles and Guidelines, 1978,* Chicago: American Library Association, 1981.

Intner, Sheila S. "Interfaces: Differences between Access vs. Ownership." *Technicalities,* 9 (Sept. 1989):4-7.

Jackson, Mary E., ed. *Research Access through New Technology,* New York: AMS Press, 1989.

Johnson, Peggy. "Dollars and Sense: When Pigs Fly, or, When Access Equals Ownership." *Technicalities,* 12 (Feb. 1992):4-7.

————. "Dollars and Sense: Collection Development Today: Coping with Reality." *Technicalities,* 12 (June 192):5-8.

Library Access Task Force, Association of College and Research Libraries. "ACRL Guidelines for the Preparation of Policies on Library Access." *College & Research Libraries News,* 51 (June 1990):548-556.

Lonsberger, Jana. "The Rise in Consumerism: The Year's Work in Serials 1990." *Library Resources & Technical Services,* 35 (July 1991):319-331.

Munn, Robert F. "Collection Development vs. Resource Sharing." *The Journal of Academic Librarianship,* 8 (Jan. 1983):352-353.

Network Development Office, Library of Congress. "Document Delivery—Background Papers Commissioned by the National Advisory Committee." Rockville, MD: ERIC, 1983. ED 221 214.

On Carl: The Quarterly Newsletter for CARL System Users, (Fall 1991). [Announcement of document delivery service, UnCover2]

Osburn, Charles, "Toward a Reconceptualization of Collection Development." *Advances in Library Administration and Organization,* 2 (1983):175-198.

Quint, Barbara. "Connect Time: Where's Your Parachute?" *Wilson Library Bulletin,* 66 (April 1992):85-88.

Roberts, Elizabeth P. "ILL/Document Delivery as an Alternative to Local Ownership of Seldom-Used Scientific Journals." *The Journal of Academic Librarianship,* 18 (Jan. 1992):30-34.

Robinson, Regan. "Ownership or Access? Just in Case or Just in Time." *Librarians Collection Letter,* 2 (June 1992):3,8.

Rottman, F.K. "To Buy or to Borrow: Studies of the Impact of Interlibrary Loan on Collection Development in the Academic Library." *Journal of Interlibrary Loan & Information Supply,* 1, no. 3 (1991):17-27.

"Rutgers and BYU test CitaDel™." *College & Research Libraries News,* 53 (May 1992):310.

Sullivan, David S. "Books Aren't Us? The Year's Work in Collection Development, 1990." *Library Resources & Technical Services,* 35 (July 1991):283-293.

A STUDY OF THE FIT BETWEEN THEORETICAL MODELS OF THE DIFFUSION OF INNOVATION AND THE DEVELOPMENT AND DIFFUSION OF THE PUBLIC LIBRARY ASSOCIATION'S PLANNING PROCESS

Verna L. Pungitore

INTRODUCTION

Between 1933 and 1966, the American Library Association (ALA) periodically issued revised editions of national standards for public libraries. Despite the acknowledged weaknesses of the opinion-based minimal standards, directors of public libraries often used them to justify budget requests, as a convenient checklist method of appraising the library, and as a general guide for improving services.

When the time came to revise the 1966 standards, the leadership of the Public Library Association (PLA) began a debate that eventually led to a total shift in direction. Instead of continuing to produce a set of national standards to

Advances in Library Administration and Organization, Volume 12, pages 39-73.
Copyright © 1994 by JAI Press Inc.
All rights of reproduction in any form reserved.
ISBN: 1-55938-846-3

be applied to all public libraries, the new approach called for user-oriented, locally developed standards that would be based on the identified needs of each community.

After a number of years of development and field testing, PLA produced a recommended planning process that it claimed could be used by any public library or public library system to set its own standards based on community needs and the self-evaluation of services. The goal was to provide public librarians, not with "rules for sameness," but with the skills and tools that would enable them to assess local needs, set objectives and priorities, make sound decisions, and evaluate results. It was assumed that the ultimate outcome of disseminating the planning process would be the development of library administrators and trustees skilled in making locally appropriate decisions and in implementing creative change.

The PLA planning manual appeared in 1980 (Palmour et al., 1980). A companion volume (Zweizig and Rodger, 1982) describing standardized procedures to be used by public libraries to measure what a library gives to its community (output) was published two years later. The output measures were designed to provide a means of evaluating the library's progress toward its long range objectives.

Between 1980 and 1984, the Public Library Association, the American Library Association (ALA), and some state and regional library organizations attempted to disseminate the planning and measurement techniques as outlined in the two self-instruction manuals. Feedback from users of the manuals was obtained and, in 1984, the Public Library Development Program (PLDP) was begun. The PLDP involved a modification and repackaging of the planning and measurement innovation. This effort by PLA eventually resulted in the 1987 publication of a new version of the planning manual (McClure et al., 1987) and a revision of the measurement manual (Van House et al., 1987). The act of publishing the self-help manuals represents only a minor part of a long, complex development and diffusion effort that began over a decade before publication of the first manual and is still continuing.

The nearly 9,000 public libraries in the United States are a diverse group of organizations, making the task of diffusing an innovation a difficult undertaking. A few statistics may help illustrate the problem. Nearly 90 percent have legal service areas of fewer than 50,000 people. Seventy-one percent of these serve populations under 10,000. They can seldom afford membership in ALA, of which PLA is a division. Nor can they afford participation in national conferences. Many cannot even afford to attend state association conferences. Often, their only access to professional journals is confined to one or two that can double as materials selection aids. Librarians in smaller institutions are effectively isolated from national professional developments. In 1990, there were 34,082 persons employed in public libraries who had the title "librarian." Of these, 21,305 had an M.L.S. degree accredited by ALA (Lynch and Lance,

1993, p. 204). Although it is the only national association devoted to the special interests of public libraries, PLA has a total membership that represents less than 20 percent of public librarians.

In 1989, a comprehensive, multiple phased study was begun of the origin and development of PLA's planning and evaluation techniques and their diffusion among smaller public libraries (Pungitore et al., 1989). One purpose of the study was to compare the process of development, dissemination, and adoption of PLA's innovation with theoretical diffusion models found in the general literature on change and innovation. This article reports on that portion of the study that examined development and dissemination activities related to the original editions of the planning and output measures manuals.

LITERATURE REVIEW

There are literally thousands of studies in a variety of disciplines that deal with organizational change. Among these, there are a number of works that focus on the process of diffusion and adoption of organizational innovations. Aspects of diffusion that are often studied include: (1) the specific attributes of a technological or managerial innovation that tend to facilitate or hinder its adoption, (2) the techniques and strategies used in the diffusion process, and (3) the characteristics of change agencies and/or their target audiences. The present study is based in that portion of the literature dealing with change agent roles and with the communication of information about organizational innovations. It subscribes to the view that the diffusion process takes place within a complex social system in which the flow of knowledge from its origination to its end use occurs through the formal and informal networking of many senders and receivers.

Several definitions may be useful at this point. A *change agent* is a person or an organized group of persons who seek to influence the adoption of an innovation. An *innovation* is broadly defined as an idea or practice that appears to be new to the organization considering its adoption. The fact that the idea may have been known to other organizations for some time is irrelevant so long as it is perceived as "new" by the potential adopter (Rogers and Shoemaker, 1971, p. 19). *Diffusion* is the process through which the innovation is spread throughout the social system. This process is defined by Katz et al. (1972, pp. 93-111) as the acceptance over time, of some specific idea, object, or practice by individuals, groups, or organizations that are linked to specific communication channels, are part of a social or organizational structure, and share a given system of values. The diffusion process involves "information use, social interaction, and behavioral change" (Bhola, 1982, p. 14). While diffusion is a *process* leading to the adoption of an innovation across many organizations, "dissemination" is perhaps more properly defined as a *communication activity* aimed at creating awareness of the innovation and its use in order to accomplish widespread diffusion. The *social system* as identified in the present study consists of the practice of public librarianship and several of its subsystems: the scholarly and research communities, the government sector, professional schools, and professional associations.

Dissemination Strategies

When an individual or organization makes the deliberate decision to introduce a new idea or practice into a social system, certain strategies for bringing about change are generally implemented. Chin and Benne (1976, p. 23) suggest that three kinds of strategies exist: empirical-rational, normative-educative, and power-coercive.

The *empirical-rational* approach assumes that people are guided by reason and will use self-interest as a basis for decisions about adopting changes in behavior or practices. Strategies falling into this category depend upon scientific investigation, research, and education in order to disseminate knowledge. Several of the strategies in this approach involve: (1) using basic research for knowledge building and general education for the dissemination of results, (2) getting the right person in the right position in order to transform knowledge into practice, (3) using applied research and planned systems for linking researchers and potential adopters, and (4) facilitating utopian thinking in order to envision a direction for planning and action (Chin and Benne, 1976, pp. 25-30).

The *normative-educative* strategies assume that people are inherently active and in search of satisfaction, not passive and dependent on the environment for a stimulus to which they can respond. This approach emphasizes re-educating potential adopters toward a desired point of view. Re-education in this case involves changing established norms, values, and cultural institutions so that value conflicts may first be resolved before attempts are made to change existing practices through the introduction of innovation (Chin and Benne, 1976, pp. 39-40).

Diffusion strategies are used to gain the acceptance of the proposed innovation by the practitioner or end user. The diffusion process begins with strategies aimed at creating an awareness of the innovation, then continues with strategies that provide sufficient information about the potential value of the innovation for the practitioner to make an adoption decision. Stein (1978, pp. 77-78) outlines six categories of diffusion techniques generally assumed to be used by change agents: telling, showing, helping, involving, training, and intervening.

Telling uses written or spoken words through such channels as newspapers, newsletters, books, articles, conversations, conferences, or speeches. *Showing* depends on structured experiences. These may include demonstrations, simulations, films, slides, displays, and the like. *Helping* includes techniques that allow the diffuser to intervene directly in the affairs of the user, but on the user's terms; that is, the user would request consultation, service, or troubleshooting. *Involving* techniques are those which include the user in the development, testing, and packaging of the proposed idea, and possibly in assisting with its diffusion. The purpose of *training* techniques is to familiarize the user with the innovation, increase skill or competency in its use, and/or change attitudes about the innovation. Workshops, institutes, apprenticeships, in-service training, and formal courses are examples of training techniques. *Intervening* is similar to helping, except that it involves the user on the differ's terms, as when certain actions are mandated or sanctions are introduced.

Diffusion Models

A number of diffusion models were examined for use in the study. It was determined that the selected model should be inclusive enough to permit examination of the life cycle of the innovation; that is, its major phases from origination and development through diffusion to adoption. In addition, the model should take into account the factors that were of particular interest: (1) the communication channels and linkages between the developers of the innovation and the practitioners at whom the diffusion efforts were aimed, (2) the diffusion techniques and methods that were used, and (3) the characteristics of the potential adopters that might facilitate or inhibit their implementation of the innovation. Finally, a flexible model was sought that would permit the application of selected components in the likely event that time and financial constraints prevented application of the entire model.

From the studies that had been conducted through the late 1960s, Havelock (1969) identifies three general models of knowledge dissemination and utilization: Research, Development and Diffusion (R,D&D), Social Interaction (SI), and Problem-Solver (P-S). The R,D&D model focuses on the activities of the originator or developer of the innovation. As the name implies, it identifies the stages in the process as: research, development, packaging, and dissemination. The SI model assumes the pre-existence of an innovation and concentrates on how the innovation comes to the attention of potential adopters and how it spreads through the social system. The P-S model views the process as starting with a perceived need by the user. The need is translated into a problem statement, alternative solutions are generated, and an optimal solution is tried and evaluated. Change is self-initiated by the user, but is facilitated by a change agent who helps with problem diagnosis and solutions.

The R,D&D model centers on the knowledge production subsystem, usually the scholarly and research community. The SI model focuses on the knowledge utilization subsystem; that is, the clients or practitioners who will ultimately use the innovation. The P-S model is to some extent a combination of the other two in that it portrays the user in the role of change agent, engaging in group problem solving with the research community. Havelock suggests that "there is a need to bring these three viewpoints together in a single perspective that includes the strongest features of each" (1969, chap. 11, p. 15). He advances the concept of "linkages" as a means of unifying and synthesizing the three models.

Linkage Model

Havelock's linkage model starts with the user as *problem solver*: "there is an initial 'felt need' which leads into a 'diagnosis' and 'problem statement' and works through 'search' and 'retrieval' phases to a 'solution,' and the 'application' of that solution" (Havelock, 1969, chap. 11, p. 15). The emphasis of the linkage model, however, is on the relationship between the user and the outside "resource system." The user seeks help from the resource system in the search for a solution. Throughout the two-way exchange of information and feedback that occurs, the user "should be learning and beginning to simulate resource system processes such as scientific evaluation and product development. Only through understanding, appreciating, and to some degree, emulating such processes, will the user come to be a sophisticated consumer of R and D" (1969, chap. 11, p. 17).

The Havelock model seemed particularly appropriate in that it stresses a series of reciprocal relationships as the resource person (with a need that is the counterpart to the user's need) draws upon external specialists as well. Eventually, these overlapping linkages form a "chain of knowledge utilization" connecting the most remote sources of knowledge with the most remote consumers of knowledge (Havelock, 1969, chap. 11, p. 17). There are a variety of roles that individuals, media, and organizations play that could be characterized as performing a "linking" function. According to Havelock, "connected to every phase, every aspect, and every problem in the dissemination and utilization process, one could conceptualize a specific role: someone responsible for retrieving knowledge from basic research; someone responsible for identifying new innovations in practice; someone responsible for writing handbooks and producing packaged knowledge for potential clients of various sorts and so forth" (1969, chap. 7, p. 2).

From a topology of linking agents suggested by Havelock, eight role types were adapted. It was assumed each of these would be found among the developers and disseminators of PLA's planning process. Table 1 lists the several role types and their functions.

Library Change Literature

Researchers in the library and information field have not shown the intense interest in diffusion studies that is found in many other disciplines. In a recent

Table 1.   Linkage Roles

Role Type	Function
A. Conveyor	to carry or transfer knowledge from producers to users
B. Consultant	to assist in identification of problems and resources; to assist in adaptation for use (tells "how" while conveyor tells "what"); the relationship between the consultee or user and the consultant is initiated by the consultee and is temporary and specific; the consultant is from a different professional discipline; role is advisory, with no responsibility for implementation; has no administrative relationship with the consultee
C. Trainer	to transfer by instilling in the user an entire area of knowledge or practice; has control over the learning environment but contact does not continue into the field setting; trainer's linking function ends after a designated training period is over
D. Leader	to create an effective link through power or influence within the receiver's own group; can be a formal leader or gatekeeper; or can be an informal opinion leader; may also function as conveyor or consultant, but is an "inside change agent" who makes new ideas and practices credible, legitimate to the group
E. Innovator	to transfer by initiating diffusion with the system; the first person to take up a new idea; the originator/advocate/champion of the innovation within the group or organization
F. Defender	to champion the user (library practitioner) against the innovation; to point out pitfalls/problems; to serve as the "quality controller" or objective evaluator who makes sure value, relevance, etc. of the innovation is adequately demonstrated
G. Knowledge Builders (basic scientists, applied researchers, experts, scholars)	to serve as futuristic planners/goal setters; to define basic values and directions; to integrate findings into theories that make sense; to retrieve knowledge from basic research, screen, package, and transmit it to the user; translate research into usable products and services and to translate practice concerns into researchable problems
H. Practitioners	to transfer benefits (derived from the innovation) to clients and end users through specialized services and products which incorporate new knowledge; practitioners (librarians) can serve as their own linkers if they have knowledge of resources, access to resources, and are able to diagnose their own needs

bibliography of diffusion studies, Musmann and Kennedy (1989) list 29 library studies, most of which involve technological innovations. In a study of innovations in public libraries, Damonpour and Childers (1984) looked at the relationship between the rate of adoption and the size of the library. They suggest that the appropriate innovation implemented at the appropriate time contributes to the good health of the organization. This is apparently because innovations tend to facilitate adaptation to the library's environment and improve the potential for the organization to achieve its goals.

Griffiths et al. (1986) used case studies to explore the process of implementing innovations in three types of libraries: public, academic, and special. Most of the innovations were technological in nature, but output measures were also included. A major outcome of the study was a tentative model of innovation diffusion among libraries. The model includes a number of factors that influence the adoption process: characteristics of the libraries and librarians, characteristics of the social networks involved, and characteristics of the innovations.

The case study method allowed Griffiths and others to develop a complex model that included interactions on the micro or individual and group level within the organization, as well as those occurring at the macro level between the organization and other organizations in its external environment. Given the broad scope of the present study, it seemed more appropriate to apply selected components of Havelock's integrated linkage model.

STUDY DESIGN AND PROCEDURES

The change agent role of the Public Library Association was a focal point of the study. Telephone interviews, supplemented by published and archival records, were used to produce a narrative description of PLA's development and dissemination activities in order to compare these activities to existing theoretical diffusion models.

The process of developing and diffusing a managerial innovation involves a complex network of relationships. When the change agency is a national professional association, the network includes a host of association committees, educators and researchers, as well as practitioners. Initially, an attempt was made to reduce this complexity to a sequential listing of events in order to better understand "what happened when," and to find an appropriate starting point in the process. But a chronology fails to capture the dynamics, the serendipitous events, the individual and institutional linkages, and the evolutionary nature of the process. These were among the aspects of PLA's development and diffusion activities of major interest in the study.

Despite the fact that PLA made deliberate and extensive use of professional journals to create an awareness and an acceptance of its innovation, the published literature provides only a fragmentary picture of the development of the innovation and it is incomplete with regard to PLA's dissemination methods and objectives. For anecdotal and other types of information that would verify and flesh out the emerging chronology, two major sources were used: (1) telephone interviews with selected individuals who had an early and continuing involvement in the development and dissemination processes; and (2) archival records and file documents housed at PLA's Chicago headquarters.

Data Collection Methods

The published literature pertaining to the Public Library Association's planning and measurement techniques was searched for names of individuals who appeared to have intimate and/or lengthy associations with the development and dissemination of the manuals. A purposive sample of nine individuals was selected from the 20 names that were identified. The following considerations were used in selecting the sample: (1) early involvement in the development process, (2) presumed knowledge of the internal structure of PLA, (3) involvement with more than one manual or more than one phase of the dissemination effort, and for practical reasons, (4) ready availability of a current address. In addition, an attempt was made to include representatives from the research and practice communities as well as those with formal ties to ALA and PLA.

Letters, with reply post cards, were sent to each of the nine individuals requesting their participation in a telephone interview. Eight agreed to participate. Because those who had consented to be interviewed matched the selection criteria, it was decided that eight persons would constitute an adequate sample for the study's purposes; and that they represented a suitable cross section of practitioners, researchers, and PLA committee members and officers.

Prior to the interviews, each participant was mailed a copy of the chronology in a flow chart format, indicating "existing conditions" that apparently precipitated the move toward community based planning, and specific "events" in the actual development and dissemination processes. Much of the information on the flow chart was revised as a result of the interviews; therefore, it will not be reproduced here. The chronology was divided into four phases:

1. Late 1960s to Mid-1970s: Awareness of the Problem and Search for Solutions
2. Mid-1970s to 1980: Research and Development of the Planning Process
3. 1980 through 1983: Initial Dissemination, Evaluation, Modification
4. 1984 through 1987: Development of the PLDP

Participants were requested to review the chronology and note omissions or discrepancies to discuss during the interviews. A number of modifications to the initial chronology emerged as the study progressed. The participants were also sent the list of possible "linkage roles" that appears in Table 1 in order to explore whether such roles could be identified as having been assumed by persons involved in developing and disseminating the planning process manuals.

The interviews were conducted during February and March 1989. Entirely by chance, it was mutually convenient to interview one individual in person;

the other seven interviews took place over the telephone. All interviews were taped and later transcribed for analysis. A list of twenty-five open-ended questions was developed. The participants were knowledgeable about behind the scene events, had an intuitive understanding of the study's goals, and were willing to discuss frankly their involvement and perceptions. As a result, little prompting was needed. The interviews tended to be informal, free-flowing discussions, each lasting approximately 75 to 90 minutes.

A three-person research team which visited PLA headquarters in Chicago examined committee minutes, memos, correspondence, and other documents dating from the 1960s. Data from the interviews, the published literature, and PLA's archives were used to compile a list of 519 keywords (including persons, places, concepts, events, and organizational entities). These were used to prepare a descriptive, sequential summary of the development and diffusion process that could be compared with existing diffusion models.

FINDINGS

A number of comments, taken directly from the interview transcripts, are included in the following discussion. When a quotation appears in the text without being attributed to a specific source, the reader may assume that the remark came from one of the interviews and that identification of the source has been deliberately withheld in order to maintain confidentiality. Some of the PLA documents that were used in the study were in the form of handwritten notes, memos identified only with the originator's name, and a date, or other items that presented similar difficulties with respect to providing a complete citation. These are not footnoted but are identified in the text as clearly as possible through parenthetical notations. Numbered references, therefore, are generally limited to citations from the published literature.

In order to examine the fit between PLA's first diffusion process and theoretical diffusion models, it is necessary to consider the origin and development of the innovation, as well as the strategies used to disseminate it. This background information allows a much clearer picture of the linkages between committees of ALA and PLA, the research community, persons in the field, government agencies, and so forth, to emerge.

Origin and Development

As the external environment of the mid-1960s began to exert an economic pressure on public libraries, a number of library directors recognized the need for change in their managerial and service philosophies. Among those librarians who were searching for an appropriate response to a changing environment, there was a growing dissatisfaction with national public library standards. The inadequacy of such standards had been recognized by the committee of PLA charged with developing the 1966 standards. The preface to this edition, published in 1967, states,

> The committee repeats the plea that research and experimentation are urgently needed as verification of these standards. In particular, quantitative measures correlated with the quality of library performance must be developed to provide the yardsticks demanded by governing and appropriating bodies. Moreover, the wide variation in levels of public service from state to state, makes the establishment of norms impossible without much more data than are presently available. The committee hopes that states will set those norms for themselves, perhaps in the form of five-year plans, for bringing their service to the level proposed in this document (Public Library Association, 1967).

It was significant that the group responsible for this final edition of national standards openly admitted that the validity of the standards was questionable. As Nancy Bolt indicates, this statement "forecasts the idea of local diversity and five-year plans, an idea that developed into the *PLA Planning Process*" (Bolt, 1985, p. 48). Although the need for a better means of self-evaluation was being expressed in a number of professional circles by 1967, the idea of community based planning as a substitute for national standards was still a long way from a fully developed concept. There was, however, a chain of circumstances occurring that would bring certain individuals and groups together into working relationships and would eventually lead to PLA's unprecedented effort to fulfill the role of change agent. These circumstances are described here because they indicate the influence of a web of linkages that will later be shown to exist in the diffusion process as well.

1. The PLA-Rutgers University Connection

An ALA-PLA project on the "Measurement of Effectiveness of Public Library Service" headed by Ernest R. De Prospo was underway during the early 1970s. This project was the outcome of joint meetings between PLA's Standards Revision Committee (SRC), ALA staff members, and De Prospo and several colleagues from the Bureau of Library and Information Science Research at Rutgers. The purpose of the meetings was to develop a PLA proposal for a federally funded effectiveness measurement project.

The PLA-Rutgers connection had begun while the SRC and ALA staff were deliberating what should be done about revising the 1966 standards. This suggests that professional networking that occurs outside the formal ALA division and committee structure allows appropriate individuals from the practice, research, and education communities to be identified and drawn into projects as the need arises.

The study's interview and documentary data indicate that De Prospo and others from Rutgers were brought into the deliberations because individual committee members had a collegial acquaintance with them and an awareness of previous work they had done on quantitative measures. Between 1961 and 1964, De Prospo, Kenneth Beasley, and Ralph Blasingame had been studying annual library statistical reports for the Pennsylvania State Library (Beasley, 1964). A report of the Rutgers study, entitled *Performance Measures for Public Libraries*, was published by ALA in 1972 (De Prospo et al., 1973). One of the elements of PLA's recommended planning and measurement process is the combined use of self-assessment techniques, measures of user satisfaction, and a marketing orientation. These same ideas are implied in the De Prospo study. Although the PLA manuals do not acknowledge a link to the earlier De Prospo work, a similar conceptual basis is present in both publications.

2. Goals-Feasibility Study

At the same time as the De Prospo study was underway, PLA was also sponsoring another project, jointly funded by the Council on Library Resources and the National Endowment for the Humanities. This work, *A Strategy for Public Library Change: Proposed Goals-Feasibility Study* (Martin, 1972), was directed by Allie Beth Martin, then director of the Tulsa (Oklahoma) Public Library and soon to become president of ALA.

According to Mary Jo Lynch, "This study grew out of a concern in the late 1960s that public libraries had lost their sense of direction. There was some feeling that a repeat of the *Public Library Inquiry* was needed. The Inquiry, a series of studies by social scientists who examined various aspects of library service in the late 1940s... had given public librarians a useful base for action in the 1950s and 1960s. The momentum was dying, however, and the questions of the day were: Do we need another *Inquiry*? If not, what do we need?" (Lynch, 1992, p. 31).

Lynch goes on to suggest that although the recommendations contained in the goals feasibility study were not effectively carried out, it provided the impetus "to an activity not mentioned in its recommendations—the development of a manual to assist public librarians in planning. It seems clear that the need for such a manual was deeply felt at the time though not explicitly recognized in the report" (Lynch 1992, p. 31). Lynch points to a statement in the study concerning consensus in the field regarding another Public Library Inquiry as an indication that the public library community at the time was ready for *A Planning Process*. The statement suggests that, if another Inquiry were to be conducted, "it should recognize that no set of goals could be universally applicable except in the broadest terms. *Each public library must set its own goals based on its own community needs*" (p. 33). According to Lynch, "this concept is essential to the reasoning which led PLA to develop *A Planning Process* rather than revise national standards" (p. 33).

3. PLA Adult Services Task Force

The chair of the PLA Standards Committee in 1972/73 was Rose Vainstein, then on the faculty of the library school at the University of Michigan. The Standards Committee was continuing its discussions on the fate of national standards while awaiting the results of the De Prospo and the goals feasibility studies. About this same time, a conference on "Total Community Library Service" was held under the sponsorship of the joint ALA/National Educational Association (NEA) Committee. This conference recommended "coordination of all library services and resources at the community level in order to provide maximum service to users" ("Community Library Services," 1973, p. 21). In order "to provide the [Standards] Committee with a conceptual framework within which to consider the philosophic implications of total community library service on any subsequent and sequential development of public library goals, guidelines, and standards" (p. 22) three Task Force groups were appointed to focus on user service needs at the community level.

Each task force was charged with developing a working paper to guide the internal discussions of the Standards Committee. One task force focused on adult services, another on young adult services, and the third on children's services. Membership "was deliberately sought from as many different ALA interests as possible, by type-of-activity division and by type-of-institution affiliation" ("Community Library Services," 1973, p. 22). Among those enlisted to serve on the Adult Services Task Force was Mary Jo Lynch, a faculty colleague of Vainstein's at Michigan. Although Lynch came from an academic library environment, she was brought into PLA's sphere of interest primarily because of her active involvement in ALA's Reference and Adult Services Division (RASD). This initial, somewhat peripheral, encounter with PLA's standards dilemma marked the first of a series of linking roles that Lynch would continue to play in the development and dissemination of PLA's innovation.

The completed Task Force Working Papers were published in the September 1973 issue of *School Library Journal* "in order to share with the profession at large the new direction in which the PLA Standards Committee is moving as it attempts to delineate goals and establish priorities that relate to a changing society. Given the wide variations in our nation's public libraries, the profession may well want to develop diversity by design, so that communities may have the choice of alternative patterns of library service" ("Community Library Services," 1973, p. 23). According to Robert Rohlf, a former president of PLA, "the papers and the apparent change of direction by the committee caused significant furor in the library press and in both committee and division meetings" (Rohlf, 1982, p. 68).

4. Design for Diversity

At the start of 1974, the PLA Standards Committee formally changed its name to the Goals, Guidelines, and Standards Committee (GGSC), indicating that a shift had indeed occurred in PLA's thinking with regard to the value of national standards as a development tool for public libraries. However, retention of "Standards" in the committee's designation also suggested that PLA was not yet ready to relinquish entirely the idea of producing national public library standards at some point in the future.

Meredith Bloss, then chair of the newly renamed committee, requested a reaction to the Working Papers from Ralph Blasingame at Rutgers. Interestingly, Mary Jo Lynch, having left Michigan to pursue her doctorate at Rutgers, was then studying under both Blasingame and De Prospo. Blasingame asked Lynch to join him in writing the reaction to the Task Force Working Papers. Their response appeared in the PLA Newsletter, June 1974, under the title "Design for Diversity" (Blasingame and Lynch, 1974).

Although Blasingame had no direct involvement with the performance measures study, De Prospo acknowledged that he was among those who "freely served as sounding boards for all our ideas" (De Prospo et al., 1973, p. iv.). Blasingame was therefore acquainted with the concepts contained in De Prospo's study, as was Lynch. In addition, Lynch understood the rationale behind the report of the Adult Services Task Force, on which she had served. Patrick Williams considers this report the most important of the working papers because it "seemed to point out the way to make the public library the kind of institution envisioned in *A Strategy for Public Library Change* (Williams, 1988, p. 110).

5. Goals and Guidelines

According to Bloss, a consolidation/synthesis of the task force reports, titled "Goals and Guidelines for Community Library Service" and published as a supplement to the *PLA Newsletter*, June 1975, "provides the conceptual framework within which the Association now intends to develop new standards for community library services" (Bloss, 1976, p. 261). He also states,

> The pioneering work in the preparation of new goals and guidelines, and in the exploration of new methods for measuring outputs, can now be the base on which standards can be empirically developed.
>
> The PLA Goals, Guidelines, and Standards Committee (GGS) now has a finished research and development proposal and is looking for ways by which the work can be carried out. The ultimate purpose of the project is to develop a process that library managers and others can use to determine standards of performance for community library service.
>
> The immediate end-product of the work described in the proposal will be a series of publications, separate but inter-dependent, on the various aspects of the standards development process. These manuals will be tools designed for use in planning, designing,

delivering, and evaluating justifiable and adequate programs. Manuals are to be based on factual evidence of actual field performance in selected library and community situations; they are not to be theoretical statements of intention or desirability. Subsequent phases of the project may develop additional publications, as the evidence is collected (Bloss, 1976, p. 1261).

The "finished research and development proposal" Bloss referred to was an initial proposal submitted to the ALA Executive Board on April 28, 1976, suggesting that user oriented standards be developed. The proposal, which was not funded, entered the minutes under the title, "The Process of Standards Development for Community Library Service: A Proposed Research Study From PLA" (ALA Executive Board Document # 56).

6. BCPL Connection

At the time PLA was pondering the direction in which it wanted to move with respect to standards, one public library was already experimenting with performance measures and planning techniques adapted from the corporate sector. In 1972, a branch librarian at the Baltimore County Public Library (BCPL) was attempting to measure performance by looking at book turnover rates. The librarian's "initiatives sparked interest at the county level" (Griffiths et al., 1986, p. 402). De Prospo gave a speech in Maryland in the early 1970s and one of his students "then came to do studies of the state system...and then interviewed County Librarians, asking how collections were used" (Griffiths et al., 1986, p. 402). Staff at BCPL began using the De Prospo manual on a trial basis in 1974. "By 1978 there was a lot of experimentation going on at different branches" (p. 403).

In 1977, BCPL adopted a five year plan that included a formal management-by-objectives process. The process and the five year plan were produced through a contract with King Research, Inc. (KRI), with Vernon E. (Gene) Palmour directing the project.

Once ALA had given PLA the authority to seek funding for its "Process of Standards Development" project, the GGSC called for proposals from the research community. Palmour's proposal was selected and it was used as the basis for developing the unsuccessful proposal that was submitted to the Office of Education. The GGSC held a number of working sessions during the time that the proposal was being revised. One of these took place at Rutgers.

Blasingame and Lynch, who was still in residence as a doctoral student, were in attendance. Also at the meeting was another Rutgers doctoral student, Charles McClure, who would later play a significant role in the development of the PLDP manuals (Lynch, 1986, p. 5). De Prospo and Bloss (chair of the GGSC) were among a number of individuals who served as consultants on the Palmour project. Thus, in a somewhat subtle manner, the connection with the earlier work at Rutgers continued throughout the development of the planning manuals.

In the fall of 1976, Mary Jo Lynch left Rutgers to assume the newly created position within ALA that involved managing the special projects of PLA, the American Library Trustees Association (ALTA), and the Reference and Adult Services Division. It was in this position that she was given the responsibility for revising the rejected proposal. The revised proposal was submitted to the Office of Education on October 13, 1976. Prior to receipt of funding in September 1977, the planning concepts developed by the consultants from KRI had already been tested in the Baltimore County Public Library. According to one of the interviews, the decision to test at BCPL was made because "they were willing to help foot the bill" at a time when PLA had no money.

When federal funding in the amount of $140,000 was finally approved, it was for an 18 month project to develop manuals, field test them, and produce a self-help publication. Additional field testing of the process occurred at several other sites. Essentially, however, *A Planning Process for Public Libraries* was based on work Palmour had done for BCPL. Palmour directed the project and BCPL director Charles Robinson served as an advisor to the research team.

During the time PLA was seeking a solution to the problem it had identified (what to do about national standards), the major change agent role was being played within the association by the Goals, Guidelines and Standards Committee. The networking between this group, the executive boards of PLA and ALA, the scholarly and research communities, the government funding agency (The U.S. Office of Education), and practitioners (including those in libraries that served as test sites for the planning process) brought the innovation to the point at which the planning manual could be produced.

Once the decision had been made to publish such a manual, however, a new committee assumed the linking role. This was the project's Steering Committee, which served in a liaison capacity between the researchers and PLA, and also provided advice and counsel to the research team. The GGSC and the PLA Research Committee were somewhat annoyed at this arrangement apparently. A letter from Shirley Mills-Fischer (9/12/82) describes the 1979 creation of an Advisory Committee for Research on Public Library Planning (ACRPLP) as a concession to complaints by the other two committees that they were "left out of the development of *A Planning Process*." The ACRPLP was composed of members from the Goals, Guidelines, and Standards Committee and the Research Committee.

The PLA Steering Committee for the Palmour project held its first meeting on November 8, 1977 in Washington, D.C. Committee members discussed performance measures as well as the development of the new planning manuals, indicating that the influence of De Prospo's work had not waned. Throughout the course of the project, Palmour made monthly progress reports, while the Steering Committee made quarterly reports to PLA. Lynch, who served as project consultant and Liaison to the Office of Education, wrote quarterly reports for the government.

7. Output Measures

The Steering Committee met with the King researchers and project consultants on January 30, 1978, to discuss the role of performance measures in the manual. Lamar Veatch suggests that, "even before the publication of the *Planning Process*, it was recognized that a weak link in the procedure for developing community-based standards was a general inaccessibility to methods for collecting and using data that describe what a library gives to a community (output), rather than what a library receives from a community (input)" (Veatch, 1982, p. 11).

The GGSC proposed to the PLA executive board that performance measures be established for public libraries by September 1982. Originally, the GGSC had planned to break the task of producing a performance measurement manual into sections assigned to members of the committee. The PLA Publications Committee approved the publication of what the GGSC was calling "Methods of Output Measures." The committee identified the measures to be included in the manual, but the actual writing proved to be too time consuming for the committee.

Meanwhile, "Charles Robinson of BCPL organized a small coalition of libraries and state library agencies to provide funds for the [output measures] work. Again King Research got the contract and this time the consultants were Douglas Zweizig and Joey Rodger" (Veatch, 1982, p. 10). While with King Research, Zweizig had worked with the Oklahoma State Library in developing performance measures, and Rodger's work had involved long range planning for libraries.

Elements from the Diffusion Models

There are obvious parallels to the R,D&D diffusion model in that the GGSC took the innovation through the research and development stages, while it became the task of the Steering Committee to see it through the "packaging" stage. There are also elements of the Problem-Solver model as well: The initial perception of the problem came from individuals in the practitioner community who were also active in PLA's committee structure. The change agent role played by librarians working through PLA was strengthened by interaction with the research community, which helped with problem solving. Without the relationships among practicing librarians, PLA, ALA, researchers and others, development of the planning process may never have occurred, thus lending support to Havelock's concept of the importance of linkages. Although the present study did not explore formally whether PLA members have become more sophisticated consumers of research as a result of their experience, a case could probably be made for a heightened awareness among public librarians in PLA of the usefulness of enlisting the aid of the research community.

Other connections may have existed between the research studies done by De Prospo and Martin and the decision to begin development of what eventually became the planning manuals. However, the significance of the links formed by Bloss, Lynch, and Blasingame between Rutgers and PLA is apparent from the foregoing description. The role of the scholarly and research community (represented by Rutgers in this instance) may be summarized as follows:

1. Research coming from that community (i.e., the early De Prospo work) was seen by the association as potentially useful in solving the specific problem PLA had identified. As a result, researchers were deliberately invited to participate in the process of what PLA was then calling the development of "effectiveness measures." The outcome of that participation was De Prospo's *Performance Measures for Public Libraries*. Although this particular form of the innovation was not developed further, the idea of measuring performance in terms of user satisfaction became a recurrent theme throughout the development of the manuals.

2. The research community was also utilized by PLA for the purpose of providing advice and counsel concerning the new direction that the Standards Committee was about to recommend. This resulted in the "Design for Diversity" paper prepared by Blasingame and Lynch, which was the catalyst for the interim document "Goals and Guidelines for Community Service." The concept of providing planning tools and techniques rather than "rules for sameness" was clearly spelled out in "Design for Diversity."

The GGSC assigned a subcommittee chaired by Carolyn Anthony to supervise the development of the planned output measures manual. Anthony had been working on performance measures at Baltimore County Public Library. Because of Palmour's pre-1978 work at BCPL, that library system may be considered an "innovator" and "early adopter" both of planning methods and performance measures. Linkages between BCPL and PLA continued as the planning process evolved into the Public Library Development Program. As staff moved from BCPL to accept management positions in other libraries, the concepts of planning and evaluation moved with them. The influence that this network of former BCPL staff has had on diffusing PLA's planning techniques was not examined in the study. However, there are indications that utilization of the manuals was facilitated in libraries were former BCPL staff had relocated. In a report on the *Diffusion of Innovations in Library and Information Science* (which considers technological innovations primarily, but also includes performance measures as one of the innovations studied), Griffiths and others identified connections to what they termed the "Maryland Mafia" as a facilitating factor in the adoption of innovation (Griffiths et al., 1986, p. 362).

Dissemination Plans

The earliest detailed description of dissemination plans found in PLA's files was contained in a letter from Lynch to the Steering Committee dated 9/25/78.

The plans were to advertise heavily in public library journals, to provide assistance to libraries in the use of *A Planning Process*, and to use conference workshops, guides to the process, and case studies for dissemination and training. According to a 1979 ALA Quarterly Report to the Office of Education, the Steering Committee was suggesting that, immediately after publication of the manual, PLA should concentrate on its dissemination, on training people in the use of the manual, and on the production of a guide to the planning process and performance measures.

At the 1979 ALA Annual Conference the Steering Committee convened for the last time. They met with the King Research team to discuss completion of the project and follow-up activities to disseminate the manual. Before them was a memo sent to the committee by Lynch two weeks before. The Lynch memo (6/10/79) suggested that PLA replicate the planned 1980 ALA conference presentation elsewhere. It also recommended that PLA get endorsements for the manual from organizations such as the International City Managers Association, and that funding be obtained for a consulting service to assist planning libraries that would be operated from ALA headquarters. Finally, Lynch's memo suggested that PLA seek funding through the Higher Education Act to produce guidelines for public libraries based on local planning that would replace national standards.

Among the other topics discussed by the Steering Committee were: (1) how to help state library agencies to use the planning process in developing state standards and (2) the advisability of sending brochures to all public libraries and state library agencies along with an order form for *A Planning Process* in the association's journal *Public Libraries*. It planned to inform the Council of State Governments, the League of Cities and Towns, the Council of Mayors, the National Academy of Public Administration, and the Organization of State Budget Directors in the hope of getting endorsements from these agencies. The objective was to further strengthen and validate PLA's efforts to get individual libraries to adopt the planning process.

The day after the final Steering Committee meeting, Lynch wrote a letter to PLA's executive board requesting that the board endorse local planning and the development of state standards based on data collected by planning libraries. She also repeated her suggestion that PLA establish a planning office at ALA headquarters to train state library agency consultants, to provide short term consultation with individual librarians, and to produce national standards based on the data collected by planning libraries.

An ALA Preconference on the Planning Process, which included informal audience interaction, was held in 1979. Robinson's keynote speech for the preconference was published in the Fall 1979 issue of *Public Libraries*. Also at this conference PLA sponsored an informal meeting including a panel discussion with the directors of the libraries chosen as test sites for the manual.

On July 20th, the date was set for a federally funded Training and Evaluation Seminar, later referred to as the "Wagon Wheel Conference" because of its location. (The seminar was held at the Wagon Wheel Resort in Rockton, Illinois, from September 23-27, 1979.) The idea was to attract selected library leaders for training in how to use the manual and how to train others to use it. It was also a chance for library leaders to evaluate the final draft of the manual, discuss its impact on the development of national standards, and exchange ideas on its dissemination and use.

Twenty-eight people were invited to the seminar and the travel costs were paid by the federal grant. Participants included library directors, state librarians, state consultants, regional library system directors, trustees, and library educators.

It was about this time that Lynch, now head of the ALA Office for Research (OFR), suggested that the OFR monitor the use of the planning process by individual libraries with the assistance of a PLA advisory committee. In a letter to the PLA executive director (10/10/79), Lynch volunteered the OFR to conduct a survey of planning libraries. The proposed survey was to be designed and implemented under the guidance of an advisory committee to be appointed by the PLA president and to be composed of GGSC and PLA Research Committee members (the ACRPLP referred to earlier). Part of the survey would involve interviews with library directors.

A letter by Shirley Mills-Fischer (10/20/79) detailed PLA's plans for dissemination of the manual. The plans included speeches at the ALTA Conference, the 1980 ALA Annual Conference, and state and regional library association conferences. Articles about the new manual were to appear in prominent library journals. Discussion groups for planning libraries were arranged for ALA's 1980 Midwinter and Annual Conferences. The discussions were to be conducted by PLA staff. After the manual's publication, PLA would hold training workshops for state library personnel and practitioners during the second half of 1980. The initial workshop would be conducted at an ALA Preconference in June. Plans for a short workshop for small libraries to be conducted by state consultants were also in the making.

The letter discussed Lynch's plans for collecting data on libraries that were using the process, with a special emphasis on data from small libraries. This letter also marked a return to the idea of developing tools for performance measurement suggesting the creation of a national database of information, including output measures, collected by planning libraries. Mills-Fischer recommended that the PLA "Statement of Principles" be rewritten to include local planning and the development of output measures as basic principles for public libraries.

The Mills-Fischer letter also included the suggestion that at supplement to *A Planning Process* be considered, with a total revision of the manual to begin in the spring of 1985. Other committees of PLA were also pursuing the idea of revising the manual or publishing a document that would provide alternatives for small libraries. The Publications Committee was considering the publication of a supplement to *A Planning Process* by the end of 1980. Lamar Veatch offered to write a "Measurement Supplement to the Planning Process." The Small and Medium-Sized Libraries section of PLA (SMLS) announced in November that a special preconference program at the ALA annual conference be devoted to the use of the planning process by smaller libraries.

Late in 1979, the PLA executive board met and approved plans for the OFR to design methods for collecting data on planning libraries and for state consultant workshops to be conducted by PLA. The OFR sent a final draft of its plans to members of the newly formed Advisory Committee in December 1979.

At the initial meeting of the ACRPLP during the 1980 ALA Midwinter Conference, the committee was given the charge to coordinate the activities of PLA in research pertaining to the planning process, to advise on such research projects, to monitor the projects, and to disseminate their findings. Furthermore, committee members were to identify additional needed research areas and projects. They discussed with Lynch what data to collect for monitoring the use of the manual and approved the plan for the OFR to design forms and procedures for such data collection.

The ACRPLP recommended that, after a few years, *A Planning Process* be revised on the basis of feedback from planning libraries and continued research into the use of the manual. They suggested that additional planning aides be developed for public libraries and discussed the role of state library agencies in disseminating the planning process. Records of these discussions indicate that this segment of PLA's leadership saw the planning manual as just the beginning of a major innovation and diffusion role for the national association.

The second meeting of the ACRPLP was held at the 1980 ALA Annual Conference. At that time the committee approved the OFR's draft document on the collection of data related to libraries that adopted the planning process. The document recommended that data from 100 planning libraries be collected through quarterly surveys, case studies, and phone interviews.

In 1980, the PLA executive board formally endorsed the move from national standards to locally based planning, supplemented by state standards or guidelines. The PLA executive director was given the charge of developing a proposal for a workshop on the manual for PLA staff and board members. This seems to be the point at which PLA made an official decision to discontinue the publication of national public library standards.

Dissemination Activities

The first large-scale dissemination activity for *A Planning Process* occurred as planned at the 1980 ALA Annual Conference. Soon after, PLA President

Robert Rohlf began giving speeches at a number of state library association meetings across the country. Charles Robinson also gave speeches during his term as PLA president. Donald Sager, Agnes Griffen, and Kathleen Balcom were highly involved in creating awareness during their terms of office as well. The interviews suggested that other presidents were less active in directly promoting the planning process, but remained supportive of the effort. Speeches on the planning process given by PLA presidents tended to be overviews of the project and largely motivational. When Nancy Bolt became president of the association, she officially set in motion the chain of events that led to the Public Library Development Program (PLDP). A list (dated 2/80) of seminars and conference programs to be conducted by the PLA president, executive director, and Mary Jo Lynch includes two regional library association meetings and numerous state meetings.

By September 1980, PLA president Robert Rohlf was scheduled to speak at more than 20 state and regional library association conferences and excerpts from his speeches were to appear in the Spring 1981 issue of *Public Libraries*. The Fall 1980 issue was to include an article advocating local standards development as opposed to national standards. Apparently, concurrent with attempts to disseminate the planning manual, PLA continued to engage in the process of re-educating practitioners in order to change their thinking about national standards. This strategy might be characterized in terms of Chin and Benne's "normative educative" approach.

Also in September, Lynch was suggesting to the ACRPLP that they revise their data collection plans because of the low rate of return of the user form that was printed on the inside back page of the manual. At an October executive board meeting, Peggy O'Donnell reported her plans for the presentation of several regional workshops across the nation. The board approved the presentation of workshops for between 30 and 60 persons, discussed the need for an advisory/resources task force, and suggested five sites for the workshops. Since the objective was training, the workshops were to be limited to practitioners from planning libraries and/or libraries that would soon implement the planning process.

The Goals, Guidelines, and Standards Committee set up a subcommittee, comprised mostly of library directors, to deal with publicity and other means of promoting use of the manual. The decision was made not to keep trying for direct dissemination to individual libraries from the national level (as with the O'Donnell workshops), but to concentrate more heavily on "training the trainers." To this end, PLA organized workshops for state agency personnel. It contracted with Barbara Conroy and Ken Fischer to conduct three regional workshops for state consultants. A task force was established to oversee the workshops. Through the use of such subcommittees and task forces, PLA was assuring that communication channels and linkages would remain in place during dissemination of the innovation.

A report from Lynch to the PLA executive board at ALA's Midwinter Conference stated that there were 35 planning libraries in 20 states by the end of 1980. The report also discussed the involvement of library schools as resources for consultants and workshop sponsors for the dissemination of the planning process. Lynch mentioned that state libraries were conducting their own workshops. Data collection and summary reports of the data collected were being planned by the OFR.

At this same ALA Midwinter Meeting in January 1981, three major avenues of dissemination for *A Planning Process* were being stressed: regional workshops, ALA and state conference programs, and articles in *Public Libraries*. Earlier, during 1980, a regular column devoted to the planning process had been started in the association's journal. At the final meeting of the ACRPLP state and regional preconference programs were planned at several sites. The ACRPLP was officially dissolved in May 1981, "because it failed to work" (letter from Mills-Fischer, dated 9/12/82).

Rohlf continued to give speeches whenever he was asked. Two programs were planned for the ALA annual conference in June. Members of the GGSC were encouraged to give presentations on the planning process whenever possible. Profiles of members willing to give presentations were compiled by PLA. These stated the conditions under which a member would conduct a presentation. Inquiries were often relayed to individual members with little coordination being attempted by PLA staff.

In addition to these channels of dissemination, it should be noted that some of the persons associated with the development of the process were hired by individual libraries as private consultants. In this way, the planning process was disseminated directly to the local level without intermediary action by PLA.

The first of the Conroy-Fischer consultants workshops was conducted in August 1981. The workshops were designed to describe and interpret *A Planning Process* as a planning tool for local libraries. The manual was presented as a "basic but flexible tool to be employed depending on the circumstances." The idea was to show the consultants how to use their skills in assisting libraries in using the planning techniques in a variety of situations. The Eastern Regional Workshop included consultants from 16 states and Canada and was sponsored by PLA, Chief Officers of State Library Agencies (COSLA), and the Association of Specialized and Cooperative Library Agencies (ASCLA). It lasted four days. The same workshop was later repeated in Indianapolis at the Fatima Retreat.

The first practitioner's workshop was conducted by Peggy O'Donnell in October 1981. Follow-up letters were sent to the participants that informed them of the availability of planning packets produced by PLA from documents that planning libraries had sent to association headquarters. Participants were also told that *Public Libraries* would be a primary source of planning news.

The follow-up letters included a survey regarding the workshops, a glossary of planning process terms, and order forms for a film strip on the planning process. The librarians were also informed of the progress being made on the development of performance measures. Several additional workshops were given by the end of the year.

The PLA Research Committee was reminded in a memo from the executive board that they were expected to take a larger role in the dissemination monitoring, and revision of *A Planning Process* and in future research. They were informed that the PLA staff was currently monitoring the progress of the dissemination effort. The memo gave approval for the creation of a survey to monitor use of the planning process by public libraries.

About this same time, ALA officially announced that the OFR was collecting documents from libraries using the manual and would make packets of them available to libraries that were just beginning to plan. Documents included in the packets were selected by the planning libraries and included user and other survey forms, goals and objectives, final reports, and similar items. In addition the OFR was exploring additional ways it might monitor libraries using *A Planning Process*.

The Goals, Guidelines and Standards Committee sent out a survey to try to identify how many libraries had implemented the planning process. PLA itself, however, was unable to sustain the necessary commitment of staff time to keep up with the collection and dissemination of data about planning libraries. Efforts along these lines were eventually abandoned.

At ALA's 1981 Midwinter Conference the first meeting was held of the PLA Planning Process Discussion Group, chaired by David Smith. The ALA Annual Conference in 1981 had two programs on the planning process. The Public Library Reporter Committee meeting discussed a condensed version of *A Planning Process* and designated a liaison for the project. The PLA Publications Committee discussed Veatch's "Output Measures and the Planning Process" and Muller's "Small Public Libraries and the Planning Process," which was to be a print version of the SMSL conference program.

The executive board asked the PLA Research Committee to look into a revision of *A Planning Process* near the end of July 1981. Mary Jo Detweiler was assigned to write a proposal for the revision. The GGSC was given the job of developing performance measures based on the planning process. Also at the end of July the OFR transferred data collected from planning libraries to PLA headquarters and discontinued its data collection activities. The PLA office staff then became the central coordinators of information collection and dissemination for the planning project. Claudya Muller's book (1982) on small public libraries and planning was published in the early part of 1982 and had sold 250 copies by May.

The PLA executive board was kept informed on matters relating to the dissemination of the planning process throughout the 1980s. It approved all

ﾑonies devoted to the dissemination of the process and funded the committees ﾑhat were established to plan and supervise dissemination. Many of the board ﾑembers had been involved in the development of the first manual and later ﾑany became actively involved in the development of the PLDP. From the ﾑearch of the files at the PLA headquarters, it became clear that much of what ﾑent on during the development and dissemination of the first planning process ﾑas facilitated greatly by the efforts of PLA's Executive Director.

ALA and PLA officers and committee members gave a considerable number ﾑf presentations after the publication of *A Planning Process* and would ﾑontinue to do so throughout 1981. The executive board members did their ﾑhare of private and informal dissemination through workshops and contacts ﾑt conferences. Several of the persons who were interviewed made mention ﾑf the fact that PLA is not highly centralized and that much of the committee ﾑork "operated in a sense outside PLA in terms of forgetting that we were ﾑully accountable to them."

Articles were published in *Public Libraries* and presentations were given at ﾑtate and national library conferences. The dissemination plans for *Output Measures for Public Libraries*, drawn up by GGSC, were submitted to the PLA ﾑxecutive board which gave its approval.

In 1982, PLA established the Database Advisory Task Force. The purpose ﾑf this task force was to work with the Library Resources Center at the ﾑniversity of Illinois to broaden the participation of planning libraries in ﾑroviding data on their planning efforts and to increase the use of the collected ﾑata by planning libraries. In August of that year, PLA distributed a flier ﾑnnouncing the availability of planning packets through the Library Resources ﾑenter at the University of Illinois. By the end of the year 146 requests for ﾑlanning packets had been received. Planning packets had been contributed ﾑrom 31 libraries that had completed a cycle of the planning process.

The researchers at the University of Illinois continued their data collecting ﾑctivities. When they developed a "computerized database of statistical ﾑnformation on public libraries," PLA's executive board became concerned that ﾑhis project, funded by the University of Illinois, might be duplicating other ﾑLA statistics gathering projects.

At the 1982 ALA Annual Conference the PLA executive board approved ﾑhe development and publication of a revision of *A Planning Process*. They ﾑlso announced the planned publication of a condensed manual within two ﾑears. The GGSC was put in charge of the production of the two proposed ﾑanuals, the revised and the condensed.

In September 1982, the PLA executive board approved the publication of *Measure for Measure*, which was to consist of the proceedings from a program ﾑiven in North Carolina. The GGSC was given responsibility for publication. ﾑhe executive board asked the Public Libraries Principles Task Force to ﾑresent a document and conduct a hearing on standards at the 1983 ALA

Midwinter Conference. It was also decided in September that the PLA Education for Public Libraries Committee would not participate in any further dissemination of *A Planning Process* due to other commitments.

In December 1982, the executive committee was still making plans for a revision of the manual. A GGSC Subcommittee had been established to revise the manual by 1985. Another subcommittee was working on a simpler version of the manual. Revisions were being discussed for *Small Public Libraries and the Planning Process* and the output measures manual. Planning packets were still being disseminated through the PLA headquarters. Plans were also being made to microfiche the planning packets and to produce a book on which libraries had adopted and adapted the manual, but these projects were never completed due to lack of funds and a switch of emphasis to the development of new manuals.

A Task Force was established in 1982 to set up a PLA planning and evaluation office. The PLA Planning Process Financial Development Task Force estimated the cost of such an office would be $250,000 over two years. The office would offer workshops and fee-based consultant services. At this time there were several committees and individuals involved in offering workshops and consulting. It was eventually decided that PLA did not have the financial or human resources to operate an office for these services without the help of urban and larger libraries, state agencies, and regional systems.

The GGSC was also pursuing the collection of output measures data for a computerized database and asked Fred Neighbors to develop software that could store, retrieve, and manipulate data resulting from user surveys conducted by individual libraries using *Output Measures for Public Libraries*. The GGSC also asked Rich Murphy to develop and publicize revised forms for collecting output measures data. The forms were to be published in *Public Libraries* and distributed at the 1983 PLA Annual Conference. Individual GGSC members were to contact state organizations and offer output measure seminars and programs, or any other assistance the states might want.

Efforts at disseminating *A Planning Process* were continued in 1983. The PLA President's Program at the ALA Annual Conference that year was to be devoted to the planning process. At the same time, however, developments were occurring that would lead to the production of new manuals, and to the abandonment of further revisions or condensations of *A Planning Process*. One final attempt was made to publish a simplified planning manual, however, as consideration was given in October 1983 to publishing a manuscript by Michael Piper called "A Planning Guide for Small Public Libraries." Nothing apparently came of this attempt.

Throughout 1983, PLA committees were involved in disseminating information on local planning. In particular, the PLA Board had given the PLA Planning Process Discussion Group the specific charge to provide new information on local planning. The Research Committee continued to monitor the development of a database on output measures and community surveys through a Public Library Data Base Advisory Subcommittee.

As late as January of 1985, the PLA executive board was still suggesting the use of the planning packets collected from planning libraries for the production of a list of recommended planning documents, the provision of microfiche copies of planning packets to libraries that were just beginning the planning process, an index to the collection of planning packets, and the production of a list of mission statements written by planning libraries. The executive board also called for the collection of more documents for the files (PLA Executive Board, Second Session Minutes, 2/2/85).

Barriers to Effective Dissemination

In the interviews, several problems were mentioned that hindered PLA as it attempted to carry out its dissemination plans. The Association lacked the funds and office personnel to accomplish all of its plans without relying on state organizations and the commitment of private consultants. It did not have the necessary resources to develop different workshops for different audiences, nor could it limit workshop audiences without reducing income.

The general workshops and presentations given at ALA conferences or state library association conferences failed to generate the expected level of enthusiasm among the attending librarians. As one of the persons who was interviewed stated, "There was this sense that everybody else would see and share our excitement. And then the people would come in and they would need to be sold." The introductory workshops did not contain enough in-depth information to satisfy people who were already engaged in planning or had seriously considered using the PLA planning process. At the same time such workshops failed to reach those who needed to be sold on the whole idea through a different type of presentation.

From the beginning, PLA saw the state and regional organizations as the proper agencies for dissemination to the local level. The developers of the planning process thought of state agencies as "important partners" with "enough clout at the local level" to be the primary disseminators of the planning process. They felt that PLA's role in dissemination was in training the trainers (state and regional system consultants), and in the refinement and further development of the planning tools. Although several agencies did attempt to disseminate the planning process to public libraries within their states, the strong partnership envisioned by PLA did not come to pass.

The perceived lack of enthusiasm for the first planning process by state and regional organizations was considered a major barrier to dissemination of the manuals by some of the people interviewed. These agencies were perceived as having the ability to work closely with individual libraries and as being in a position to deal with the problems libraries might encounter in applying the planning process. The interviews indicated that those involved with the innovation recognized early on that small libraries could not set up planning committees and do community needs assessments without the help of state or system consultants. Without state level cooperation, dissemination directly from the national level would be extremely difficult for PLA to accomplish. Interviews indicated that the developers felt that it was the job of the state libraries to help individual libraries "and what PLA should be doing is training the trainers. That we should do workshops for state library staff, which we did. We should do workshops for regional library consultants so that they can go out and provide this assistance free."

At one time it had been hoped that federal monies would be made available for libraries wishing to implement the planning process. It was envisioned that this money would provide a "great groundswell of people who needed consultants," but neither the money nor the groundswell materialized. Private consultants, many closely associated with PLA or King Research, were paid by individual libraries to conduct workshops on the planning process; but the demand for such consultants was not high.

Although numerous workshops were conducted, some sponsored by PLA and some presented by private consultants, not all of the workshops were well received. "California, for example, did not participate at all in the first wave of the planning process. And apparently, what we understood was, it was the way it was presented to them...Some of the presentations did not go over well. And [this was particularly the case in] some of the western states."

Smaller libraries, according to our interviews, were simply not interested in adopting the planning manual. "They weren't doing [planning] at all. I just never got the impression that there was that much demand by the smaller libraries to do it. I mean, I think most of them were just too intimidated by it." The manual was "difficult to read." Librarians "felt that they needed to go literally from the first step to the end and got bogged down." They "used surveys right from the book without regard to their appropriateness to local conditions." They "never understood the need to plan, nor the benefits of planning." There was nothing "to motivate small libraries" to use the planning process and they generally thought that "things were working fine in the library as it was."

PLA had also hoped that the process would be adopted by the "leading libraries" and their use of the process would influence other libraries to adopt. The feeling was that "there was a kind of dynamism about what was going on that would spread even if only a few libraries went through it."

Interviews indicated that the consequences of the development of the concept of local planning extended beyond the publication of the manuals and their dissemination. The innovation has had an impact on the general attitude and activities of PLA, "more than any other division of ALA has experienced," according to one of the developers interviewed. "I can't think of another division [of ALA] that is as strongly affected by a project it's done as PLA. So while the organization may not have changed, certainly the whole mood, the whole way of thinking, the whole set of activities have changed."

Another of those interviewed suggested that the image of PLA has improved and that it is now seen as a national association that is nonetheless concerned with what is going on at the level of the individual library. The prolonged commitment to its innovation has invoked within the membership and the committee structure of the association "a spirit...that's also driving so much else at PLA and it all comes together to make it certainly more visible, and I think [it has produced] a very positive feeling among public librarians about the association."

Much of the enthusiasm, excitement, and commitment that was initially generated among the developers of PLA's innovation, and that eventually spread throughout the association's formal structure, was still obvious in the voices and the comments of most of the people that were interviewed. When a national professional association assumes the role of a change agency, the faith that it has in its innovation and the strength of its commitment to dissemination seem to be among the attitudinal and behavioral factors that will have a bearing on the success of the diffusion effort (which must be sustained by an association leadership prone to natural change over an extended period of time). One of the most fascinating aspects of PLA's development and diffusion endeavor is that it was undertaken and maintained by a relatively small group of individuals. Although the number of people involved expanded and contracted periodically, a small core group apparently kept the goal and the concept alive.

DISCUSSION

The development and diffusion of PLA's managerial innovation represents a unique situation in that the concept originated with the director and staff of a larger public library system that had been experimenting with planning techniques adapted from the private sector. Instead of spreading on this local level, however, the idea was diffused upward to the level of the national professional association. There it combined with compatible ideas that were then being debated in the Standards Revision Committee and other committees of PLA. The subsequent merging of the concept of long range planning with the idea that national standards should be replaced with a method for measuring local library effectiveness, became the seedbed for PLA's planning and evaluation techniques.

PLA recognized that the notion of long range planning was potentially useful in solving the major problem it had been confronting—that of redefining the public library's purpose in a changing society. The Standards Revision

Committee of PLA saw the concept as an opportunity to "do something" about the credibility of national standards: give them a research base by using data collected from planning libraries in order to develop the standards. In accepting the recommendation that the standards not be revised but be replaced with an instruction manual on how to engage in community based planning, the association assumed both an innovation development and an innovation diffusion role.

Through telephone interviews and the examination of published and unpublished documents, three phases in the life cycle of the innovation were explored: its origination, its development, and the planned attempt to disseminate it. Of major interest was the fit between what had occurred in actuality and the existing theoretical models of the development and dissemination of innovations. A number of conclusions were drawn from the study. The major ones are briefly summarized below.

Comparisons with General Diffusion Models

One of the study's conclusions was that elements similar to those found in general diffusion models can indeed be identified in the development and diffusion of PLA's innovation: (1) networks or linkages among a number of different social subsystems, (2) specific types of linking roles assumed by individuals, (3) approaches that contain characteristics of the three general change strategies, and (4) combined use of the several general categories of dissemination techniques.

1. *Linkages* were discovered among (a) the federal government sector (which provided development funds), (b) the library education/scholarly community (which provided resource people to aid in problem solving and scientific research), (c) the private research sector (which conducted applied research in the form of field studies, then developed and packaged the results), (d) practicing public librarians (some of whom were originators and developers of the innovation, while others were the target audience for diffusion efforts), (e) state library development agencies (which were cast in the role of target audience with respect to adopting the conceptual foundation of the innovation, as well as partners in the dissemination of the innovation to the local level), (f) the professional media (which performed an information dissemination role in publishing articles about the innovation), (g) the Public Library Association (which served as futuristic planner and goal setter throughout), (h) its parent organization, the American Library Association (which provided advice along with administrative, financial, and other types of support), and (i) state and regional library associations (which like state agencies were both targets of the dissemination process and disseminators of the innovation).

2. Specific *types of linkage roles* included: (a) conveyors (who transferred knowledge from the research community to librarians in the field and to PLA

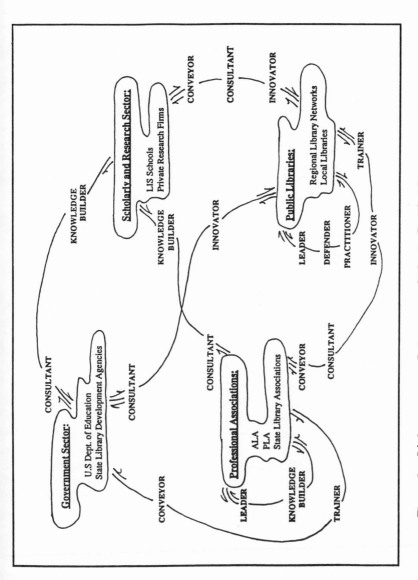

Figure 1. Linkages among Subsystems within the Public Library Social System

members who were seeking solutions to change related problems), (b) consultants (who helped PLA to identify the planning techniques from other disciplines that could be adapted to the public library environment), (c) trainers (who conducted workshops), (d) leaders (who served to influence the opinions of others), (e) innovators (who initiated the search for solutions and brought new concepts into committee discussions), (f) defenders (who protected the interests of smaller libraries with regard to the innovation), and (g) knowledge builders (who served on PLA committees and were the project's goal setters and visionaries).

For illustrative purposes, Figure 1 provides a partial model of the linkages within the public library social system. It should be noted that, for the sake of clarity, not all of the linkage roles among the several subsystems are shown in the model. Nor does each linkage role represent a unique individual. A number of the same people assumed different linkage roles at various times as the innovation evolved from *A Planning Process for Public Libraries* and *Output Measures for Public Libraries* into the Public Library Development Program.

3. Characteristics of two of the *general types of dissemination strategies* were found with regard to PLA's innovation:

1. The rational-empirical approach dominated the development of the first set of manuals in that much of the emphasis was on utilizing the services of resource persons for applied research and field testing of the manuals and for "packaging" the results.

2. The normative-educative approach was also utilized from the start as proponents of community based planning within PLA tried to "re-educate," first the leadership within the association itself (to accept the diversity of public libraries and hence the inadequacy of national standards, regardless of how "scientifically" derived); and later the librarians in the field (to manage with user needs and user satisfaction in mind rather than national standards). Once PLA made the official decision to dispense with any further editions of national standards, it began in earnest to apply normative-educative techniques via the professional literature, conferences, and workshops in order to convince librarians to buy into the rationale behind the concept, so that they would more readily adopt and use the manuals.

4. *Dissemination techniques* that were used by PLA may be categorized as: telling, showing, helping, involving, and training. As the innovation moved through its initial development stage, during which time a considerable amount of problem identification and problem solving were occurring, practitioners and leaders within public librarianship were interacting with PLA and ALA officials as well as with the scholarly community and the private research sector.

Helping, telling, and involving techniques characterized much of this interaction. When the innovation began to be diffused among potential adopters, showing and training techniques were added to the mix. Members of each sector (subsystem) within the social system utilized more than one of these techniques often concurrently. The only technique that was not used to any extent was intervening; that is, mandating use of the innovation, invoking sanctions, or otherwise forcing adoption. ALA and PLA were obviously not in a position to intervene on the local library level. Some state library development agencies, however, have recently begun to require that local libraries submit a written five-year plan of service and include selected output measures in their annual reports to the state (Ballard, 1989).

The second conclusion is related to the first: The development and dissemination process evidenced characteristics of each of the three general diffusion models as described by Havelock. The progression of events and activities identified in this investigation of PLA's innovation could easily be divided into the stages outlined in the R,D&D model of knowledge production and utilization: research, development, packaging, and dissemination. Similarities to the SI model were also discovered in that dissemination was heavily dependent upon networking activities (social interaction) between PLA, state agencies and associations, private consultants employed to train the trainers, regional library systems, and local libraries.

The P-S model views the adoption of innovation as an extension of the classic approach to problem solving: problem identification, generation of alternative solutions, selection and implementation of the optimal solution, and evaluation of the results. This model was appropriate as well, in that it describes the user as the initiator of change, with the help of outside change agents and other resource persons in problem diagnosis and in selecting and applying solutions. Much of what occurred from the early 1970s through the mid-1980s was the result of networking between PLA (as both user and change agent) and the various resource people from the practitioner, scholarly, and research communities whose help PLA had enlisted in order to solve the problems of what to do about national standards and how to measure library effectiveness.

Events and activities in the development and diffusion of PLA's managerial innovation combine to reveal a complex network of interrelationships among individuals, formal and informal groups, and the various organizations that comprise the public library social system. There is no single path through this maze from innovator to user. Instead the innovators were at times both the users and the developers, interacting with outside resource systems as the need arose. Resource persons who were drawn into the project engaged in research, consulting, fund raising, development, and packaging. State agencies and the federal government provided money for development. Even prior to the publication of the first set of manuals, practitioners provided feedback that led to the decision, almost immediately after initial publication, to redesign and repackage the innovation.

The concept of linkages is not completely explained by the analogy to the "links" in a "chain" of knowledge utilization. Linkages in the diffusion process are not static relationships. The functional role assumed by a single linking agent may undergo several transformations over time. The same "linker" could easily appear at different nodes in the knowledge chain—perhaps a better simile would be the "web" of knowledge use—conveying, telling, training, consulting, or performing other linkage functions between various subsystems. What should be noted, perhaps, is that the entire process from origination through diffusion depends upon such linkages to maintain a reciprocal exchange of information and an environment conducive to the transfer of knowledge.

ACKNOWLEDGMENTS

The author wishes to gratefully acknowledge the support of the United States Department of Education under the Higher Education Act, Title II-B, Library Research and Demonstration Program, Project No. R039A80012. She also wishes to acknowledge the important contributions of research assistants Jay Ed Wilkerson and Lanju Yoon, who were active in project planning and data collection for the broader study on which this paper is based.

REFERENCES

Ballard, Thomas H. "Planning and Output Measures." *Public Libraries*, 25 (1989): 292-95.

Beasley, Kenneth E. "Statistical Reporting System for Local Public Libraries." Pennsylvania State Library Monographs, No. 3. University Park: Pennsylvania State University Institute of Public Administration, 1964.

Bhola, H.S. "Planning Change in Education and Development: The CLER Model in the Context of a Mega Model." *Viewpoints in Teaching and Learning*, 58 (1982): 1-35.

Blasingame, Ralph, and Lynch, Mary Jo. "Design for Diversity." *PLA Newsletter*, 13 (June 1974): 4-22.

Bloss, Meredith. "Standards for Public Library Service—Quo Vadis?" *Library Journal*, 101 (June 1, 1976): 1259-62.

Bolt, Nancy. "Performance Measures for Public Libraries." In *Public Libraries and the Challenge of the Next Two Decades*, edited by Alphonse F. Trezza. Littleton, CO: Libraries Unlimited, 1985.

Chin, R., and Benne, K.D. "General Strategies for Effecting Change in Human Systems." In *The Planning of Change*, edited by G.W. Bennis et al. New York: Holt, Rinehart, and Winston, 1976.

"Community Library Services—Working Papers on Goals and Guidelines." *School Library Journal*, (September 1973): 21-28.

Damonpour, Fariborz, and Childers, Thomas. "The Adoption of Innovations in Public Libraries." *Library and Information Science Research*, 7 (1984): 231-46.

De Prospo, Ernest R., et al. *Performance Measures for Public Libraries*, Chicago: American Library Association, 1973.

Griffiths, Jose-Marie et al. *Diffusion of Innovations in Library and Information Science*, Final Report. Rockville, MD: King Research, Inc., 1986.

Havelock, Ronald G. *Planning for Innovation through Dissemination and Utilization of Knowledge*, Ann Arbor: University of Michigan Institute for Social Research, 1969.

Katz, E. et al. "Traditions of Research on the Diffusion of an Innovation." In *Creating Social Change*, edited by G. Zaltman et al. New York: Holt, Rinehart, and Winston, 1972.

Lynch, Mary Jo. "The Public Library Association and Public Library Planning." *Journal of Library Administration*, 2 (Summer 1992): 29-41.

Lynch, Mary Jo. "Planning and Measurement of Library Services." Typescript draft of a speech given at McGill University, Montreal (dated August 26, 1986).

Lynch, Mary Jo and Lance, Keith Curry. "M.L.S. Librarians in Public Libraries: Where They Are and Why It Matters." *Public Libraries*, 32 (July/August 1993): 203-07.

Martin, Allie Beth. *A Strategy for Public Library Change: Proposed Public Library Goals-Feasibility Study*, Chicago: American Library Association, 1972.

McClure, Charles R. et al. *Planning and Role Setting for Public Libraries: A Manual of Options and Procedures*, Chicago: American Library Association, 1987.

Muller, Claudya. *The Small Public Library and the Planning Process*, Chicago: American Library Association, 1982.

Musmann, Klaus, and Kennedy, William H. *Diffusion of Innovation: A Select Bibliography*, Westport, CT: Greenwood Press, 1989.

Palmour, Vernon E. et al. *A Planning Process for Public Libraries*, Chicago: American Library Association, 1980.

Public Library Association. Standards Committee. *Minimum Standards for Public Library Systems, 1986*, Chicago: American Library Association, 1967.

Pungitore, Verna L. et al. *A Study of the Development and Diffusion of the Public Library Association's Planning and Evaluation Manuals*, Final Report. Bloomington: Indiana University School of Library and Information Science, 1989. (ERIC document ED317217)

Rogers, Everett M. and Shoemaker, F. *Communication of Innovations*, New York: The Free Press, 1971.

Rohlf, Robert H. "Standards for Public Libraries." *Library Trends*, (Summer 1982): 65-76.

Stein, Nancy Helburn. "Causal Attributes and Effectiveness of Diffusion Techniques as Perceived by Physical Education Department Chairpersons." Ph.D. Dissertation, Indiana University, Bloomington, 1978.

Van House, Nancy et al. *Output Measures for Public Libraries: A Manual of Standardized Procedures*, 2nd ed. Chicago: American Library Association, 1987.

Veatch, Lamar. "Output Measures for Public Libraries." *Public Libraries*, 21 (Spring 1982): 11-13.

Williams, Patrick. *The American Public Library and the Problem of Purpose*, Westport, CT: Greenwood Press, 1988.

Zweizig, Douglas L. and Rodger, Eleanor Jo. *OutPut Measures for Public Libraries: A Manual of Standardized Procedures*, Chicago: American Library Association, 1982.

LIBRARIES, ACCESSIBILITY AND THE AMERICAN WITH DISABILITIES ACT

Willie Mae O'Neal

People with disabilities or handicaps are used to being over looked. They are among the minorities and have been either pushed or lost in the cracks. However, thanks to the new Americans with Disabilities Act (ADA), as of July 26, 1992 this is becoming a behavior of the past. People with handicaps and disabilities are no longer treated as second class citizens.

This document will address the problem of accessibility in libraries and what they must do to comply with the ADA. Accessibility is defined as making existing facilities usable for people with disabilities. Compliance must be met by reasonable accommodations which means the administration has a responsibility to see that the law is followed.

DEFINING DISABILITIES

The ADA (Schneid, 1992, p. 25) refers to disabilities as a" physical or mental impairment that substantially limits one or more major life activities. A record or history of such an impairment, or a perception of such an impairment also qualifies one as having a disability or handicap." The points brought out in this definition of disabilities have been broadened and cover more than the

Advances in Library Administration and Organization, Volume 12, pages 75-84.
Copyright © 1994 by JAI Press Inc.
All rights of reproduction in any form reserved.
ISBN: 1-55938-846-3

obvious definition of what used to be considered as the only way to distinguish who was disabled, such as a wheelchair or walker, missing limbs, blindness and/or deafness. Disabilities that are not as noticeable include but are not limited to: speech, vision, hearing impairments, as well as mental retardation, specific learning disabilities, emotional learning and repetitive stress injuries. Many diseases which limit one or more of a person's life activities—palsy, epilepsy, multiple sclerosis, arthritis, kidney, asthma and diabetes—may be considered disabling.

People with contagious diseases are protected, including those who test positive for the HIV (AIDS) virus. Alcohol and drug addition are considered disabilities and are protected by the ADA. However, an individual must be in a supervised rehabilitation program and must have successfully completed the program and be drug free in order to be covered by the ADA. AIDS or HIV is clearly stated as being protected by the ADA. It is difficult to keep a list of all the conditions because of new specifics that may develop in the future.

PURPOSE OF THE LAW

The purpose of the American with Disabilities Act is to increase employment to the millions of disabled working age people who until this Act was passed were without employment rights. Evan J. Kemp Jr. (Schneid, 1992, p. 29) of the Equal Employment Opportunity Commission said:

> A staggering 58 percent of all men with disabilities and 80 percent of all women with disabilities are unemployed. So long as two-thirds of disabled Americans are unemployed, we will be unable to break the terrible cycle of dependency and segregation. And, if people with disabilities cannot break the grip of economic dependence, our society is doomed to spend $160 billion a year on benefits that most recipients would be willing to trade for a good job.

The ADA provides a clear understanding of the law for people with disabilities and give them an equal opportunity in the job market. By mandating, the law enforces standardization throughout the land.

The ADA is re-enforced by the Rehabilitation Act of 1973 and the Civil Rights Act of 1964, laws which already protect millions of employees.

EMPLOYMENT AND ATTITUDES

Employers can now take advantage of the flexibility that the new ADA gives them for employees with disabilities. The issue of stereotyping people can now be addressed. Disabled people have not been given the opportunity to demonstrate what they can or cannot do. They are perceived as unemployable because of handicaps and have therefore been discriminated against. Disabilities should not be labeled or categorized, for example, if you're blind you're also deaf and dumb. Each person's disability must be treated as a separate condition.

Almost all employers will be affected by the ADA's hiring practices. The article in Employee Benefit Plan Review (1992, p. 100), states:

> the act specifically prohibits discrimination in job application procedures, hiring, advancement, or discharge of a qualified individual because of a disability.

Confidentiality is important and must be kept by managers and supervisors. Supervisors are not told what the medical problems are, but only what the work restrictions of the person are. Most employers are ready to comply with the ADA, but want clearer guidance of the law. Fletcher and Harty, (1992, p. 100) said:

> The ADA doesn't provide any bright lines or safe harbors about what are the essential functions of a job or what would be a reasonable accommodation.

Researchers have studied attitudes toward the handicapped for many years and found that the problem of resistance still exists. They also concluded that even though we are in a more enlightened era, we continue to stereotype individuals. The only change researchers have been able to uncover was that people no longer laugh or make fun of people with disabilities. School and public librarians have been credited with educating the public about people with disabilities by the selection of books for libraries that have helped reduce some of the misinformation related to the disabled. Legal strategies could cause problems for employers if they are not kept abreast of the law with regard to their employees. The ADA guarantees equal rights to people with disabilities. The handicapped are also protected by their constitutional rights the same as any "normal" person. According to Benshoff and Souheaver, (1991, p. 29):

> Counselors will be increasingly called upon to act in an active advocacy role for clients. They will have the task of assisting companies to screen in candidates based on ability, rather than screening out based on disabilities.

The ADA lists a number of modifications that fall within the framework of reasonable accommodations:

1. Modifying the physical layout of a job facility so as to make it accessible to individuals who use wheelchairs or who have other impairments that make it difficult;

2. Restructuring a job to enable the person with a disability to perform the essential functions of the job;
3. Establishing a part-time or modified work schedule (for example, to accommodate people with disabilities who have treatment needs or fatigue problems);
4. Reassigning a person with a disability to a vacant job;
5. Acquiring or modifying equipment or devices (such as buying a hearing telephone amplifier for a person with a hearing impairment);
6. Adjusting or modifying exams, training materials, or policies (for example, giving an application examination orally to a person with dyslexia or modifying a policy against dogs in the work place for a person with a service dog);
7. Providing qualified readers or interpreters for people with vision or hearing impairments.

The goal is to look at all aspects of the job to identify what might cause a problem for a disabled person and to modify the job for that environment.

ACCESSIBILITY

Library services and facilities must be barrier free and accessible to the disabled. Some of the problems are related to the exterior of the library building and architectural interior barriers. Gunde (1992, p. 90) states:

"Probably the most frequently encountered exterior barriers for the United States libraries include:
1. Lack of appropriate accessible parking;
2. Failure to locate accessible parking spaces on the most direct accessible route to the accessible library entrance;
3. Lack of curb ramps with appropriate slope connecting accessible parking to accessible routes;
4. And, the absence of signs indicating which entrances are accessible if all or not at least one entrance must be accessible to people who use wheelchairs or walkers.

Architectural barriers found in the libraries are common problems said Gunde (1992, p. 90). He cites the most common problems as:

1. paper towels dispensers over 48" high (for forward approach) or 54" (for side approach);
2. supposedly "accessible" toilet stalls that are too narrow, lack sufficient grab bars, or have toilet seats that are not between 17"-19" high;
3. urinals that have a rim that is more than 19" from the floor;
4. mirrors whose lowest reflecting edge is higher than 40" from the floor;
5. perhaps the most common, faucet hardware that cannot be operated effectively without twisting of the wrist.

Modifications are needed in most existing buildings to comply with the ADA's new law. Existing libraries may elect to provide an alternative service to accommodate the disabled person. According to the Uniform Federal Accessibility Standards all newly built state and private colleges or university facilities must be barrier free. A few other common problems in the libraries include (Gunde, 1992, p. 90):

1. lack of sufficient visual and audio fire alarms;
2. floors only accessible by stairs;
3. operating controls that are mounted higher than 48" from the floor;
4. failure to erect braille and raised letter signs to mark permanent rooms and spaces or to provide otherwise accessible information and directional signs;
5. and, inaccessible door hardware doors that are too heavy or provide insufficient clear width for passage through the door.

Other problems librarians should look for are in the service areas, such as:

1. The height of the circulation desk and other service counters which includes computer desks;
2. Aisles that are wide enough for wheelchairs in the stack area and free of obstructions such as book carts or foot stools that may prevent the disabled person from access to the stacks;
3. Listening systems, public pay phones, and card or online catalogs that may be inaccessible to the handicapped.

Guidelines to assist in making corrections or information can be located in The American with Disabilities Act Accessibility Guidelines for Buildings and Facilities (ADAAGC) attached to the ADA handbook.

ACCOMMODATIONS

Libraries in colleges and universities can comply with the ADA by modifying the existing buildings for accessibility for the handicapped. Title III requires that all facilities be "readily achievable." This is to remove any structural, architectural and communication barriers from existing buildings that are easily accomplished with little difficulty or expense. Title III prohibits an institution from denying access to goods and services to disabled who have the need for auxiliary aids. The ADA refers to auxiliary aids as:

*   qualified interpreters or other effective methods of making aurally delivered materials available to individuals with hearing impairments;
*   qualified readers, taped text, or other effective methods of making visually delivered materials available to individuals with visual impairments;

- acquisition or modification of equipment or devices;
- and other similar services or action.

Two years ago we moved back into a newly renovated library that was completely renovated and expanded. After evaluating the accommodations at the library facility, it was brought to the attention of the administration that the library was not in compliance with some of the new ADA requirements for the handicapped. Some of the problems that had not been addressed were:

1. A person in a wheelchair could not open the doors;
2. Little or no signage was available for directing the disabled around the library;
3. There were some areas that could not clearly hear emergency announcements or fire alarms;
4. Elevators were not equipped for emergencies.

Actions taken by the administration resulted in the following improvements:

1. Hand pushed controls were installed on one set of the entrance doors;
2. More directional signs were posted;
3. More speakers were installed;
4. All elevators were equipped with telephones lines connecting directly to the public safety department.

Some of the problems mentioned above were detected before occupying the facility and others like hearing the warning alarms were detected only after moving back into the building and using the facility.

COMPLIANCE

There are eight steps to a barrier free environment leading to compliance with the ADA. Management must keep in mind that areas not open to the public are not required to be updated by law. This may affect employees with disabilities, but employers would not be violating the ADA. Schneid's (1992, pp. 46-58) eight steps to comply with Title III are:

Step 1. Facility evaluation—the initial step in achieving compliance with Title III is to evaluate your facility and operations.
   A. Parking areas
   B. Walks, curbs and stairs
   C. Entrances, corridors and stairs
   D. Public restrooms
   E. Public telephones, water fountains and elevators.

Step 2.   Evaluate policies, procedures and practices.

Step 3.   Auxiliary Aids—if requested covered employers are required to provide auxiliary aids needed by the individual with disabilities. There is no requirements that the covered employer offer auxiliary aids to customers, and so forth.

Step 4.   methods of accommodations—the ADA does not specify which auxiliary aids need to be provided in a given circumstance.

Step 5.   Evaluate accommodations for undue burden expectation covered employers may decline to provide auxiliary aids if it should cause an undue burden to the employer. An "Undue Burden" is defined as on accommodation causing significant difficulty or expense as listed in the ADA section 302 (B)(S) (A).

Step 6.   Evaluate accommodations for safety and health threat.—An employer may require that an individual not pose a direct threat to his or her own safety or health, as well as to the safety and health of others.

Step 7.   Evaluate contracts and leases—covered employers should evaluate any and all rental agreements, leases or other contracted arrangements to insure the facility meets the requirements of the ADA.

Step 8.   Evaluate for tax benefits—last but not least, sources of funding to assist in the cost of modifying a work-place to achieve compliance should be expanded.

Accessibility is expensive to the organization if the facility doesn't meet the ADA requirements. Schroeder and Steinfeld (1979, p. 151) stated:

> that costs for accessibility in new construction are only 1 percent of the total. Even modification to existing facilities can be as low as 2 percent of the adjusted original cost to the facility.

MYTHS

Exceptional understanding and empathy is one of the myths that affects disabled people. The assumption is that people with a handicap have better knowledge of other people with the same or similar condition. But the reality is that anyone who wishes to understand people with handicaps must put forth an effort to learn how they can be of assistance to them.

WHAT THE AMERICANS WITH DISABILITIES ACT MEANS TO THE NONDISABLED

The ADA will change the way nondisabled people think about disabled people. Next, we will see people in the work force who have not been seen before.

Hopefully, through training, attitudes will change. People will not look upon the handicapped with the need to treat them any differently than normal people. They will not receive special consideration when hired, but successfully gain employment by being the best person qualified for the position. Training must be ongoing to help the staff learn how to deal with their own feelings, and how to make the person with the disability feel at ease. Training must be creative and unique for each work environment. Flexibility needs to be addressed so that both the nondisabled and the disabled feel comfortable on the job. Supervisors and managers set the examples for the employees. We must not leave library patrons out of the picture. They are an important part of the library and if they see how well the staff is treating the handicapped, they may be encouraged to participate in the program as well.

SOLUTIONS AND SUGGESTIONS TO COMPLY WITH THE ADA

- Compliance—Accessibility for the disabled is attainable with modification of existing facilities or can be included in construction of a new facility.
- Funding—Funds are available to support the cost if assistance is needed. For information, contact the Internal Revenue Service (1-800-Tax Form (voice) or 1-800-829-4059 TDD), and request a copy of publication 907, Tax Information for Persons with Handicaps or Disabilities.
- Planning—This process is done by evaluating the library to identify what problems need to be addressed. The eight steps outlined earlier in this paper can be followed to identify what problems need to be addressed.
- Reasonable accommodation—Develop a plan and procedures to assist the administration, supervisors, and employees with the hiring, advancement, and the discharging of employees.
- Services—Implement an incentive program to help supervisors educate and disseminate information about the ADA and the disabled throughout the library. Keep a directory of services for the disabled conveniently available for students requesting information about services, equipment and accessibility to the library facilities.

SUMMARY

The purpose and background of the Americans with Disabilities Act (ADA) and library services to the disabled and physically handicapped population were discussed. Library education, training of staff and the re-training of librarians about the Americans with Disabilities Act were reviewed. Some suggestions on how to comply with the new law and meet its requirements for employers, employees, and patrons that use the library facilities were given.

Accessibility was the focus of this paper and is just one of the possible areas for future research. Other topics include areas such as technology, drugs, acquired immunodeficiency syndrome (AIDS) and repetitive stress injuries which are also covered by the ADA. One area for future research is the marketing of librarians with information on ADA to assist managers in evaluating and redesigning library environments for compliance to the ADA. It is hoped that this paper will provide librarians with an overview of the American with Disabilities Act and encourage future research.

WHERE TO FIND INFORMATION ABOUT THE ADA

Equal Employment Opportunity
Commission
1801 L. St., N.W.,Rm. 9024
Washington, DC 20507
Voice 800/669-3362

JAN (Job Accommodations
Network)
West Virginia University
PO Box 6122
Morgantown, WV 26506
VoiceTDD 800526-7324

Employment Policy Foundation
Employment Advisory Services
1015 15th St. N.W. Ste. 1200
Washington DC 20005
202789-2166
202789-8685 (for information on
publications
Publications include:
*Disability Etiquette in the Work-
place by Patricia Morrissey
*A Complete Legislative History
of the Americans with disabilities
Act
*A Compliance Guide to the
Americans with Disabilities Act
Solomon, C.M.

Desk Reference

Small Business Legislative Council
1156 15th St., N.W., Ste
510 Washington, DC. 20005
202639-8500

National Leadership
Coalition on Aids
1730 M St., N.W. Ste. 905
Washington, DC 20036
202429-0930

Architectural and Transportation
Barriers
Compliance Board
1111 18th St., N.W. Rm 254
Washington, DC 20036
VoiceTDD. 202653-7834

Federal Communications
Commission—Office of
Public Affairs
1919 M St., N.W., Ste. 254
Washington, DC 200554
Voice 202632-6999

REFERENCES

"ADA Accessibility Guidelines for Buildings and Facilities Appendix B." *The Americans with Disabilities Act Handbook*, U.S.Department of Justice 202-514-0301.

Benshoff, J. J., and Souheaver, H. G. "Private Sector Rehabilitation and The Americans With Disabilities Act." *Journal of Applied Rehabilitation Counseling*, 22 (1991): 27-31.

Crispen, J.L. (Ed.) "The Americans with Disabilities Act: Its Impact on Libraries: The Library's Responses in "Doable" Steps." Chicago: ALA, 1993.

Employee Benefit Plan Review, 46 (1992): 97-100.

Feldblum, C.R. "Employment Protections." *Milbank Quarterly*, 69 (1991). 81-110.

Fersh, D. and Thomas, P.W. "Complying with the Americans Disabilities Act: A Guide for Management and People with Disabilities. London: Quorum Books, 1993.

Fletcher, M. and Harty, S. J. "Most Employers Ready to Comply with ADA Rules; But Many Want Clearer Guidance to Follow the Law." *Business Insurance*, 28 (1992): 3-10.

Gunde, M. "Working with the Americans with Disabilities Act." *Library Journal*, 00 (1992): 90-91.

Hearne, P. "Employment Strategies for People with Disabilities: A Prescription for Change. *Milbank Quarterly*, 69 (1991): 111-128.

Nagler, M. "Perspectives on Disability," Palo Alto: Health Markets Research. Evan J. Kemp, Jr., 1990.

Schneid, T. D. "The Americans with Disabilities Act: A Practical Guide for Managers." New York: Van Nostrand Reinhold, 1992.

Schroeder, S. and Steinfeld, E. "The Estimated Cost of Accessible Buildings. Washington, DC: U.S. Department of Housing and Urban Development 9HUD-PDR-398), 1979.

Solomon, C. M. "What the ADA means to the Nondisabled." *Personnel Journal*, 71 (1992): 70-79.

Wright, K. C. and Davie, J. F. "Library and Information Services for Handicapped Individuals." Englewood, Colorado: Libraries Unlimited, Inc., 1989.

SOME THOUGHTS ON THE FUTURE ACADEMIC LIBRARY

Murray S. Martin

For some years what librarians and others say about the future of the library (Curzon, 1989, Dowling, 1984, *Farewell to Alexandria*, 1976; *Academic Library in Transition*, 1989, and others cited in the list of references) seems to have been predicated by automation and electronics. There has been comparatively little about library buildings as such in that writing. Apart from David Kaser's "Academic library Buildings: Their Evolution and Prospects," which concludes

> no radical departures in architectural style appear on the horizon that are likely to aid in library building enhancement over the next couple of decades (1988, p. 160).

The annual *Library Journal* issue devoted to buildings seems to show libraries as usual. The first issue of *Library Administration & Management* (June, 1987) which treated buildings was limited and technical. The next buildings and equipment issue (Spring 1990) was much more adventurous and included a very interesting article by Phil Tompkins on new structures (Tompkins, 1990). An issue of *Library Trends* (Fall, 1987) discussed library buildings and paid most attention to public libraries but has an excellent bibliography.

Advances in Library Administration and Organization, Volume 12, pages 85-108.
Copyright © 1994 by JAI Press Inc.
All rights of reproduction in any form reserved.
ISBN: 1-55938-846-3

The *Canadian Library Journal* (October, 1990) carried a short note on the new public library in Rotterdam and there have been notes here and there on new national libraries, or on disasters that have overtaken other libraries, but there has been almost nothing substantive about design issues. The very useful manual *Library Space Planning* by Ruth A. Fraley and Carol Lee Anderson. (New York: Neal-Schuman, 1990) touches on some of the issues but concentrates on the traditional elements in discussing the needs of a library move. Given this background, it is heartening to read Margaret Beckman's article on cost avoidance in library planning (1990) based on her presentation at an IFLA post conference in 1989. She questions all the old space standards, takes account of the new technologies, and recognizes that many library users will not need to come to the library at all. A special issue of *Library Hi Tech* (1987) did contain several articles on the design impact of the new technologies. Others, notably Richard W. Boss (1987) have emphasized the new user needs for space in which computers can be used effectively. It is all the more surprising, therefore, that William Dix, speaking at a seminar on "Accommodating Technology: Space Planning for the Modern Library," sponsored by PALINET, should conclude that

> Architects, even as they make all of the necessary provisions for new technologies, should still be designing comfortable and humane spaces where people can browse among the stacks and curl up with a good book. (1990, p. 20)

The same *Library Journal* issue reports awards given to library buildings which honor traditional values. Two of the standard architectural books, Godfrey Thompson's *Planning and Design of Library Buildings* (2nd ed., 1977), and Michael Browne's *Libraries, Architecture and Equipment,* (1970), are now more than 20 years old. Even Mickey Palmer's *Architect's Guide to Facility Planning* (1981) is still behind current trends. On the face of its, given the other comments about the future, this is a startling lack.

Kaser suggests that we are currently in a design limbo, waiting for a new paradigm to emerge. He attributes that hiatus not only to uncertainty about the ways libraries will function but also to a general uncertainty about the academy—its goals, its components, its style. He may be right, but it raises the concern that we are likely to go on building old-style libraries well past the time when we should have found a new paradigm. The result may well be some kind of dinosaur that fossilizes or it may lead to having the library bypassed in favor of smart or expert systems. Professors and college administrators are as responsible as librarians, for they continue to place their emphasis on owning books, often at the expense of almost everything else, regardless of the financial problems or of the future implications for building construction.

This problem surfaced in a different way when the ACRL Committee was working on a revision of the University Library Standards. After considerable discussion the Committee decided that no quantitative standards could possibly be either adequate or universal (*Standards,* 1989). The old formulas for collections, reader spaces and budgets were developed in pre-electronic days and could, at best, be only partial guides to the future. The committee ended up with a librarians' version of the architect's dictum "form follows function." That implied that each university would have to work out its own destiny with its institutional officers, and the standards provided guidelines and questions to be used in the process. Many librarians felt that they had been sabotaged— without figures to refer to they felt helpless—yet the committee felt that there was no other way in which to address the startling differences among universities and their libraries. This is in line with the Critical Theory application to library planning supported by Ernest DeProspro, revisited in several of the essays in *Library Performance* (1990), which reminds us that there are no prescriptive ways of planning.

For several generations of library buildings, the principal determinants have been the numbers of volumes and the numbers of readers to be incorporated into the plans. Staff and workspace needs were derived from those two factors. Projections were based on models established in the 1950s and 1960s, for example a collection-growth goal of 5 percent a year, or 50,000 volumes per doctoral program. No-one, as far as the author can tell, has ever pointed out the implications of such models at the extremes: Harvard, for example, to meet the 5 percent figure should be adding 1,000,000 volumes a year and building a new library every couple of years to hold them, while small, special purpose universities, or polytechnics should be able to get along on 5-10,000 volumes a year. Neither figure makes sense in relation to need or to financial capability. Rather it encourages the large to grow larger and the small to remain small, despite the fact that faculty and students at either institution need the same kind of library support to do well. Moreover, librarians have begun to refine these definitions anyway. They have become more specific in defining volume equivalents—films, archives, microforms, maps—but nowhere has there been a systematic attempt to incorporate these into planning guidelines. Each medium has its own space requirements, both for storage and for use, and each has a role to play within the library, but from the two major statistical annuals (from ARL and ACRL) one would never suspect this diversity.

Similarly, librarians now have to think differently about "readers." In fact the term "user" may be more accurate, since people using the library may be looking at microforms, watching films, or using computer terminals, consulting the catalog, asking reference questions or any number of other activities. This range suggests a different approach to use than is inherent in the word "readers." The computer has introduced another factor which finally calls into question the volume and the reader as building determinants. If an index or text is online and the would-be user has an office or home terminal must he or she come to the library to use either. As the author pointed out over 10 years ago in a wrap-up address at the RTSD "Preconference on Acquisitions for the Eighties" (ALA, New York, 1980), information has become fluid. At the ACRL, New England Regional Conference at Providence, in 1984, he enlarged on this idea, (Martin, 1984) pointing out that when almost all information was in codex form it was simpler and more efficient to bring the user to the information, since the latter required a great deal of space and had to be organized. Now, at an increasing rate, it is becoming possible to move the information to the user.

In addition, librarians have begun to realize that the most serious library users take their books away with them, unless they are fortunate enough to have a library room or carrel of their own. Browsing and consulting reference books and bibliographic tools are still activities carried out in the library, though even these functions will be changed by the computer, but they need different accommodations from reading. Those multitudes of seats are mostly being used by students doing their homework, using their texts, or simply socializing, and who may *sometimes* use library resources and services. There is nothing wrong with having comfortable space for those purposes, but it has less to do with the function of the library than with its centrality on campus, and library space is far more costly to build and maintain than study space. None of this is meant to imply that the author does not read books (an average of four a week) or that libraries in the future will have not have books and readers, only that librarians have to think more clearly about these components in relation to the new ones that are emerging, if they are to design effective libraries.

If this thesis is even partly correct, what new factors will come into play? These factors, none entirely new, will be service-oriented. They will be less concerned with what the library is than with what is does, perhaps more correctly with what it enables people to do. In this sense they reflect the concern with performance measures that has resulted in *Measuring Academic Library Performance* (1990). In general terms they are:

- Access to information
- User training
- Specialized assistance to users.

ACCESS AS A FACTOR

Access includes not only physical access, but electronic access, whether from within the library or elsewhere. It includes the traditional concepts of reading, browsing, and borrowing, but extends them to include database searching, photocopying, electronic transfer, telefacsimile, telecommunications in general, and assistance in finding and using resources and services. In addition, as librarians have become increasingly aware, access is not the same as ownership, it may mean sending people elsewhere, using machines, or bringing in materials from other libraries for use by local users. The increasing complexity of information storage requires multiple forms of access, often mediated by machines or people, and may take place in a variety of settings ranging from an individual workstation to media-viewing rooms and computer classrooms. Not all of these may be in the library, though they will be linked to it by a number of telecommunication networks. Access is no longer, to put it starkly, entering the library through a door.

TRAINING AS A FACTOR

The multiplying kinds of information sources imply more sophistication in their use and also a much higher level of training in what is often referred to as "library literacy." Whereas, in the past, a faculty member could, and often did, bring a group of students into the library, introduce them to a few key reference works, show them the card catalog, show them the relevant portion of the stacks, and refer them in passing to the reference and interlibrary loan staff. Now that is scarcely the beginning. As graduate students they would also have to familiarize themselves with the bibliographic requirements of their discipline, but they seldom came to grips with the entire world of bibliography. As we have come to realize, there are innumerable bibliographic systems, each with its own peculiarities, and they must somehow be made accessible to all. The variations in entry, access codes, and search strategies are legion. New users of libraries and systems require help with this jungle and even regular users need to be brought up-to-date from time to time. (Turner, 1990) There are many ways of meeting such needs. Some require training space (perhaps academic libraries should also emulate public libraries in providing literacy training), others require individual attention, and some can be met by expert systems or by including more assistance programs in the OPAC. There is some truth in the suggestion that librarians resist expert systems, as having the power to replace them, but all would gain by their incorporation into library design (Aluri, 1988).

SPECIALIZED NEEDS AS A FACTOR

Some idea of the range of possibilities can be gained from Figure 1. This figure divides functions, somewhat arbitrarily perhaps, into automated and personal. The intention is to emphasize the degree of personal interaction needed. We do have to remember both that automated services are developed by people, and that people providing direct services often use automated products. The difference, however, is that most automated services are designed to be used

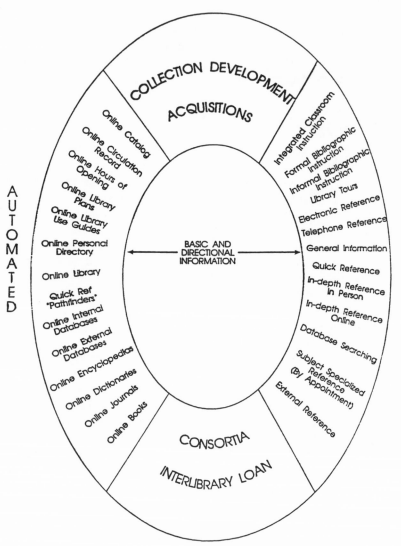

Figure 1. Reference and Information Functions

without personal intervention, while personal services depend on individual personal skills. Many of the latter relate to instruction, where most still find direct personal communication more persuasive (though interactive TV or Computer programs may change this), but many relate to the kinds of specialized knowledge that people accumulate over time. There is still the inescapable fact that the majority of human knowledge remains in printed format and may never be computer-analysed to the degree where people become superfluous in its location and interpretation.

Planning Implications

The library implications of these kinds of needs are twofold. First, effective automation depends on people, and those people require somewhere to work. It also requires space for the central computer equipment, though this may not always be in the library. And it is not always recognized that Local Area Networks require machine and people room. Some of these issues are ably covered by Boss (1987).

Those workrooms have become much more sophisticated and complex. All of us have noticed, for example, how many boxed books of programs, software, and instructions accompany computers, while the space for work encompasses much more than the computer table (Cohen, 1981). Second, the increase in automation has not decreased the need for people, though it may have changed job assignments and skills, and may have caused physical movement by relocating activities. It has also changed many spatial relationships. On a very simple level, it is no longer essential for catalogers to be near the card catalog and reference librarians with a terminal have access to bibliographic information on a level never before possible. How librarians can or should deal with such newly acquired flexibility is a perplexing problem.

The physical requirements of the workplace are no longer the only determinant of location. Because universities are investing in Wide Area and Local Area Networks it is possible to carry on the same or related activities in different locations with equal ease. An interesting series of administrator, librarian, technologist interactions is reported in Layton (1989), which uses case studies to explain the extensive use of new information technologies and their effects. None of these, however, address completely the need for personal interface. As Sheila Creth said at the ACRL NEC Fall Conference in Worcester (1990), she now expects librarians to be more mobile, to move to the classroom, or work with faculty in their own offices, so even more walls and divisions are being lowered or abolished. If people are expected to move about it would seem imprudent to place their home offices on the 10th floor, or to put them where they must traverse the whole library while on the way to an appointment.

Now we need to see what these new factors mean for library buildings. The old emphases on collections and seats implied a building based on the library as a warehouse. The new emphasis on use implies designs based on what users need and want. This has, of course, always been the theoretical basis for library buildings, but it has been turned upside down by the removal of one of the basic elements, the enormous dependence on physical access to the stacks. The millions of volumes had to be central to the building, but now we find that personally based services are more central. As Lyman put it:

> A book is something in a fixed graphic form in a fixed location. It is the book's nature for the author to dominate its reader. Programmers, however, want the reader to dominate the author (*Considerations in Planning*, p. 18).

The same applies to the resulting buildings. Book-derived buildings dominate the user. Computer-derived buildings, if properly designed, allow the user to dominate. Lyman is striving to convert the thought into substance in the teaching library being installed at the University of Southern California.

QUALITY OF THE WORKPLACE AS A FACTOR

Given this kind of shift, there will be much more emphasis on the quality of workspace, not only for staff but for users. Over the past few years we have learned more than we ever wanted to know about productivity and health, in the process creating a new science—Ergonomics—which has become a driving force in building design. A brief overview of developments up to ten years ago can be found in *Ergonomics* (1984). The new machines involve far more than the eyes, though we have now discovered that our old ways were not too good, even for simple reading. For those who have to spend hours at a terminal posture is important, and the placement of equipment. Lighting has become much more important and we need more attention to glare, reflection, and shadow. Machines are also noisy and give off heat. They have wires and cables attached and make any room, no matter how attractive it was, into an appalling mess unless carefully handled. Extensive consideration is given to these concerns in Cohen (1983). A simple but significant preautomation example comes to mind. At one library we had bought 40 single pedestal well desks for typists and secretaries, only to find that, three months later, when the typewriters ordered at the same time finally arrived, they would no longer fit in the wells! By great good fortune the desks could, however, accommodate terminals until they too changed, and the library had to cope with all the other paraphernalia that comes with automation. Most standard furniture is no longer appropriate for libraries, and suppliers have not yet developed the necessary substitutes. It is significant to note that one of the better texts in the field (Pierce, 1980), though published barely a decade ago, has only two pages devoted to computer equipment.

Traditional

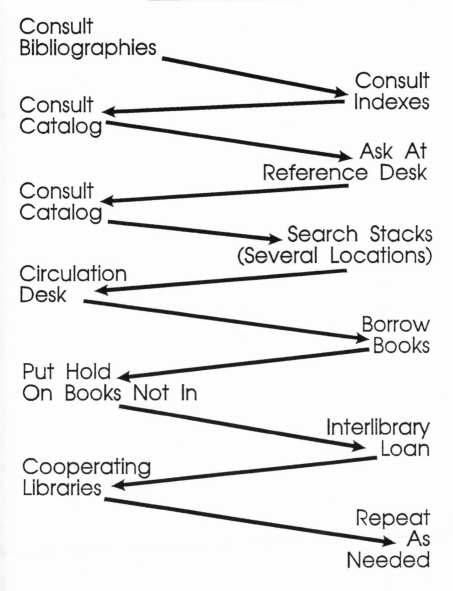

Consult
Bibliographies

Consult
Indexes

Consult
Catalog

Ask At
Reference Desk

Consult
Catalog

Search Stacks
(Several Locations)

Circulation
Desk

Borrow
Books

Put Hold
On Books Not In

Interlibrary
Loan

Cooperating
Libraries

Repeat
As
Needed

Figure 2. Library User Search

Emphasis on users and workflow implies user-friendly design. Architectural statements are no longer relevant if they get in the way of good working conditions. Library stacks have always been obstacle races. The size of research libraries implies an inordinate amount of walking around. With automated catalogs one of the major sites has lost its importance, though research libraries will still, for some time, have to cope with card catalogs for unconverted items, often in sites that have long been inadequate. Circulation desks may soon go the same way, as we introduce self-charging techniques and the circulation area is likely to become more of a problem-resolution area. Ease of movement will still be important, but it will take on different patterns. Reading rooms, with rows of long tables will become obsolete, replaced by smaller areas of work-stations. Functional differences will become blurred, as users expect to find the same help at any service location. When the stacks were a predominant feature, everything else tended to be put where it did not interfere with that central fact. Now it is no longer good enough to have media rooms, microforms and the like in spare corners.

TECHNOLOGY AS A FACTOR

All of this is conditioned by the massive incorporation of technology. Terminals, database workstations, COM files and the like intermingle with books and journals. The new reference area is no longer composed of bookstacks and index tables. Instead it may principally be directed towards electronic tools, each needing its own accommodation—and a degree of isolation. Buildings which did not have an electrical core are finding it difficult to handle these changes, especially those with poured concrete pillars and solid concrete floors. Expansion has become a much more serious problem, since now it means not only setting up a new stack but providing for electrical fitments and chairs where such were never before contemplated. Moving such equipment is a great deal more difficult and more expensive even than moving stacks, Microform rooms without expansion space simply have to be relocated, since it is impossible to work in conditions where material has continually to be transported to be useable. Though these may sound like constraints as serious as those of the old bookstack, they arise only because we have continued to build libraries with the book first in mind. The three foot bookshelf has dominated modular planning, even though that measurement is no longer useful for other media, and is counterproductive in terms of computer workspaces. Nor is it possible to shift items like microform cabinets or map-cases to areas not built to carry such loads. The 150 lb per sq ft that suffices for books in open stacks is incapable of bearing other heavier loads, which reduces flexibility almost to zero. This point is emphasized by Beckman (1990). To help people use the library most effectively such barriers must be removed.

The modern library most closely resembles a maze. The novels of Eco and Borges are a realistic appraisal of their condition. The numbers of activities and things that have to be accommodated are many, so it is not surprising that directional information should take up a lot of time. Still, we should be able to do a better job of directing people. The structure itself should help in this task, impossible when so many departments and services are squirrelled away in corners. It is impossible always to have clear lines of sight in a very large building, but every effort has to be made to ensure that corners, pillars and stacks do not intrude on frequently travelled paths. Librarians have tended to be very discreet in their use of signs and may have to learn from department stores and similar places. These kinds of directional needs are discussed in Levine (1982). Even worse, far too many libraries do not update such information. The author has only too often looked at very well designed maps and brochures, only to discover that they are outdated. Yes, it costs money to print new editions, but it costs even more money to have people wandering around asking for directions.

How often have you been in a lobby where the lines of people waiting to be checked out have interfered with those of people trying to get in? Most lobbies were not designed with security in mind and libraries have become overconscious of the need for such protection. It costs money to keep two entrances open, but the institution should be made aware that congestion at one entrance also costs the institution much in terms of time lost by users. These and other issues must be addressed if the library is to become a truly user-friendly place. Among the most important of the other issues is accommodating the handicapped. Most traditional library designs are impossible for them to use. Though many barriers are attitudinal, barrier-free building design is essential. With the passing of the Americans with Disabilities Act, even more pressure can be expected to be placed on libraries to provide equal access. No-one is yet entirely sure what the effects are likely to be, but new libraries and redesigned libraries will be the first to feel them. Useful suggestions are given in Velleman (1990), and there have been several conferences and special sessions on the topic.

SPATIAL RELATIONSHIPS AS A FACTOR

The changes in information technology have also changed spatial relationships. Since the card catalog no longer has to be in a central location, must its replacement occupy the same prime space? This mode of replacement is common largely because the layout of most libraries included a central space for the card catalog, a space that was difficult to reuse for any other purpose. The combination of location and tradition has kept most users in the habit of starting their library work in the catalog area regardless of whether that

Manual

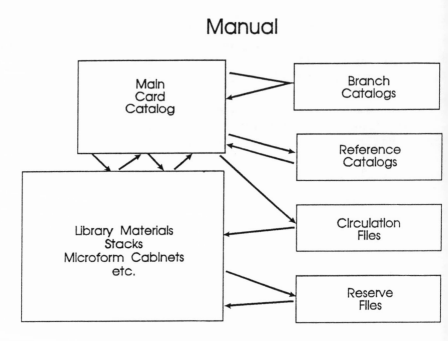

Automated

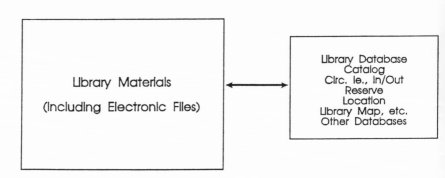

Figure 3. Motion and Time

is, in fact, the best place to start. Figure 3 indicates some of the changes involved by the switch to automated catalogs.

Since the catalog now can, instead, be distributed through the building, it is no longer necessary to start from a central location. That means helping users to develop new strategies, but it can also free space for a central information service area, something that is sadly lacking in most libraries. Staff economies are forcing most libraries to reduce the numbers of service points, which means that, in a large library, most of the space is depersonalized. To compensate, it may be necessary to provide peripatetic staff. It is certainly necessary to put much more information on the terminal, for example maps, directories, staff locations, and directional help screens.

Now that technical services staffs do not need to worry about keeping the cards filed, or consulting the card catalog, their location can be off-center, and indeed can be removed from the main building altogether. As self-service becomes possible for circulation, does the circulation desk still need to be so large or in so prominent a location in order to provide the needed services? Before too long it will be possible to provide electronic substitutes for reserve reading collections, which can result in a lot less library traffic and less congestion. Figure 4 suggests ways in which this might be done and their effects on library activity would be substantial. The Reserve Reading Room may become a thing of the past. Instead, there are likely to be many more spaces for intensive study, using hypertext and similar aids.

ARCHITECTURAL CONCEPTS OF THE LIBRARY

The architectural implications of these changes affect the whole concept of the library building. A very interesting study of architectural attitudes to libraries was produced by Jones (1982) discussing the concepts behind the work of Walter Netsch at Northwestern and The University of Illinois, Chicago Circle. Of Northwestern he says,

> Although stylistically elegant, users complain that the complicated layout, extensive use of interior corridors, and inadequate lighting lead to a building that prevents users from finding their way within it, (p. 208)

and concludes that

> Librarians need to be alert to the consequences of accepting designs that depart from conventions by which much of the world judges buildings, and they should ask themselves how the design promoted the uses to which a building will be put (p. 220).

The situation at Chicago is further explored by Daugherty (1989), who follows the building through its three stages. An interesting revisitation by an architect

Manual

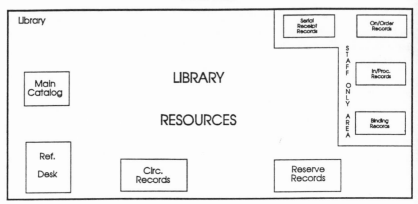

Automated

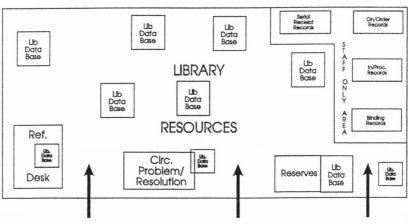

Personal Workstation Access: Office; Classroom; Dorm

Figure 4. Bibliographic Information Location

is provided by Oringdulph (1990), who is particularly concerned about monumentality, and failures to provide adequately for workspace.

When the central fact was the collection in its stacks, it was relatively simple to develop a plan that would place all other areas round them, though, as Kaser has remarked, too often the stacks were simply fitted into spaces left over after the architect had expressed his own ideas in monumental reading rooms and the like. On the other hand many libraries are cursed with separated stacks having little or no connection to the rest of the library. This kind of architectural thinking is exemplified by the stack areas at the library of the Central Connecticut State University, where the building exemplifies a divisional approach. Each floor consisted of a high ceilinged reading room, with back-up book stacks on two levels. No interconnections were provided between floors so, as the collections grew beyond the capacity of each level, the building interrelationships have become actual barriers to study.

The idea of open access intermingled reading rooms with books, and in doing so made much more difficult the logical arrangement of the contents. Divisional arrangements, which seemed to meet the wishes of the faculty, usually resulted in overcrowding or hard to use annexes as the original spaces were filled. As libraries filled up, it became more and more difficult to maintain classified arrangements without imposing a lot of travel between floors. Many libraries then resorted to compact storage on-site or distant storage buildings for older material, both of which solutions interfere with browsing capacity and result in a sort of shuttle traffic in materials. None of these problems will go away, and we will have to find some means of reconciling access to collections with access to all the other necessary services. Some idea of the changes involved can be gained from Figure 4, which outlines some of the changes that have occurred.

USER-STAFF INTERACTIONS AS A FACTOR

Early libraries relied on the user to provide self service and offered only skeletal staff support. Consequently, they provided little workspace for staff members, often in otherwise unuseable corners. Typical was the reference office behind a little desk, which was supposed to cope with the highly varied types of transactions that took place. Other reference staff members might well be hidden away on another floor, and new activities, such as database searching, might be placed in yet other locations. Circulation desks tended to be fixed in place and monumental in nature, often because in that way they were part of the construction cost and not of furniture and equipment costs, but they could not be used to house terminals because no provision had been made for electrical support.

With the advent of electronic information, user-staff interaction has become the rule rather than the exception, requiring totally new working conditions.

Whereas the old emphasis was on the "quiet" library, the modern library is likely too full of conversation, machine noise, and movement. High, echoing rooms are inappropriate, as is having consulting areas next to quite study areas. The workspaces themselves have changed in nature. High desks and chairs do not function very well (quite apart from inducing many health problems) because of the need for personal interaction as machine records are examined and explained. The cables, telephones and keypads that are now standard do not fit into standard desks, and the cables can be hazardous if they are not covered. The same, incidentally, is true of user tables, desks, and carrels. The old 2 × 3 table does not accommodate a terminal, a printer and the books or paper being used. In the same way as new equipment had to be designed for microform areas, new equipment has to be developed for computer areas. Some attempts have been made, but so far none has been totally successful. Only too often, furniture designed for general office purposes is used for the library where it is not capable of meeting the work needs of the users.

Modular Planning

Modular planning seemed to be the answer, since it seemed to mean that area use could be switched with minimal difficulty. This has not always been the case, and, since libraries are in constant change, it has been difficult to exchange books for people, switch microforms with periodicals, or to move computers into an unwired area. For one thing the floor load factors are different. For another the HVAC and other support needs differ. The lighting patterns appropriate to stack areas are different from those needed in a computer study area or a microform area. In many ways what was practiced was not modular planning, where the modules could be interchanged, but block planning, with the shape of the blocks deriving from the size of a standard bookstack. A truly modular building will have all factors in common. That, of course, increases the construction price, but it does mean that re-use of space is simpler. That solution is not, of course, available for existing libraries, and the adaptation of existing spaces to new uses will continue to be an architectural challenge.

ENVIRONMENTAL CONCERNS

Librarians have become increasingly aware of the problems associated with preservation. The temperature and humidity needs of library materials differ greatly from the needs of people, which suggests that, in some instances, libraries may need to return to closed stacks, at least for rare and brittle books. More attention is being given to mechanized, automated book storage systems, but so far these have proved somewhat expensive unless receiving heavy use, and most research collections are not so used. They may, however, be useful for core collections or for annexes. A partial exception is offered by the example of the California State University at Northridge and that model could well be further explored by architects. The new public library at Bordeaux, France, makes extensive use of electronic retrieval, though that appears to respond to a different style of library use more common in Europe than in the United States. Delayed access, like delayed gratification is not an American way. Nevertheless, the high cost of open library stack space and the problems of preservation may well force a rethinking of this style, at least in the major research libraries.

Microforms, computers, films, artwork, all need specific environmental treatment which in turn means much more complicated HVAC controls, leading to the smart building. The addition of large numbers of computers, printers and other such devices upsets the balance of most HVAC systems and the building design is mostly such that only palliative treatment is possible. Better understanding of the health needs of workers has led to calls for extensive changes in office layout. Concern for the internal environment will therefore have to be much greater in the future.

Electrical needs have recurred in earlier paragraphs, but their importance in the library of the future cannot be over emphasized. These kinds of issues are addressed in several articles in *Library Hi Tech,* for example Kapp (1987) and Novak (1987). Buildings where the only power sources are on columns, or where offices have to exist in a jungle of power poles simply frustrate both workers and users. They also make the effective re-use of space either impossible or prohibitively expensive. Even recent buildings have not taken advantage of the developments in Local Area Networks. The author remembers being told that we could not have all that wire, it simply wasn't in the estimates, besides what would we do with it, weren't people going to read books anymore. Retrofitting proved expensive and could not meet all the needs anyway in a poured concrete building. All staff need to be linked, with one another, with users, and with outside resources, such as the computer center or a bibliographic utility. In many cases, Interlibrary Loan for example, more traffic is likely to come in online than by mail and the needs include FAX machines (the newest models, again computer-related, copy onto real paper), terminals, laser printers and optical scanners. An entire collection may be on disk (one of several varieties) and must support several simultaneous users, together with the means for producing floppy disks or paper printouts. The total power requirements of libraries will increase dramatically.

All these changes imply changes in the proportions allocated to different functions, as suggested by Beckman (1990). They also imply a new way of planning, which begins from what the user needs and how the library plans to meet those needs, rather than from figures about size. The people space, now mostly allocated to "reading,' may increase, or may remain the same, but its uses will change and with those uses the nature of the space required. There are likely to be many more rooms for teaching or group activity, and all spaces will have to be wired. The old reading rooms with long tables and green lampshades, no matter how nostalgically they may be remembered, are now out of date. As Oringdulph remarks,

> In these formal libraries [the Bibliotheque Nationale], acoustics were impossible, and lighting was monumental... Library designers still have difficulty in deciding on appropriate spatial volumes, and acoustics continue to be compromised by the desire for "architectural" spaces (p. 72).

Environmental needs may move us away from rows of carrels lining the stack walls. We may need automatic retrieval systems, and better internal delivery systems, to make up for restricted access. These systems all take up room and have to be planned carefully, since they are also relatively immovable, and also control the location of many other spaces. A vertical transportation system, for example, requires that access to it be in a standard location on each floor. Too often elevators or stairways were located peripherally and created internal traffic problems, as well as personal security risks. On the other hand a central transportation core may enhance security but adds rigidity to the building design. Such situations work against totally flexible buildings, and must be taken into consideration in planning.

There are also many implications for librarians in these changes. The first, which has been widely covered in the literature, is openness to change. How this is handled will vary from library to library, but the underlying theme is that the library of tomorrow will probably not resemble the library of today. With an emphasis on library literacy we can expect to have a more mobile staff, working with groups and individuals both inside the library and outside. Continuing attempts to reduce the barriers between Technical and Public Services have not yet been reflected in library design, and the space needs of the two kinds of activity are different. What has happened is a rapid increase in the proportion of non-librarian staff in Technical Services, working in teams with totally redesigned workspaces. Terminals instead of typewriters are the most obvious aspect of this change. Their appearance, however, disguises the fact that little has changed. As Brown said,

> Almost everything we've done in libraries, and much of what we've done in the use of automation technologies, has been the automation of what we are comfortable with, of our traditional ways of doing things. We've automated the catalog, we've automated the library. In effect, we make more efficient what we traditionally do (*Considerations in Planning*, p. 24).

The workspaces are the same and for the most part set up in the same fashion, even though the technology demands a totally new approach. Of course that was probably inevitable when old space was simply being retrofitted, but we are in danger of reproducing the same space in new buildings, unless we look closely at the possibilities offered by change.

WORKING RELATIONSHIPS

The transfer of much information to electronic or micro format suggests a very different library space allocation. In fact much of the information is no longer even in the library. The "catalog" for example may actually be in the Computer Center, and the files that support database searching are often hundreds or thousands of miles away. Even the access terminals will not all be in the library, though they will be part of the network the library supports, an extension like and yet unlike a branch library. In most libraries OPAC terminals simply replaced the card catalog, perpetuating the idea of a single access point. If some card cabinets remained because retrospective conversion was incomplete this made sense, but when everything is online does the central catalog space still make sense? Of course nothing changes more slowly than habit, and most of us still think in terms of going to the catalog, to reference and the stacks. The patterns involved are sketched out in Figure 3, along with the potential inherent in the OPAC terminal. Can we work with this? How do we reconcile the existence of electronically stored data with the still dominant idea of the stack? The first means an emphasis on the individual workstation, the second on shared access. These emphases are not incompatible, but ignoring the difference may stultify library design.

The workstation exemplifies the new emphasis on people, since it provides a total service in one place, rather than scattered points of access and use. The future reference area will undoubtedly require many such workstations. Do they need to be in one place? What are their relationships to older print collections, the reference service point, or to the circulation area? How much help needs to be provided and in what way? These and similar questions will shape the future library. A further problem is that most reference information will continue to be available only in book format, with the corollary that many users, hooked on electronic information, may not be willing to use them. Librarians may find that they will be expected to carry out actual information searches, in much the same way as is now done in many special and public libraries.

Library staff can thus expect to enter new relationships with users, as guides and mentors, not always in person, and sometimes only through the design of expert systems. If many simple reference questions can be answered through the machine, how do we provide for the more sophisticated research question? The old reference desk seems ill-suited to that task. Instead we will need better designed offices for extended contact. Many users will also want help from a distance, and we will have to develop a new model for the telephone reference desk. Teaching the use of the new technology requires properly designed space, and so far computer classrooms resemble nothing so much as the old lecture room, only with lots of equipment. How many people can participate at the same time? We will learn the answer to that one pragmatically, and it may turn out to be fewer than the traditional classroom. A medical friend once said to the author that most courses in Medical Schools depended heavily on a large printed syllabus and she opined that most students could pass by memorizing it instead of going to class. If, as is commonly suspected, most of the data would change by the time the student graduated, what was the use of the syllabus and how could you keep it up to date? The same instrument online could become an interactive teaching tool, could be used with windows, and could be updated with ease. Medical curricula are changing to overcome that dilemma, and are instead emphasing problem-based study, which teaches how to learn and involves the library directly. The same model could be applied to many other disciplines and would radically change the role of the library and librarians. (Tompkins, 1990 and Lyman, 1990) It is likely that, in the future, many librarians will spend more time out of the library than in it, and, with electronic support, will not have to feel isolated, are more than the teacher feels lost away from the office.

Combined, these factors suggest that there is a need for much more attention to workflow, both on the part of the staff and also the users. The contrasting movement patterns implied in Figure 3 place this in perspective. A building designed around the workstation will be very different from one based on collections and seats. Industrial models are not particularly helpful, since they have tended to perpetuate space models derived from the production line. Successive actions are no longer predominant, at least in the sense that they will be carried out by different people in different locations. Instead one person at a console will be able to complete a task. There is one significant drawback, in a library context, that is. Since each workstation occupies a good deal of room and stands alone much more space will be required to provide the same level of access as is represented by the current index table. They are also not ideal for use by groups, and, so far at least, have not reached the sophistication that would enable a user to duplicate the common scholarly situation of consulting many texts at once. These are real limitations and eventually they will be solved by technology, but in the meantime libraries will continue, as they always have, to incorporate yet one more element into their resources in a manner that is helpful to the user. We may expect to find the equivalents of the projection room and cinema, the individual video-station, and the headset becoming regular features of the reference service area. Architecturally it will require some skill to fit them in without turning the library into a factory or office. They also imply much more extended time in the library on the part of the user, who will consequently bring in other needed support—food, drink, more baggage—with all the associated space and health implications.

In effect, libraries will have to seek new organizational models for space as well as for staff. Some of these will have to reflect environmental needs as well. It is simply not possible to interfile all materials formats, because of their differing HVAC needs, and the different ways in which they are used. But the advent of electronic systems has made it necessary to provide better linkages, better ways of using or finding all that is needed, whatever format or location it is in. There will be problems of "turf" since many constituencies have vested interests in *their* part of the library. A prime example relating to the change in location of periodicals is discussed by Butcher and Kinch (1990). No matter how sensible a change may be there will always be opposition and care must be taken to explain the benefits.

SOCIAL AND BEHAVIORAL CONCERNS

Although there have been numerous references to behavioral and social implications above, it seems appropriate to gather them together in a separate statement. The first, and most important fact to be recognized is the need to include users in the planning process. The process itself is important. The library exists to fulfill user needs and, unless these are studied and understood, the library may very well hinder rather than help users, as suggested by Jones. It may be impossible to meet all needs, for example study space, but it is essential that all constituencies have input into the planning process. Second, organizational needs must be downplayed. In the past we have tended to look at ways in which to reflect the organization rather than at ways in which to make it more effective and productive. This reconsideration must also look at whether the individual units are appropriate, how they should be linked— the architectural term is adjacencies—and what their role is in relation to the whole. All this should be carried out with the user firmly in mind.

Examination of the ways in which staff and user interact should determine the ways in which spaces are designed, rather than precedent or existing patterns. The kinds of spaces needed for specific interactions must be acknowledged, since there are wide differences between transactions and the ways in which they are conducted. In addition traffic patterns should play a larger part than they have in the past.

Automation has changed many traditional activities and this should be recognized. The library is no longer a closed building but has connections that extend throughout the campus and into the external world. As a result it cannot be conceived as a closed system, but has to be constructed as part of an open network. This implies not only more attention to electrical work, but also a recognition that the work taking place within the library will be advanced or hindered by its design. The multiple information formats now common have special spatial requirements and the ways in which they are used require closer attention by planners or to user work habits.

The library staff, in adapting to these changes, has also developed different work styles, and the older work areas are inadequate. Work areas must now pay closer attention to health, productivity, privacy and the like. Many architects and administrators have tended to impose their own ideas on others, and in today's social climate that is no longer acceptable. Emphasis on individual space is important, but so is the fact that most library activities are the result of team effort. Quality of workspace is likely to become an issue in the very near future, if indeed it has not already become a factor in union negotiations. Despite the development of ergonomics, we have barely begun to grapple with the issues involved in planning workspace, and much more attention is needed, particularly in libraries which epitomise the information age.

Health, security and privacy issues have come to the fore. It is no longer acceptable to design buildings which present health and security hazards, especially for the handicapped. HVAC systems have not been very responsive, and buildings without windows or means of escaping from the closed environment of the office are counterproductive. Open, modular office landscapes have failed to consider the individual's concern with private space, with a resultant drop in productivity. Many layouts have equally failed to provide for the need for socialization, with the result that socialization took place in inappropriate areas. Unless these and similar concerns are addressed in building plans the resulting buildings will still prove inadequate.

SUMMARY

A library is a busy productive workunit. It is not a statement of architectural space, nor the embodiment of the library as the heart of the university. Rather it is an expression of the information-centered nature of society. Any plans should begin with this concept and go on from there. Unfortunately, most architects and administrators seldom use libraries. If they did they would see the inappropriateness of the immense atrium in the New York University's Bobst Library, or the problems caused by a plan which provides the Central Connecticut State University with its unconnected series of two-level stacks. More attention to staff and user input would help reduce such preconceptions.

Quite apart from the new libraries likely to be needed over the next 20 years (the life cycle of a library building) there are many libraries which desperately need to be improved and made useful in the new information age. The field is large and those involved should be trying to find answers to the many questions that remain unresolved. Then we can indeed find the new library paradigm that can take us into the twenty-first century.

REFERENCES

The Academy Library In Transition, edited by P. Lynch. New York: Neal-Schuman, 1989.

Association of College and Research Libraries. New England Chapter. (1990 Fall Conference) Worcester, MA.

Beckman, Margaret, "Cost Avoidance" in Library Building Planning, *Canadian Library Journal,* (1990). 47(6): 405-409.

Boss, Richard W. *Information Technologies and Space Planning for Libraries and Information Centers.* Boston: G.K. Hall, 1987.

Brown, Roland C.W. "Programs and Services." *CWRU Report,* (1990). 24

Browne, Michael. *Libraries, Architecture and Equipment.* New York: Praeger, 1977.

Butcher, Karyle E., and Michael P. Kinch, "Who Calls the Shots? The Politics of Reference Reorganization," *Journal of Academic Librarianship* 16(5) (Nov 1990): 280-284.

Cohen, Elaine, and Aaron Cohen. *Automation, Space Management and Productivity.* New York: Bowker, 1981.

_____. *Planning the Electronic Office.* New York: McGraw-Hill, 1983.

Creth, Sheila. Keynote speech at the Association of College and Research Libraries. New England Chapter. (Fall 1990 Meeting), Worcester, MA.

Curzon, Susan C. (1989) *Managing Change.* New York: Neal-Schuman.

Daugherty, Allen, "University Library Building," in *The Academic Library in Transition.* Beverly P. Lynch, ed. New York: Neal-Schuman, (1989). 282-304

Dix, William, *Reference in article "Accommodating Technology: Space Planning for the Modern Library" reporting a PALINET seminar in Library Journal* 115(21): (1990). 20

Dowling, Kenneth E. *The Electronic Library.* New York: Neal-Schuman, 1984.

Ergonomics: The Science of Productivity and Health. John L. Burch Ed., (Lawrence, KS: The Report Store.) which provides capsule reviews and tables of contents of books up to that time, 1984.

Farewell to Alexandria: Solutions to Space, Growth and Performance Problems of Libraries. edited by Daniel Gore. Westport, CT: Greenwood, 1976.

Fraley, Ruth A., and Carol Lee Anderson. *Library Space Planning.* New York: Neal-Schuman, 1990.

Integrated Planning for Campus Information Systems. edited by Daphne N. Layton. Dublin, Ohio: OCLC, 1989.

Jones, William G., Academic Library Planning: Rationality, Imagination, and Field Theory in the Work of Walter Netsch-A Case Study, *College & Research Libraries* 51(3) (May 192): 207-220.

Kapp, David. Designing Academic Libraries: Balancing Constancy and Change. *Library Hi-Tech* 5:82-5. (Winter 1987)

Kaser, David. Academy Library Buildings: Their Evolution and Prospects, *Advances in Library Administration and Organization,* Vol. 7 edited by Gerard B. McCabe and Bernard Kreisman. Greenwich, CT: JAI Press, pp. 149-160, 1988.

Levine, Marvin, "You-are-here Maps: Psychological Considerations," *Environment and Behavior* 14(2) (March 1989): 221-237.

Library Administration & Management. Issues for June, 1987 (1:3), and for Spring 1990 (4:2).

Library Architecture: Striking a Balance, *Library Journal* 115(21) (Dec. 1990): 20.

Library Performance, Accountability, and Responsiveness: Essays in Honor of Ernest R. DeProspo. (Norwood, NJ: Ablex). Particularly apposite are the concluding remarks by Ellen Altman, 1990.

Library Trends. "Thematic Issue on Library Buildings," Fall, 1987 (36,2), edited by Anders Dahlgren.

Lyman, Peter. "Considerations in Planning the Library of the Future." *Report of an Invitational Conference Held at Case Western Reserve University* (September 1989). (Cleveland: Office of the President, May 1990), p. 18. The whole report is essential reading.

Martin, Murray S. (1984) "Library Relations in Electronic Times," *ACRL NEC Newsletter*, 33:2-5.

"The Model Research Library: Planning for the Future,' *Journal of Academic Librarianship*, 15(3): 132-138, 1989 and "Reactions to The Model Research Library: Planning for the Future,' *Journal of Academic Librarianship*, 15(4): (1989). 196-203.

Novak, Gloria et al. "The Forgiving Building: A Library Building Consultants' Symposium on the Design, Construction, and Remodelling of Libraries to Support a High-Tech Future," *Library Hi Tech*, 5 (4): (1987). 77-99

Oringdulph, Robert E., "Thoughts on Library Buildings and Their Parts," *Library Administration & Management*, 4(2): (1990) 71-73.

Palmer, Mickey A. *The Architect's Guide to Facility Planning*, Washington , DC: American Institute of Architects, 1981.

Pierce, William S. *Furnishing the Library Interior*. New York: Dekker, 1980.

Standards for University Libraries and Evaluation of Performance, Chicago: ACRL, 1989. Reprinted from *College & Research Library News*, Sept. 1989.

Thompson, Godfrey. *Planning and Design of Library Buildings*, 2nd ed. New York: Nichols, 1977.

Tompkins, Phillip, "New Structures for Teaching Libraries," *Library Administration & Management*, 4(2) (Spring 1990): 77-81.

Turner, Ann, "Computer-assisted Instruction in Academic Libraries," *Journal of Academic Librarianship*, 15(6) (Jan. 1990): 352-354.

Van Horn, Nancy, et al. *Measuring Academic Library Performance*. Chicago: ALA, 1990.

Velleman, Ruth. *Meeting the Needs of People with Disabilities: A Guide for Librarians, Educators, and Other Service Professionals*. Phoenix, AZ: Oryx, 1990.

LIBRARY STORAGE:
ACHIEVING SYSTEMATIC CONSIGNMENTS

Cordelia W. Swinton

INTRODUCTION

A familiar household word for the final answer to the accumulation of superfluous artifacts and debris, "storage" has acquired a special connotation in academic and research libraries. Like the typical householder—and partly because our very profession involves collecting and shelving and preserving—librarians show a reluctance to weed or discard materials. To express it positively, we have a desire to keep as much material as possible covering as many subjects as possible available to as many users as possible.

The acquisitive behavior that results also reflects a need to rely on volume counts to achieve or retain accreditation; a need to maintain large collections so as to join various professional associations like the Association for Research Libraries; a natural, professional inclination to accommodate some scholar in search of some particularly arcane document; and a desire to save the cost and time it takes to borrow materials from another library.

For all these understandable reasons, academic libraries now bulge at the seams—often to the point where librarians find it difficult to locate materials crammed into crowded shelves. For students and researchers and librarians

Advances in Library Administration and Organization, Volume 12, pages 109-123.
Copyright © 1994 by JAI Press Inc.
All rights of reproduction in any form reserved.
ISBN: 1-55938-846-3

too, our collections must remain both accessible and easy to use. A majority of academic and research libraries continue to maintain open stacks, and to keep these collections easily usable, the shelves should remain no more than 80 percent full. To reduce the overcrowding, then, we must finally resolve to move some materials. But move them where?

Recognizing the need to confront overcrowding merely starts a long sequence of decisions that can collectively alleviate the pressure. For example, where do you plan to store the excess materials? On site? Off site? In a remote depository? Will your storage facility be a newly constructed unit? Will you own it or rent it? Can you suitably renovate an existing facility? Can you share space with any other academic or research unit? The list of considerations is long, but luckily it is finite. It is also based on a good deal of actual experience. Appendix 1 lists 14 colleges and universities that responded to an informal survey I conducted during 1991 over an E-Mail listserve. All of the respondents have consigned or are planning to consign large quantities of their lesser used materials to storage, and all have confronted the kinds of general choices this chapter sets forth.

FOUR GENERAL TYPES OF STORAGE FACILITIES

Meanwhile, having collected and examined moving procedure and storage destination options, and having chosen those that appear suitable under the prevailing circumstances, one must consider such additional, general issues as the politics, philosophy and planning of library storage. More specifically, one must consider the provision of an actual storage facility, the ease of access such a facility provides, the cost of storage, the type of shelving to use, and the environment attainable in the available facilities. While one can attach various weights or priorities to each of these factors, one should consider all of them carefully. The next four sections discuss the four general types of storage facilities research and academic libraries select.

The On-site Storage Facility

Extra space within the current library presents the ideal storage choice for both librarians and users. It usually means they can get what they want pretty much when they want it. Furthermore, librarians find the selection and justification for storing materials away from open areas much easier to defend when the materials remain on site. The new facility at Northridge California is an example of high-density, on-site storage. At Northridge, a user can select an item from the online public access catalog (OPAC) and activate a retrieval process from the Automated Storage and Retrieval System (AS/RS) with just a few keystrokes. The procedure is ideal, and if the system works as planned it may well become the model for future storage facilities.

Unfortunately, a far more common on-site storage method involves boxing materials and shoving them into some closet, classroom or steam tunnel, with a faint and fading paper trail and problematic access. Such informal storage methods obviously inconvenience a patron requesting the material, to say nothing of the material itself—classrooms, closets and steam tunnels rarely providing the climate controls appropriate for preservation.

The Off-site Storage Facility

Off-site storage raises different and more complex issues than on-site storage raises. Both the most difficult and the most important is the need to select the materials to be moved out into storage. Almost as important, however, is the distance between the storage facility and the main library. Distance here equates to time as well as cost. A walk across campus is quicker and cheaper than a twenty-mile round-trip truck drive. On the other hand, a nearby off-site facility may require staffing and its attendant costs.

Librarians should also weigh the cost per volume of materials stored off site against the cost of resorting to interlibrary loans, remembering as they do so that students and faculty members rarely concern themselves with such matters. They want and can sometimes demand fast access or at least a convenient method of recovering what they need for their research. To patrons like these, retrieving materials from a storage building on campus is preferable to waiting for materials from an off-campus facility or from another library. Instinctively, they consider materials housed off campus to be "out of the loop" even when the turn-around service time is quick.

The New Storage Facility

A facility constructed for the specific purpose of storing overflow library materials under optimum conditions at maximum density with easy retrievability and transferability—now here we have a solution far superior to an abandoned building meant for some entirely different purpose and requiring a complete overhaul.

But the architect of this new storage facility has, of course, made certain that its floors can withstand the extraordinary weight of books and shelving. The climate control system will, of course, be keeping the temperature between 55 and 65 degrees and the relative humidity between 45 and 55 percent in all weather and without short-term fluctuations. The lighting will minimize or eliminate ultra-violet rays. The air will be filtered and circulated throughout the collection—let us say (taking Harvard's Depository as an example), six times an hour (Kennedy and Stockton, 1991).

Patrons will no doubt gain access to materials housed in this new building either through a document delivery service or at a designated visitation site.

The shelving just alluded to will be high-density, mechanically assisted mobile shelving, and robotically equipped for retrieving material, thus accommodating the greatest possible number of volumes per square foot.

A librarian would be wise to make sure requests can be telefaxed or E-mailed to such a facility for quick retrieval and delivery. The delivery service could include digitization capability for articles and documents, a telefacsimile service, or Ariel™ transmission to the requesting library or patron. If the library decides to permit or encourage patron visits, it should provide an area where walk-in visitors can use the materials with some semblance of solitude. On-site photocopying should also be installed (whether or not patrons are invited) with "preservation copiers" featuring slanted copier edges to avoid the cracked bindings that result when the spines of old books are held against the flat edge of the standard photocopiers.

The Used Storage Facility

Those libraries—all too many—without the resources for a new storage building may find themselves renting abandoned warehouses, classrooms or even grocery stores, in which case they should take special note of several additional considerations.

Can (for example) the floors withstand the weight of books and shelving, far heavier than widgets, students, or canned goods and cereal boxes? (Spacesaver estimates that a filled, single-tiered book stack weighs 35 pounds per cubic foot, and that the floor load for a filled range may reach 150 pounds per square foot. Compact shelving produces floor loads of between 200 and 250 pounds per square foot.)

Does the roof leak? (The flat roofs of low, single-floor warehouses often do.) Is the building accessible to trucks or moving vans, ideally offering a traditional loading dock? If it has more than one floor, does the building include a suitable heavy-duty freight elevator? Are its pipes and wiring sound? Does the heating and air conditioning work satisfactorily—which is to say, reliably and in season? Can you detect any sign of invasive insects or rodents? Do the windows require caulking and sun shielding? Are all the entrances securable? Do the fire alarms and sprinkler systems work? What kinds of communication capabilities exist? How safe is the surrounding neighborhood, and how reliable are the fire and police services there? Do the zoning ordinances permit the storage of library materials in that area?

Here's a particularly important question: Do you expect to share the storage building with anyone else? If so, take the time to discover what else will be going on around and among your library materials. The Pennsylvania State University's on-campus Library Annex at University Park established a compact storage facility on the ground floor of a building that also houses a combustion laboratory, an Anthracite Institute, and the Theater Arts

Production Shop where students paint the scenery flats and props for their dramas and reviews. This shop is located directly—and ominously—above the library storage area, and on one occasion, the incipient thespians left a faucet dripping over a long weekend. Luckily, no materials suffered damage, but stains still mark the walls and floor where the water seeped in from above.

Penn State is currently preparing an off-campus facility, a former A&P grocery store to be precise, for additional storage. We expect to share this building with University Police Services, which intends to use its share of the space to store pieces of evidence too large and cumbersome for its on-campus office to accommodate. This evidence could include anything from beer kegs to auto wrecks. As you can well imagine, we have agreed to maintain discretely sealed and secured areas of our reclaimed grocery store.

In *The Great Divide: Challenges in Remote Storage* (1991, pp. 37-46), Wendy Pradt Lougee describes a library storage building at The University of Michigan that shared space with an amphibian lab, a cricket ranch, and a colony of brown recluse spiders. The moral here is to pick your neighbors carefully if you can, and in all cases reach some kind of understanding beforehand about your respective research and security needs.

STAFFING CONSIDERATIONS FOR ALL TYPES OF STORAGE FACILITIES

Meanwhile, some important storage facility considerations center on the staffing storage requires. If you plan to allow the public to use materials in a stored collection, you will want to station a staff member at this walk-in location. The expertise level of your staff and the associated labor expenditures will naturally depend upon the types of materials you store there and the extent of the service you expect to provide there. If you have installed compact, motorized shelving, you need someone who is handy with a screwdriver and can spot and fix (for example) a jammed microswitch. If you have an automated storage and retrieval system, you may want a person on hand who can address mechanical failures and perform routine maintenance chores.

In other words here is the ideal person for staffing an off-site storage facility: an accomplished artisan who (1) understands how to interpret bibliographical information from an on-line public access catalog; (2) knows the filing or shelving system in the storage area; (3) knows how to retrieve materials from the storage area; (4) is sensitive to the need to preserve often fragile materials and handles them gently; (5) is alert to such environmental danger signals as damp walls, excessive humidity, and temperature fluctuations; and (6) is, in general, a tractable, trainable person with a personal interest in and appreciation for the collection.

Both my reading and experience tell me that water is the commonest library storage problem. It can enter surreptitiously through leaky roofs, sweating walls, burst pipes, spring thaws, and undetected aquifers. Therefore, even with an on-site staff person, a storage area should include a water detection system connected to an alarm at the local fire department or police station. A person on hand who can detect a problem before any damage occurs is preferable to a mechanical alarm system. But leaks usually happen at the most inconvenient of times—which is to say, late at night and over long vacations.

Before renting a storage facility, if that is the choice you make, settle all these issues and arrange for all these needs well in advance. There is no point in storing materials if you thereby place them in danger of damage. You might as well discard them.

My research for this chapter uncovered a near paradigm of an off-site library storage facility. The University of Kentucky rents 32 acres of storage space twenty miles south of Lexington near Wilmore. The space is an abandoned underground rock quarry equipped with modern office accommodations, sodium lights, and a temperature and a humidity held constant in part by a subterranean stream. Utterly pest-free, the Kentucky facility is managed by a certified records keeper and employs a round-the-clock guard.

PLANNING FOR COOPERATIVE STORAGE

We earlier discussed the problems that arise when library materials must share space with different units and activities altogether—with a theatrical production shop or an entomology lab, for example. By contrast, "cooperative storage" refers to storage space shared by several different libraries, that space being remote from one, or most, or all of the cooperating libraries.

Participation in an arrangement like this requires careful planning and as the name of the arrangement implies, close, continuing cooperation. The University of California's Northern and Southern Regional Library Facilities, the New England Depository Library, and the new Harvard Depository are three current and prominent examples of cooperative storage arrangements. The newest, Harvard Depository, employs a storage and management firm to maintain the collections and keep them secure. Built in 1986, it uses an automated storage and retrieval system. A staff member on a mechanical lift (rather than an automated robotic "picker") retrieves the trays from their shelves. An excellent discussion of this and other remote cooperative storage facilities appears in *The Great Divide: Challenges in Remote Storage*, edited by James R. Kennedy and Gloria Stockton (American Library Association, 1991). A particularly strong contribution to this volume is the chapter by Barbara Graham entitled "Firmitas, Utilitas, et Frugalitas: The Harvard Depository" (Graham, 1991, pp. 27-39).

Claire Q. Bellanti, Director of Access Services at the University of California's Research Library in Los Angeles, takes responsibility for the University of California's Southern Regional Library Facility—a cooperative depository. In correspondence, she succinctly appraised the stored ownership she has experienced this way:

> The University of California has a philosophy of
> 'one university, one library.'

In general, however, with regard to the University of California's cooperative storage, the depositing library "takes credit" (for accreditation purposes) for owning the volume it forwards into storage while the other cooperating libraries use the volume as they need it. The California system has a regular program of shared purchases for expensive items and is looking into designating the remote storage facility itself as the owner of at least some of the shared purchase items.

A major problem with cooperative storage that has arisen in California and elsewhere is that two or more of the libraries may want to store the same title. Under these circumstances, the depository ideally retains the best copy, and certainly not all of the copies. At California, for example, the members originally chose to keep just one copy of each title forwarded. But the selection process became so cumbersome that the depository currently retains everything it receives. Although Claire Bellanti reports that the duplicate rate remains low, one suspects the depository will confront a weeding task in the near future.

THE ELEMENTS OF PLANNING

No doubt that planning qualifies as the most silent and unobtrusive but crucial aspect of any library storage project. In a perfect world, with enough lead time and adequate funding, one could select appropriate materials for storage, reassure and assuage nervous faculty members and other users, prepare the storage facility, smoothly transfer the selected materials, and provide responsive access to them.

But what is enough lead time? Actually, there is never quite enough of it, but less than a year would be unreasonable except for the smallest of collections. How does one appease the nervous users? One can offer constant reassurance personally and through the available media; however, one must also constantly remind one's self that all people resist all change most of the time but most people adjust to most of it most of the time. The following sections address some of the more objective issues a library storage planner faces.

Designating Materials for Storage

Selecting the materials to be stored is an agonizing but unavoidable step. You must first agree upon the criteria to use in choosing what gets stored. The criteria commonly include usage records, dates of publication, the language of the publications, the condition of the publications, and their classification (books under the Dewey system, for example, making likelier candidates for storage than Library of Congress materials, provided your library uses both classifications).

Firm criteria become particularly important and useful when faculty members and other users involve themselves in the selection process. I have yet to meet or hear of a subject specialist free from qualms about sending materials in his or her area off to storage. But this resistance appears especially strong in the social sciences and humanities, where the date of an article or book is not as relevant a factor as it is in the applied sciences, where age and relevance can be inversely proportional.

Unless you enjoy a sophisticated circulation system that can prove what materials have neither circulated nor been targeted by casual browsers in the building, you will find it difficult to convince some users that the material is best consigned to storage. Nor will pleading the dust factor work with faculty members and special users—unless you can convince them that a storage facility will help preserve their materials.

Incidentally, periodicals make ideal candidates for storage, especially earlier volumes. But it can also be problematic to pick uniform cut-off dates (like all volumes before January, 1960) because some titles start their volumes in September and end in May, and their bound collections tend to reflect their volume numbers rather than their publication dates.

Ease of Physical Access

Users need to know that if they require materials in storage, the library can retrieve them quickly. To dispel the natural skepticism, consider providing a few users doubtful of your efficiency with some stored materials for their extended use. Or consider offering to copy a few requested articles and telefaxing them to their requestors. As you carry out such services, however, remember that the main library may well retain equally suitable or even more relevant materials—the purpose of a storage service in the first place being to remove less relevant and lightly used titles.

Transfer Sheets: The Need for a Paper Trail

The Pennsylvania State University found it invaluable to fill out transfer sheets in triplicate for each individual call number scheduled for a transfer into storage. (Appendix II shows one of these transfer sheets.) Such a sheet would include space for the call number, a location or shelf assignment. (In Penn State's instance a specially assigned locator number indicates the actual section in storage), and the height of the material (Penn State shelves by volume size in its Annex.) If the call numbers include, as they often do, more than one volume, the transfer sheet can also indicate the width of the set. It can include the name of the transferring (or "owning") library if branch libraries or a cooperative system are involved. Finally, the transfer sheet should also include the date of transfer.

Transfer sheet drafts can serve as preliminary screening documents for users to examine. Also, librarians who decide to shelve by height or width or some other specified criterion can pull the appropriate sheets, arrange them in the desired order and actually place them in the material destined for the storage site. Once the materials have been moved to storage, transfer sheets provide (1) on-site shelf lists, (2) references for the staff responsible for changing the catalog, (3) a public notice for users (a point to be discussed further shortly), and (4) the "paper trail" essential for anyone concerned with the current whereabouts of a volume in transit.

Bibliographic Access in the Main Location

In addition to the actual physical access to materials in storage, users require bibliographic access to the materials. Consequently, a librarian should update the bibliographic record as quickly as possible to show the current location of stored materials accurately. One must coordinate this important service with those responsible for keeping the bibliographic records, particularly since this record keeping is labor-intensive work. The quantity of materials being transferred to storage may be great and the speed of the transfer may exceed the ability of the records staff to keep up. Plan well ahead to track the probable locations of the materials during their transfer phase.

Keeping Patrons Apprised of Location Changes

If you plan to transfer a large block of materials into storage (for example, all the books and serials classified in the Dewey Decimal System—assuming you use both Dewey Decimal and Library of Congress systems), consider posting signs until the individual records reflect the location change. If your library uses an online catalog, a "global" (or blanket) change in the record of the location may be feasible. Unfortunately, transfers to storage generally involve small blocks of materials, or even individual titles, transferred piecemeal.

One way to notify patrons of what has been transferred to storage is to keep a loose leaf notebook at a service desk that includes copies of the transfer sheets for all titles being moved. As we have seen, a copy of this transfer sheet has accompanied the title to storage, a particularly important step if the books are to be shelved in any way other than some strict classification order. When a title reaches its shelving location, an annotation is added to the transfer sheet. A copy goes to those responsible for changing the bibliographic record and the original serves as a shelf list in the storage area until the record has been updated.

If this blizzard of transfer sheet paper seems troublesome, one can (for example) enter the call number and location from the original transfer sheet into a strictly internal, local computer program showing the location of the call number in storage before sending the sheet on to those responsible for adjusting the catalog record.

Arranging Materials in Storage

I alluded earlier to decisions regarding the arrangement of materials in the storage facility, and it seems appropriate here to point out that these decisions all incur associated costs, some more obvious than others. Arranging materials by size, for example, provides the most efficient use of space. In order to shelve materials in storage by size, however, you need to know first how many linear feet of volumes fall into the height classifications you have chosen—that is to say, how many volumes between eight and 12 inches tall (for example) you have consigned to storage.

You need these measurements in order to pre-set the shelves before moving the materials. Pre-setting the shelves is particularly crucial if you have purchased double-faced industrial shelving. Cantilevered shelving, by contrast, provides more flexibility by offering an off-setting shelving arrangement on either side. But both shelving types require a great deal of lead time and careful record keeping. Also, if you plan to arrange the materials by (Library of Congress, or Dewey Decimal, or Superintendent of Documents) classification, you will sacrifice some flexibility later on if you must add to the stored collection. On the other hand, knowing both a book's size and call number encourages ease of access right away.

You can also arrange materials by accession number, which means you need not shift the collection every time you add new material and you will always know how much space you have left in the storage facility—assuming, that is, the stored materials are never recalled to a permanent residence back at the main library.

Once you have decided upon the arrangement of materials, you must decide how to deploy those materials physically on the storage shelves. Will they be shelved in the familiar upright fashion? on their fore-edges? or two deep on their fore-edges? Do you plan to use drawers or trays for an automated retrieval system? and if so, how do you propose to arrange the materials in the drawers or trays? Have you taken into account your preservation needs? For example, how do you plan to cope with brittle books? At the Pennsylvania State University, we decided to shrink wrap our brittle volumes so they survive the transfer undamaged. We will also shrink wrap, as time permits, some of the endangered materials that remain in the main library, particularly those materials that cannot be rebound. If someone wants to use one, we remove the wrap and shrink wrap it again when the book comes back. We also intend to shrink wrap books that show signs of mold. During 1991 it cost Penn State 39 cents to shrink wrap a volume.

Finally, as John Kountz has observed, compact shelving uses space effectively and is particularly desirable in a closed-stack operation:

> The cost per square foot for conventional bookstacks with a capacity of ten books per square foot is $111.90. For 'moving aisle' bookstacks with a capacity of 40 books per square foot, the cost per square foot is about $175.00 Finally, for the industrial technique with a capacity of 140 books per square foot, the cost per square foot is estimated at $375.00 ....However, when the cost per book stored is used for comparison, the industrial unit has no competition (Kountz, 1987).

Table 1 shows that the cost per book for the conventional book stack is $11.29; for the moving aisle book stack, it is $4.38 per book; and it is $2.68 per book for those who use the industrial AS/RS technique. Although these are 1987 prices, the comparisons remain valid and indicative.

CONCLUSION

In the perfect world I hypothesized earlier, the need to shift library materials into storage would set in motion a regularized, efficient procedure featuring predetermined weeding criteria and reasonable financial parameters all forged in open and collegial negotiations. The storage facilities themselves would keep all materials inviolate, would never leak, would all be economically maintained by dedicated employees, and would provide conscientious users with instant access.

In this perfect world, no dean would treat the library as a private preserve and a personal sanctuary, no influential donor would insist upon the sight of useless leather-bound tomes arrayed in pretentious rows throughout public areas, and graduate students would never throw tantrums at the idea of borrowing through interlibrary loan the monographs they need for tonight's seminar.

When we discuss library storage, however, the general area of human experience we enter is resistance to change, with all its political and logistical and psychological ramifications. One would like to present a chapter that details a procedure reliably applicable on all occasions when libraries find it

Table 1.

Construction Type	Cost per Square Foot	Books per Square Foot	Cost per Book
Conventional Book Stack	$111.90	10	$11.19
Moving Aisle Book Stack	$175.00	40	$ 4.38
Industrial Technique	$375.00	140	$ 2.68

Table 2.   Cost Category and Estimate

Storage Type	Open Stacks	Industrial Shelving	Compact (Motor)	Industrial Technique
Area (Sq Ft)	$ 60,000	$ 40,000	$ 20,000	$4,000
AC Light	63,000	42,000	10,000	863
Janitor	81,420	54,000	13,570	1,115
Reshelv Oper.	24,000	24,000	24,000	27,170
Power			2,700	7,642
Equipment			3,000	4,000
Total Cost	$168,420	$120,280	$ 53,770	$ 40,790
Cost per Unit	0.281	0.200	0.090	0.068

Notes: AC/Lights = $1.05/sq ft/year; Janitor = $1.357/sq ft/year; Reshelve/Operate = $8.00/hr; Industrial operator area = 822 sq. ft.

Source: From Kountz (1987).

necessary to weed their collections and consign parts of those collections to storage. Until that chapter gets written, I hope that this discussion—based on both my research and my experience at The Pennsylvania State University— serves to alert other librarians to most or at least many of the considerations likely to arise when materials must be moved into storage.

APPENDIX 1

- Brigham Young University at Provo has storage in an old grocery store with 24 hour turn-around service.
- Canisius College in Buffalo NY uses four converted classrooms in an adjacent building. The environment is unsatisfactory. The books are in several call number sequences. They have lost books and some have been misshelved.
- Drexel University in Philadelphia PA has two on-campus facilities with retrieval twice daily.

- Knox College in Galesburg IL has stored archives off-site with retrieval on request.
- Missouri University in Columbia rented a former furniture store. It offers once a day delivery.
- Northwestern University in Evanston IL has an off-site warehouse.
- Oberlin College in Oberlin OH has a Carnegie Library off-site with 24 hour service.
- University of California System has two cooperative storage facilities. The Southern Regional facility is in Los Angeles serving the southern campuses, and the Northern Regional facility in Richmond California serves the northern campuses of the University of California.
- University of Georgia is building an off-site storage. University of Hawaii is in the planning stages.
- University of Indiana at Bloomington is in the planning stages.
- University of Iowa in Iowa City has on-site storage.
- University of Kentucky at Lexington rents space in an underground rock quarry. Delivery is once a week.
- University of Pittsburgh in PA has an off-site storage with 48 hour delivery. They are planning for a second off-site storage.

APPENDIX 2

Candidate for Transfer to Bigler Road Annex

1. Present location of title: _____

2. Call Number:

3. Section Number: [   ]
   (To be completed
   by Annex Team.)

4. Main entry:
   Author: _____
   Title: _____

5. List actual holdings on self to be transferred.
   e.g. V. 1-10, V 13-16;
   1910-11920, 1923-1926 (from spine).

6. If barcoded, list volume number and correspond-
   ing item number:

Vol.	Barcode	Vol.	Barcode

7. Currently received serial or set? Yes ____ No ____

8. Dow we have holdings in microforms? Yes: ____ No: ____
   If "Yes", indicate Call number and holdings.

9. Justification for transfer:
   a. Little-used: ____   c. Preservation: ____
   b. Have in microforms: ____   d. Other: ____

10. Holdings and Measurements: (Linear measurements in inches)
    (See example below)
    Height of largest   Depth of largest   Width of
    book in set.   book in set.   complete set.

Requested by: _____

Date: _____

Approved by: _____

Date: _____

LIAS updated _____
                    initials/date

ICP updated _____
                    initials/date

REFERENCES

Graham, Barbara, "Firmitas, Utilitas, et Frugalitas: The Harvard Depository," In *The Great Divide: Challenges in Remote Storage*, Chicago: American Library Association, 1991.

Kennedy, James R. and Gloria Stockton, eds. *The Great Divide: Challenges in Remote Storage*, Chicago: American Library Association, 1991.

Lougee, Wendy Pradt, "A Remote Shelving Facility Retrofit: The University of Michigan Experience," In *The Great Divide: Challenges in Remote Storage*, Chicago: American Library Association, 1991.

SLAVIC AND EAST EUROPEAN LIBRARIANSHIP:

PROBLEMS, ISSUES, AND OPPORTUNITIES IN THE POST-SOVIET ERA

Mark J. Bandera

In light of the revolutionary changes that are today faced by Slavic librarianship in both East Europe and the West, it is appropriate to recall that "Not all change is beneficial, but all growth and progress come from change."[1] In East Europe, the demise of the Soviet Union is necessarily imposing transformations on an ideologically based system of librarianship. In the West, the mission of Slavic librarianship has traditionally been fueled by the Cold War and technological races. As these threats recede, the *raison d'etre* of the Slavics library also comes into question. In East and West, the role of Slavic librarianship faces change in terms of both mission and ideology.

In this paper, a broad spectrum of related problems and issues concerning Slavic librarianship will be explored. What began as a survey of East European librarianship, has over time expanded to include also parallel issues in Slavic librarianship in the West. Therefore, a broad range of literature and related information sources have been considered. Traditional authorities of library

Advances in Library Administration and Organization, Volume 12, pages 125-142.

literature have been sourced through CD-Rom and article citations. Apart from the library literature, some relevant criticisms of present day Slavic and East European studies will be applied to Slavic librarianship. In addition to traditional print sources, professional association through the Slavic and East European section of the ALA and a Slavic librarian's E-Mail forum operated through the University of California at Berkeley have provided a vehicle for observing trends in the field as well as discussion of the topic under consideration. The author also brings to this paper personal experience and insights gained through work in a Slavic library, as well as recent graduate work in librarianship and Slavic studies at the University of Illinois and the University of Alberta.

In North America, Slavic librarianship has evolved due to distinctive language, subject area, and peculiar acquisition needs of libraries and their clients. As a result, Slavic librarianship has developed into a specialty defined by overlapping subsets of both academic librarianship and Slavic and East European studies. An examination of Slavic librarianship in the West suggests several disturbing problems and issues. To begin with, the scholarly foundations of traditional Slavic and East European studies on which much of Slavic librarianship is based come into question. Furthermore, the relevance of Slavic librarianship's traditional mission is suspect. Lastly, opportunities for renewal of the Slavic Libraries mission exist, but are not being universally pursued.

In East Europe, problems and issues facing libraries begin with ideology, but extend to mainstream library practices, technological gaps, and historical conflicts. The current and future problems of the former Soviet bloc began with the formation of the Soviet Union, but have not disappeared with the dissolution of the empire. A sound understanding of problems inherent in East Europe requires de-mythologizing many Soviet as well as Western precepts and interpretations of the Soviet library. While the dissolution of the Soviet Union is a positive first step in the reformation of the library, it comes fraught with dangers, twists and turns that are not always self-evident given the inherited precepts of the Soviet Union.

SLAVIC LIBRARIANSHIP IN THE WEST

Discussions among Slavic librarians and a survey of institutions would indicate declining status and diminished financial support for many Slavic libraries. Given a mission defined by the Cold War and technological race that traditionally has served a narrow range of Russian and Sovietological perspectives and interpretations, Slavic librarianship's importance in the academic libraries has weakened. This decline may reflect real lack of relevancy, and is paralleled by related problems in Slavic and East European Studies.

Scholarly Foundations

A special issue of *National Interest* carefully delineates the basic problem.[2] Traditional areas of Slavic and East European Studies have been built on "Russophile" and "Sovietological" perspectives and interpretations of "reality." Points of views by non-Russian East European groups and opposing scholars such as Richard Pipes, Robert Conquest and Zbigniew Brzezinski have been persistently dismissed. However, their scholarly alternative interpretations are now actively challenging the *status quo* and attempting to de-mythologize and redefine the field. For example, at the University of Alberta a recent lecture and discussion titled "Cultural Turf Wars: Slavic Studies and the New World Order," led by prof. Oleh Ilnytzkyj, sought to identify and challenge traditional precepts of the field. His analysis has since been published as "Russian and Ukrainian Studies and the New World Order."[3]

The problems of perspective and bias in North American Slavic Librarianship are by no means new. As Andrew Turchyn noted back in 1980, the Library of Congress has traditionally exhibited a pro-Russian bias when it comes to the cataloging and classification of Slavic materials.[4] This bias extends to questions of language, historical interpretation, and nomenclature. With great foresight, Turchyn suggested that "The Library of Congress should finally remove all traces of misconceptions based on the outdated assertions that all Eastern Slavs are Russians, and that the USSR is Russia."[5] But, efforts to challenge the ingrained LC standards have met with little success over the years. Perhaps in the interest of international cooperation, LC has been reluctant to challenge Soviet ideological interpretation in sensitive areas. And yet, this is a good example of problems caused by competing interests in our field. In any case, for too long non-Russian or non-Soviet viewpoints have been effectively trivialized by the system. Furthermore, there is little evidence that the demise of the Soviet Union has modified in the overall hegemony of "the Russian" over other Eastern Slav groups. It would appear that in the realm of Slavic librarianship, convenience and the status quo too often take precedence over scholarly standards and objectivity.

Mission: Old and New

To proceed beyond questions of perspective and bias, Slavic librarianship's traditional subservience to Slavic and East European Studies has impeded its adaptation to changing realities and opportunities. While the Cold War and technological races have diminished, the new frontier is being expanded into economic opportunities and trade in East Europe and the entire restructured Eurasian region. In this context, the Slavic library and librarians could and should be a natural source for much needed information. For instance, as noted by Maja Jokic, 8.9 percent of articles indexed in Medline are in Slavonic languages,[6] and Ingrid Chambert recently drew attention to the wide range of business information and general news of Eastern Europe available on Dialog.[7] Tania Konn has also published reviews of on-line information sources related to Eastern Europe.[8] A survey of these literatures suggests that Western Europe has the jump on North America when it comes to information brokerage. Especially in Germany and Great Britain, there already exist many on-line information brokers prepared to give companies interested in doing business in East Europe a competitive edge.

Instead of expanding and refocusing their services, Slavic librarians in the West have been slow to recognize changing realities, and are in danger of losing competitive advantage to other information specialists. As noted by Liz Parcell, "Soviet and East European affairs are no longer the sole preserve of the 'Slavonic specialist'."[9]

Even traditional activities in the Slavic library face new challenges. Acquisitions have always been a special problem for the Slavic specialist, with a customary reliance on bureaucratic centralized purchases from the Soviet Union and specialized dealers in the West. After the fall of the Soviet Union, traditional centralized sources such as *Mezhdunarodnaia kniga* [International Book-Chamber] in Moscow have collapsed, and a number of book dealers in the West have gone bankrupt. In the aftermath, Slavic libraries have had to scramble and develop new acquisition sources and relationships in order to protect the integrity of their collections.

Several brief case studies help define the pressures of the field. For instance, until recently, the Slavic library at the University of Manitoba employed a number of librarians and related technicians. Upon the head librarian's retirement, the three positions were reduced to one librarian, and the acquisition budget virtually eliminated. This downsizing occurred at a time when the province is actively seeking to expand its marketing of agricultural technology and expertise into Eastern Europe. In this case, the failure to meet changing demands has resulted in the slow and perhaps unnecessary decline of Slavic librarianship at the University of Manitoba.[10]

Similarly, with budget pressures, Ohio State University recently eliminated a Slavic cataloging position and decided instead to contract the work out.[11] As noted by Sally Rogers, Slavics librarianship is by its very nature highly specialized and labor intensive.[12] Slavics librarianship is thus relatively expensive.

An example of a successful evolutionary track of Slavic librarianship is the case of the University of Illinois Slavic Library.[13] This library grew greatly in the 1960s. In the 1970s, the greater library decentralized into special cataloguing, reference and acquisitions functions that served to concentrate Slavic expertise in one area.[14] In the intervening years, the Slavic library has forged alliances not only within the university community, but has broadened its base to include outside governmental and private interests. Each summer, the University of Illinois hosts a series of East European conferences for academics, newspeople, governmental officials and business men and women from the United States and abroad. Keeping up with trends, summer conference topics have ranged from traditional Sovietological themes, to *glasnost* and *perestroika* and to the implications of the post-Soviet era. In parallel, the library has developed a unique reference and research service available to virtually everyone in North America, adopted new technologies and capabilities, and invested in unique direct contacts with East Europe and Newly Independent States. The ability of this library to continually adapt and market itself in response to changing service needs of customers has made it a central conduit for Slavic and East European information access second to none in North America.

As can be seen, successful response to the challenges of the changing geopolitical and cultural international environment requires active library strategies that could market services beyond the traditional Slavic and East European sector to include political, economic and international trade dimensions of the field. Similarly, traditional subject, language and library skills should expand to incorporate technological know-how such as online services of such areas as economics.

Fortunately, the needed renewal of mission has started on many levels. Professional associations, and tools such as the Internet are allowing for the pooling, sharing, and growth of ideas and expertise. The growth of professionalism is facilitated by an active body within the Slavic and East European Section (SEES) of the Association of College and Research Libraries. Apart from traditional activities such as conferences and publication, continuing education and increased levels of cooperation between libraries and librarians should become a new priority. The University of Illinois in 1993 hosted a workshop for librarians as part of its annual Slavics conference.[15] A new tool in the library is the formation of a Slavic Librarians' E-Mail Forum hosted by the University of California at Berkeley. Begun in the spring of 1991, the forum currently boasts over 150 members. It allows interested colleagues to actively network and access resource materials and people.[16]

East European Librarianship

The history of the Soviet Union reflects some incredible technological and military advances, but at terrible costs to its people. A look at Soviet librarianship reflects some of the paradoxes that helped define the Soviet Union. In order to understand Soviet librarianship and its transition in the post-Soviet era, it is important to understand that while some of its recognizable structures parallel those found in the West, the underlying philosophy and objectives of the two are worlds apart. Whereas in the West, librarians concentrate on universal availability, the Soviet librarian was a vigilant watchdog behind ideological barriers.[17] With the demise of the Soviet empire, old problems have not disappeared, but exhibit themselves more openly and in new manifestations that are at times mistaken for new problems of the so-called new order.

Soviet Ideology and Library Practice

The ideological role of libraries was recognized very early by the Soviets. Particularly important in this regard were Lenin and his wife Krupskaya who defined much of the ideological foundations of librarianship. Krupskaya believed that the specific task of libraries was to deliver communist ideology to the masses and that all library work as subordinate to the political and economic tasks of the Soviet Union was as defined by the Communist party.[18] The political role of libraries was defined by the 1922 Congress of the Political Education Committee, stating that "the library must stop being an institution for storing books, and for lending them; it must rather become a weapon for the propaganda of communism."[19] Through the era of Brezhnev, most library literature cites Lenin at the beginning of any publication. Not surprisingly, Chubaryin exhulted that, Lenin's works contain "270 pertinent articles, reports, speeches, letters, telegrams, drafts of government decrees and other documents," which deal with the subject of libraries.[20]

Axel lists five areas, based on the ideas of Lenin and Krupskaya which the Soviets identified as especially important:[21]

1. Libraries should build socialism as defined by the communist party.
2. Keeping in mind party ideology, librarians should guide leaders to self-education through reading.
3. Librarians should actively investigate readers' habits through conversations and readers cards.
4. Differentiation of forms of library service requires extensive library networks and special libraries.
5. The role of bibliography is stressed both in order to guide readers, and to impress visitors from western countries.

In the West, a number of works dealing with Soviet librarianship appeared in the late 1950s and early 1960s. Western interest in Soviet librarianship coincided with concerns about Russian technological advance, specifically as reflected by military buildups and the space program. Paul Horecky, provides a realistic and comprehensive description of the Soviet library system, covering both ideological and structural issues. While confirming the ideological strictures of this institution, he also describes an intricate system of libraries and bibliographic service which goes beyond anything a North American might envision.[22] He notes that "operational efficiency and dynamic activity are combined with bureaucratic regimentation."[23]

Horecky's work is complemented by Melville Ruggles and Raynard Swank who documents the results of an exchange program between the United States and the U.S.S.R. They note the degree of centralization in all aspects of librarianship and contrasts it with the individual initiative and relative decentralization in the U.S. system.[24]

A more up-to-date and very comprehensive look at Soviet libraries and librarianship is provided by Axel Andersen. Based on first hand study tours and extensive use of library literature, this work more clearly defines the various aspects of librarianship and types of libraries available in the Soviet Union. Here again, the continuing primary ideological functions of library institutions are confirmed.[25] Library training is more rigorous and developed than in the West. Educational choices include "institutes of librarianship," "*library tekhnika,*" technical information institutes," and "in-service training courses." At an institute of librarianship, the curriculum may take up 4,000 hours of study time, including over 1,000 hours devoted to questions of the party, Marxist-Leninism and physical training and civil defense.[26] Thus, at the end of their programs, students are well trained to fulfill vigilantly the guiding function of librarians.

The Transition of *Perestroika* and Beyond

Of note is Paul Lisson's recent sketch of Soviet librarianship. Lisson's work provides a readable overview of Russian and Soviet Librarianship up through the 1980s. Of particular interest is his observation that although several thousands of books have been removed from *spetskhran* [secret stacks] by 1988, a significant percentage under considerations were still being hidden. Moreover, there was no indication of the total number of books still held in secrecy. It should be noted that during *glasnost* and *perestroika,* although censorship rules were relaxed, they were by no means dismantled.[27] It is not certain how much of the current problem is due to this heritage of censorship, practical considerations of physically cataloguing and transferring books, or attitudes of library workers themselves.[28]

Jenny Brine identifies low morale, inferior pay, poor working conditions, and poor prestige as chronic problems of the Soviet library profession during the period of *perestroika.*[29] Yet, she errs in prematurely heralding the end of censorship. While there has been a formal abolition of censorship, it is unlikely that structural impediments to freedom of information institutionalized during decades of Soviet library practice can be erased overnight. Instead, it has been suggested that term "censorship" does not adequately relate to the Soviet era. Choldin offers the term "omnicensorship" to describe the acknowledged all-pervasive control of information by the state."[30] Genieva further suggests that omnicensorship has been followed by newer forms of censorship that are defined by lack of funds for buying foreign materials, old bureaucracies controlling information access, library closure due to lack of funding, and discarding of "Soviet-materials." Therefore, there currently exist continued tensions between democratic forces and the "omni-censor."[31]

A deeper definition of the problems of *perestroika* are presented by Kasinec. While the term *perestroika,* indicating "reconstruction," has been popular in the West for several years, it should be noted that present changes also involve *zastroika,* which defines pre-Gorbachev stagnation and post-Gorbachev *rasstroika* which defines dismantling of old structures. With *rasstroika* comes "confusion, deconstruction, excitement, opportunity, frustration, and a future that seems somewhat unpredictable."[32]

Thus, unresolved questions abound. For instance, it has not been universally decided which classification system(s) post-Soviet libraries should adopt. Axel provides a good explanation of *BBK,* the traditional Soviet classification system based on Marxist-Leninism. Main subject headings include natural sciences, applied sciences, and technology, with one-tenth of the subject headings being devoted to Marxist-Leninism.[33] A more detailed and comprehensive description of bibliographic practices may be found in Whitby, who details a simple structure with central bibliographic control that evolved into a very complex bibliographic system.[34] A more up-to-date overview and analysis of Soviet classification theory and practices can be found in Gurevich.[35] While Gurevich indicated the uncertain future of the Soviet classification system during the Gorbachev era, available literature has not identified the directions that will be followed in the fragmented Soviet Empire. It would appear that some libraries are converting to new systems, while others have adopted a wait-and-see attitude.[36]

A survey of technology in libraries suggests inequitable gaps in application across the former empire. Technology has penetrated privileged large academic and technological centers, particularly in Moscow and Leningrad (now St. Petersburg), where cooperation with the West has led to modernization and computer technologies allow the searching of databases. Unfortunately, the technological change to date still reflects the anomalies of the inherited Soviet system. Generally, most libraries lack basics such as duplicators, typewriters, telephones, copying machines and paper. Although the advantages of technological innovation are understood in the former Soviet Union, there will be not quick fixes, given economic constraints and uncertainties that pervade the system.[37] Perhaps the best chance for improvement in the technological area is contingent upon Western investment and foreign aid. Indeed, the major problem for the present and near future is their lack of hard currency.[38]

Another major issue linked to technological innovation and funding issues is the labor intensive nature of Soviet librarianship. Adoption of technology will lead to massive displacement in the library work force. For instance, in 1970, there were 300,000 professional librarians and bibliographers in the Soviet Union.[39] In the 1980s, there were 7,000 professionals and 14,000 technicians trained a year.[40]

Recent journal articles begin to interpret some of the confusing post-Soviet library systems in transition. Jenny Brine provides an overview of many issues involved in the reorganization of libraries in the transitional period of *perestroika*.[41] She accurately notes that libraries were overtaken by the pace of change. Uncertainties created by marketization, rampant inflation, and breakdown of old administrative structures are intensified by new commercial priorities and shifts in library policy.

Although primarily concerned with the fate of foreign publications in the Soviet Union, Marianna Tax Choldin provides an interesting view of the journal *Bibliotekar'* from 1923-1989. The article indicates changes in attitudes during the reigns of Stalin, Khrushchev, Brezhnev, and Gorbachev. Still, she believes that a solid ideological thread underpinning has remained resistant to change at least through 1988.[42]

A glance at more recent issues of *Bibliotekar'* suggests that old habits are hard to break, since biased articles expanding anti-religious and pro-communist topics persisted into the 1990's. Erastova still writes about "propaganda and children,"[43] Brodskii about "aetheistic propaganda."[44] While the U.S.S.R. was breaking up into the Newly Independent States, *Bibliotekar'* seemed to cling to the Communist party's leading role in librarianship."[45] Uporova's article actually defends the *status quo* in Soviet librarianship.[46]

Nonetheless, some winds of change are already evident in the monolithic post-Soviet librarianship as reflected in recent writing of Evgenii Kuz'min available in English.[47] Being familiar with Western library practices, he offers new insights in his analysis regarding the status and needs of the Soviet library system and its successor in Russia. Further dialog with other reformed experts in East Europe, and the Newly Independent States is essential if their library systems are to be expedite their reforms.

A Non-Russian Case

Since non-Russians made up just over 50 percent of the former Soviet Union's population, it is worth considering the effect of Soviet librarianship on the national entities which formed independent countries on the basis of former Soviet republics. A case in point is Ukraine, the largest non-Russian republic with a population of 52 million.

In 1971, Babijcuk, Minister of Culture of the Ukrainian S.S.R. wrote an article praising the development of library systems in Ukraine. After quoting Lenin and defining Ukraine, as "an outlying district of Russia,"[48] Babijcuk presents an idyllic picture of library development under the Soviets. To the uninitiated, the republic's 69,513 libraries, 466 million volumes, and 27 library schools is proof positive of the success of Soviet librarianship.[49]

While Babijcuk's article was being published, the Soviets were pursuing a massive repressive crackdown on books, authors and libraries in Ukraine. As reported in the underground *Ukrainian Herald,* libraries in Ukraine made virtually all literary and scholarly books from the 1960s "unavailable" to the public. Moreover, books were banned, writers were forbidden to publish, authors imprisoned and held in psychiatric institutions.[50] Further analysis of Soviet cultural policy toward Ukraine may be found in Ivan Dziuba's work,[51] while descriptions of political trails in which books are prominently featured can be found in the writings of Chornovil.[52] Unfortunately, the West has chosen to largely ignore the fate of libraries and librarians in Ukraine since the 1970s, and only in 1990 the Library of Congress found it possible to host librarian Hanna Mykhaylenko, a former political prisoner.[53]

Given the degree of Soviet repressions of the Stalin and Brezhnev eras, it should come as no surprise that change in Ukrainian librarianship has lagged behind that of Russia. The legacy of the Soviet period for non-Russian countries is that libraries outside Russia are better supplied with books in Russian than the local language, even in rural areas where people do not speak Russian.[54] Very often books that are available in native languages do not address relevant technological and social concerns as much as ideological needs of the state. Also, the library profession entrenched itself in Russian scholarship, where journals in the field like *Bibliotekar'* are in Russian. Thus, as was noted previously, it may prove difficult to change attitudes of librarians and adapt the inherited institutions to the needs of the Newly Independent States given the monolithic structure of the former Soviet system. An example of a positive project is the George Soros Foundation's project to establish a law library in Kyiv.[55] An attempt is being made to train staff in Western legal and library norms, provide open access, train the West (partially at the University of Alberta), and provide funding of such a venture. Given the legacy of Soviet librarianship and dependency on Russian norms, such a project will entail a sharp break with previous Soviet library tradition. This should be better understood in the United States and Canada where library leaders now have access to funds intended to encourage exchanges and joint projects with East Europe and the newly independent countries in order to support the difficult democratization process in the former Soviet empire.

Entering the World Stage

While Eastern bloc countries struggle to constitute themselves as independent national entities, they are also struggling to assert themselves in the international arena. In Russia, competing interests are debating the directions libraries should pursue in relation to the "outside world." An example of the problem is the status of "trophy" library and archival collections purloined from East Germany, East Europe, and the non-Russian republics after World War II. There is currently a debate raging within the Russian library community as to the ultimate disposition of millions of these "confiscated" materials. Should they be returned or not? Many librarians favor selling materials back. Some materials have already been sold on the open market in the West. Others have suggested returning the books on an individual basis when individually requested. There is even a question as to whether materials from some collections that have been split up can even be tracked down. Ultimately, it is not even certain who is in charge: librarians, government bureaucrats officials, or both?[56]

At a recent international conference, Russian delegates expressed a fear of "cultural imperialism" being imposed from the West (specifically from the U.S.).[57] However, when some delegates suggested that Russia look to the third world for working models of librarianship, "Agitated Russian delegates rose from their chairs to say they considered such a comparison ridiculous given their country's proximity to Western Europe and the advanced technology and high level of culture that exists in their societies."[58] As Russia comes to grips with the contradictions of a developed military-industrial nation with third world economic status, it will eventually have to face and resolve its inherent xenophobic and colonial *weltanschauung*.

Conclusions

Soviet librarianship, as defined by the literature, differs greatly from Western norms in terms of centralization and ideological definition. Yet, while Western literature has done a good job in defining the monolithic structures of the Soviet library system, it has largely ignored its role in suppressing freedom of information and the brutal national and colonial cultural implications of imperial library policy. The demise of the Soviet Union marks the end of a colonial empire. Both academicians and leaders in the West largely failed to predict the demise of the USSR, and have yet to define and come to terms with the new geopolitical order.

Obstacles to progress in East Europe and the larger Eurasian region include problems of labor and technology, decentralization, ideology, and national assertiveness and cultural diversity. In the struggle between old and new, some librarians and institutions are exhibiting resistance to changes that must ultimately and irreversibly alter the monolithic, bureaucratic structures and ideological intractability of the old Soviet order.

When we consider the place of non-Russian nationalities in the scheme of Soviet and post-Soviet librarianship, we observe large gaps in coverage, shortsightedness, and plenty of prejudices. It is understandable that Russians would neglect to document the role of the library as a tool of ruthless repression in the Stalin and Brezhnev eras. It is however puzzling that these issues have been largely ignored or misinterpreted in the West. Perhaps in the spirit of detente, there has been reticence to ruffle Russian sensibilities. Nonetheless, in the post-Soviet era, both Russia and the West will have to deal with newly emerged countries. It will be especially important to watch and encourage non-Russian nations to develop democratic traditions of librarianship while attempting to overcome many decades of Soviet repression and Russian domination.

This survey has offered a broad overview of some of the problems faced by Slavic librarians. It would be worthwhile to delve deeper into the individual issues discussed within. Such studies should include more formal surveys of Slavic libraries in North America as well as alternate emerging sources of information. In addition, this paper has relied heavily on Western sources for literature concerning East Europe. More direct study of East European library literature and discussions with active librarians of the Newly Independent States is indicated for the future. Especially interesting, and here-to-for neglected, are the cases of the non-Russian nations.

While East Europe and such newly constituted countries as Russia, Ukraine and Belarus expand their horizons beyond the strictures of dogmatic librarianship, Slavic librarianship in the West faces parallel challenges. While support for traditional Slavic and East European research wanes, new conditions in that part of the globe require a broadening of technological and subject area skills. This offers exciting possibilities. At the same time, the Slavic librarian in the United States and Canada also faces new challenges from competing information brokers in Europe and the successor states. To reiterate, "Not all change is beneficial, but all growth and progress come from change."[59] This insight is now especially applicable to Soviet librarianship in both East and West. Surely, the Slavic sections in major North American libraries should not be weakened but strengthened and restructured.

NOTES

1. Herb White, *Library Personnel Management* (New York: Knowledge Industry Publications, 1985), 15.

2. Richard Pipes, Robert Conquest, Peter Rutland, Martin Malia, et al., "The Strange Death of Soviet Communism: An Autopsy,' *National Interest* [Special issue], 31 (Spring 1992):1-79.

3. Oleh S. Ilnytzkyj, "Cultural Turf Wars: Slavic Studies and the New World Order," Lecture presented at the University of Alberta, 15 March 1993; and Oleh S. Ilnytzkyj, "Russian and Ukrainian Studies and the New World Order," *Canadian Slavonic Papers/Revue canadienne des slavistes* 34 (1993): 445-58.

4. Andrew Turchyn, "Slavic Publications: Their Cataloging and Classification in American Libraries," in *Cataloging and Classification of Non-Western Material: Concerns, Issues and Practices,* ed. Mohammed M. Aman (Phoenix, Arizona: Oryx Press, 1980), 297-320.

5. Ibid., 320.

6. Maja Jokic, "Information Value of Papers Written in Slavonic Languages in the Medline Database," *Online Review* 16 (1992):21.

7. Ingrid Chambert, "Eastern European Information on Dialog," *Online Review* 16 (1992):313-22.

8. Tania Konn, "Eastern European Online Information," *Aslib Information* 18 (November/December 1990): 352-53.

9. _____, "Eastern European Online Information- II," *Aslib Information* 19 (July/August 1991): 265-66.

Elisabeth Parcell, "Focus on the Soviet Union and Eastern Europe," *Library Association Record* 92 (November 1990): 852.

10. The author of this paper has lived in Winnipeg for several years and familiarized himself with many of the library's workings and politics through informal observation and discussions.

11. "Cataloger for Slavic Materials," [Advertisement] *American Libraries* 24 (May 1993): 404; and subsequent discussions with Sharon Sullivan, Personnel Librarian at Ohio State University.

12. Sally Rogers, "Backlog Management: Estimating Resources Needed to Eliminate Arrearages," *Library Resources & Technical Services* 35 (January 1991):31-2.

13. First hand observations were made while working as an assistant cataloger at the University of Illinois Slavic Library, 1988-1989.

14. Bingham, Karen Havill. "Management of Original Cataloging Activities in a Decentralized System." *Cataloging & Classification Quarterly,* 8 (1987):49-63.

15. Victor Gorodinsky, "Meeting," Slavic Librarians' Electronic Mail Forum, Posted:8:55am MDT, Monday 14 June 1993.

16. "Slavic Librarians' Electronic Mail Forum," *Association of College & Research Libraries Slavic and East European Section Newsletter* 9 (1993): 48-9.

17. Axel Andersen, et al., *Library and Information Centres in the Soviet Union* (Forlag: Bibliotekscentralens, 1985), 28.

18. Boris Raymond, *Krupskaia and Soviet Russian Librarianship, 1917-1939* (Metuchen, New Jersey: Scarecrow Press, 1979), 180.

19. _____, "Libraries and Adult Education: The Russian Experience, *The Journal of Library History* 16 (1981): 398.

20. O.S. Chubaryin, *Libraries in the Soviet Union* (Memphis: J.W. Brister Library Monograph Series, 1974), 22.

21. Axel Andersen, 30.

22. Paul L. Horecky, *Libraries and Bibliographic Centers in the Soviet Union* (Bloomington, Indiana: Indiana University Publications, 1959).

23. Ibid., 150.

24. Melville J. Ruggles and Raynard C. Swank, *Soviet Libraries and Librarianship: Report of the Visit of the Delegation of U.S. Librarians to the Soviet Union, May-June, 1961, under the U.S.-Soviet Cultural Exchange Agreement* (Chicago: American Library Association, 1962).

25. Axel Andersen.

26. Ibid., 73-81; Maxine K. Rochester, 5-6.

27. Paul Lisson, "History, Change, and Libraries in the Soviet Union," *Canadian Library Journal* 48 (February 1991): 47-50.

28. Jenny Brine, "Perestroika and Soviet Libraries," *Libri: International Library Review* 42 (April 1992): 156.

29. Ibid., 157-58.

30. Marianna Tax Choldin and Ekaterina Genieva, speakers. "SEES Program: "Is There Still Censorship in the Former Soviet Union?"," *Association of College and Research Libraries Slavic & East European Section News* 9 (1993): 6.

31. Ibid., 6-7.

32. Edward Kasinec, "Zastroika, Perestroika, Dostroika, and US," *The Serials Librarian* 21 (1991): 59-67.

33. Axel Andersen, 67-70; also Paul L. Horecky, 152 notes that between 1918 and 1956, 365,000 copies of Marx, Engels and Lenin were published in 84 languages in the Soviet Union.

34.   Thomas J. Whitby, and Tanja Lorkovic, *Introduction to Soviet National Bibliography* (Littleton, Colorado: Libraries Unlimited, 1979).

35.   Konstantin Gurevich, "Russian/Soviet History in Library Classification," *Cataloging and Classification Quarterly* 12 (1990): 63-86.

36.   Jenny Brine, 152-153.

37.   Ibid., 151-52.

38.   J.T. Chiang, "Management of Technology in Centrally Planned Economies," *Technology in Society* 12 (1990): 397-426; T. Konn, "Glasnost and the Business Information Sector: Soviet Problems and Perspectives," *Online* 15 (February 1991): 19-26.

39.   George Chandler, *Libraries, Documentation and Bibliography in the USSR 1917-71: Survey and Critical Analysis of Soviet Studies 1967-1971* (London: Seminar Press, 1972).

40.   Maxine Rochester, "The Impact of Economic and Social Trends on Education for Librarianship in the USSR," *International Leads* 5 (Winter 1991): 5-6.

41.   Jenny Brine, 144-66.

42.   Marianna Tax Choldin, "Access to Foreign Publications in Soviet Libraries," *Libraries and Culture* 26 (Winter): 1991.

43.   N. Erastova, "Chto napisano perom ..." [What is written down with the pen ...], *Bibliotekar'* [Librarian], 4 (1990): 22-7.

44.   M. Brodskii, "Slovo mirskoe i bozhe." [God's word and the world's]. *Bibliotekar'* [Librarian], 6 (1990): 38-40.

45.   "Navstrechu ocherednomu partiinomu s'ezdu," [Towards the next Party Congress], *Bibliotekar'* [Librarian], 11 (1989): 2-4.

46.   Uporova, V. "Ne prenebregat dostignutym." [Without ignoring our accomplishments]. *Bibliotekar'* [Librarian], 6 (1990): 10-4.

47.   Evgenii Kuz'min, "At a Crossroads: Russian Libraries Face the Future," *Wilson Library Bulletin* (January 1993): 52-58.

48.   R. Babijcuk, "Development of Librarianship in the Ukrainian S.S.R.," *Unesco Bulletin of Librarianship,* 25 (July-August 1971): 223.

49.   Ibid., 223-225.

50.   Maksym Sahaydak, comp, "The Prohibition of Ukrainian Scholarship and Culture. The Persecution of the Intelligentsia, *"The Ukrainian Herald Issue 7-8. Ethnocide of Ukrainians in the U.S.S.R. Spring 1974. An Underground Journal from Soviet Ukraine,* trans. and ed. Olena Saciuk and Bohdan Yasen (Baltimore: Smoloskyp, 1976), 131-51.

51.   Ivan Dziuba, *Internatsionalizm chy rusyfikatsia* [Internationalism or Russification] (Munich: Sucasnist, 1968), 168-204.

52.   Vyacheslav Chornovil, *The Chornovil Papers* (New York: McGraw-Hill, 1968).

53.   Natalie Gawdiak, "Ukrainian Librarian, a Former Soviet Prisoner, Speaks at LCPA Program," *Library of Congress Information Bulletin* 7 May 1990, 179-81; _____, "Ukrainian Librarian Hanna Mykhaylenko Honored at the Library of Congress, *International Leads* 4 (Summer 1990): 5.

54.   Jenny Brine, 155.

55.   "Ukrainska Pravnycha Fundatsia/The Ukrainian Legal Foundation," Proposal Approved by George Soros and the Soros Foundations. April 23, 1992, TMs [photocopy], (A. Rutkowski, Government Publications, Cameron Library, University of Alberta, Edmonton, Alberta).

56.   "Europe East and West: New Resources for North American Libraries" Symposium papers and discussions at the 112th Annual Conference of the American Libraries Association—Slavic & East European Section, New Orleans, Louisiana, 28 June 1993.

57.   Ron Chepesiuk, "Information Policy an Cultural Policy: A Conference for a New Europe." *American Libraries* (February 1993): 162.

58.   Ibid., 163.

59.   Herb White, 15.

REFERENCES

Andersen, Axel, ed., et al. *Libraries and Information Centres in the Soviet Union,* Forlag: Bibliotekscentralens, 1985.

Babijcuk, R. "Development of Librarianship in the Ukrainian S.S.R." *Unesco Bulletin of Librarianship,* 25 (July-August 1971): 223-25.

Balzer, H. "From Hypercentralization to Diversity: Continuing Efforts to Restructure Soviet Education." *Technology in Society,* 13 (1991): 123-50.

Bingham, Karen Havill. "Management of Original Cataloging Activities in a Decentralized System." *Cataloging & Classification Quarterly,* 8 (1987):49-63.

Binnington, John P., ed. *Mutual Exchange in the Scientific Library and Technical Information Center Fields: A Report from The Special Libraries Association Delegation to the Soviet Union 1966,* New York: Special Libraries Association, n.d.

Bowden, Russell. "The Library Association and Eastern Europe: Programmes of Co-operation Continue to Develop." *Library Association Record,* 93 (March 1991): 111.

Brine, Jenny. "Perestroika and Soviet Libraries." *Libri: International Library Review,* 42 (April 1992): 144-66.

Brodskii, M. "Slovo mirskoe i bozhe." [God's word and the world's]. *Bibliotekar',* [Librarian], 6 (1990) 38-40.

Chambert, Ingrid. "Easter European Information on DIALOG." *Online review* 16 (1992): 313-22.

Chandler, George. *Libraries, Documentation and Bibliography in the USSR 1917-1971: Survey and Critical Analysis of Soviet Studies 1967-1971,* London, Seminar Press, 1972.

Chepesiuk, Ron. "Information Policy as Cultural Policy: A Conference for a New Europe." *American Libraries,* 24 (February 1993): 162-63.

————. "An Interview with Evgenii Kuz'min." *Wilson Library Bulletin* 67 (January 1993): 52-53, 57.

Chiang, J.T. "Management of Technology in Centrally Planned Economies." *Technology in Society,* 12 (1990): 397-426.

Choldin, Marianna Tax. "Access to Foreign Publications in Soviet Libraries." *Libraries and Culture,* 26 (Winter 1991): 135-50.

————, and Ekaterina Genieva, speakers. "SEES Program: "Is There Still Censorship in the Former Soviet Union?"," *Association of College & Research Libraries Slavic & East European Section News,* 9 (1993): 6-7.

Chornovil, Vyacheslav. *The Chornovil Papers,* New York: McGraw-Hill, 1968.

Chubaryin, O.S. *Libraries in the Soviet Union,* Memphis: J.W. Brister Library Monograph Series, 1974, 22.

Denisiuk, V. "Lish pravda Lenina." [Only Lenin was right]. *Bibliotekar',* [Librarian] 10 (1985) 54-5.

Didur, V.C., comp., et al. *Biblioteky Ukrains'koi R.S.R.: Dovidnyk,* [Libraries of the Ukrainian S.S.R.: A Finder]. Kharkiv: Knyzhkova palata URSR, 1969.

Dobbs, Michael. "Even Lenin Censored in 'Special Collection'." *Edmonton Journal,* 8 August 1993, 3 (D).

Dziuba, Ivan. *Internatsionalizm chy rusyfikatsia?* [Internationalism or Russification?]. n.p.: Suchasnist', 1968.

Eames, Patricia. "The Russian-American Genealogical Service." *Prologue: Quarterly of the National Archives,* 25 (Summer 1993): 176-181.

Erastova, N. "Chto napisano perom ... " [What is written down with the pen ...]. *Bibliotekar'* [Librarian], 4 (1990): 22-7.

Felbrugge, F.J.M. *Samizdat and Political Dissent in the Soviet Union,* Leyden: A.W. Sijthoff, 1975.

Francis, Simon, ed. *Libraries in the USSR,* London: Clive Bingley, 1971.

Gawdiak, Natalie. "Ukrainian Librarian, a Former Soviet Prisoner, Speaks at LCPA Program." *Library of Congress Information Bulletin,* 7 May 1990, 179-81.

_____. "Ukrainian Librarian Hanna Mykhaylenko Honored at the Library of Congress." *International Leads,* 4 (Summer 1990): 5.

Gorodinsky, Victor. "Meeting." Slavic Librarians' Electronic Mail Forum. Posted:8:55am MDT 14 June 1993.

Grimsted, Patricia Kennedy. *Archives and Manuscript Repositories in the USSR: Ukraine and Moldavia,* Princeton, N.J.: Princeton University Press, 1988.

Gul'chinski, Victor. "Libraries in the U.S.S.R.—A Time of Restructuring." *Canadian Library Journal,* 48 (February 1991): 55-56.

Gurevich, Konstantin. "Russian/Soviet History in Library Classification." *Cataloging and Classification Quarterly,* 12 (1990): 63-86.

Horecky, Paul L. *Libraries and Bibliographic Centers in the Soviet Union,* Indiana University Publications. Slavic and East European Studies Series Volume 16. Washington, D.C.: Council on Library Resources, 1959.

Humeniuk, M.P., ed. *Knyha i biblioteka na sluzhbi nauky: Zbirnyk naukovykh prats',* [The book and library in the service of scholarship: A compilation of scholarly works]. Kyiv: Naukova dumka, 1978.

_____, et al. eds. *Knyha i biblioteka na sluzhbi nauky,* [The book and library in the service of scholarship]. Kyiv: Naukova dumka, 1978.

Igumnova, N.P. "The Problems of Retrospective Conversion in the Research Libraries of the Socialist Countries: A Survey." *IFLA Journal,* 16 (1990): 91-6.

Ilnytzkyj, Oleh S. "Cultural Turf Wars: Slavic Studies and the New World Order." Seminar presented at the University of Alberta. 15 March 1993.

_____. "Russian and Ukrainain Studies and the New World Order." *Canadian Slavonic Papers/Revue Canadienne des Slavistes,* 34 (1993): 445-58.

Inkova, Ljudmila, and I. Osipova. "Librarianship in the USSR: The Reality of Transformation.' *IFLA Journal,* 17 (1991): 115-27.

Ilyina, Emilia. "A Russian Critique of Russian History." *Ukrainian Echo,* 15 February 1989, 7-8.

Jokic, Maja. "Information Value of Papers Written in Slavonic Languages in the Medline Database." *Online Review,* 16 (1992): 17-25.

Karetzky, Stephan. "The International Ideology of Library and Information Science: The Past Three Decades." *The Reference Librarian,* 33 (1991): 173-81.

Kuz'min, Evgenii. "At a Crossroads: Russian Libraries Face the Future." *Wilson Library Bulletin,* 67 (January 1993), 52-55, 57.

Kasinec, Edward. "Library and Archival Developments in Eastern Europe—and US." *Research Libraries Notes,* 4 (1992): no. 3: 7-8.

_____. *New Resources from Eastern Europe,* Paper presented as part of a symposium "Europe East and West: New Resources for North American Libraries." At the 112th Annual Conference of the American Libraries Association—Slavic & East European Section, New Orleans, Louisiana, 28 June 1993.

_____. *Slavic Books and Bookmen: Papers and Essays,* New York: Russica Publishers, 1984.

_____. "Zastroika, Perestroika, Rasstroika, Destroika, and Us." *The Serials Librarian,* 21 (1991): 59-67.

Kimmage, Dennis, ed. *Russian Libraries in Transition: An Anthology of Glasnost Literature,* Jefferson, North Carolina: McFarland, 1992.

Kohl, E. "The Challenge of Change in Eastern Europe to the Parliamentary Libraries in the West." *IFLA Journal,* 17 (1991): 128-34.

Konn, Tania. "Eastern European Online Information." *Aslib Information,* 18 (November/December 1990): 352-533.

————. "Eastern European Online Information—II." *Aslib Information,* 19 (July/August 1991): 265-55.

————. "Glasnost and the Business Information Sector: Soviet Problems and Perspectives." *Online,* 15 (February 1991): 19-26.

Krol, Ed. *The Whole Internet User's Guide & Catalog,* Sebastapol, California: O'Reilly & Associates, 1992.

Kubijovyc, Volodymyr, ed. *Ukraine a Concise Encyclopaedia,* Toronto: Ukrainian National Association, 1817. S.v. "Libraries," by V. Doroshenko and B. Krawciw.

Kuzmin, Evgenii. "At the Crossroads: Russian Libraries Face the Future." *Wilson Library Bulletin,* 67 (1993), No. 5: 52-58.

Lastovskaia, G. "S veroi v cheloveka." [With faith in mankind]. *Bibliotekar',* [Librarian] n.s. 10 (1986): 48-9.

Lisson, Paul. "History, Change and Libraries in the Soviet Union." *Canadian Library Journal,* 48 (February 1991): 47-50.

Makuch, Andrew. "A Critique of Exclusion Categories for Translations in the Acquisitions Policies of major Research Libraries." *Collection Management,* 15 (1992), no. 3/4: 381-87.

Markiw, Michael. "Searching of East Slavic Materials in Library Catalogs." *The Reference Librarian,* 22 (1988): 309-316.

Mikhnova, I . "... Litsa neobshchim vyrazhenem." [... Faces with unsocial expressions]. *Bibliotekar',* [Librarian] 6 (1990): 15-7.

Mironov, Georgii Efimovich. Mokhov, N. J. "Libraries as a Means of Education and Enlightenment. International Federation of Library Associations, 1970." Eric Reports Washington, D.C.: U.S. Department of Health, Education, and & Welfare, 1970.

Mokhov, N.J. *Librarians as a Means of Education and Enlightenment,* Seven Oaks, England: International Federation of Library Associations, 1970.

"Navstrechu ocherednomu partiinomu s'ezdu." [Towards the next Party Congress]. *Bibliotekar',* [Librarian] 11 (1989): 2-4.

Parcell, Elisabeth. "Focus on the Soviet Union and Eastern Europe." *Library Association Record,* 92 (November 1990): 852.

Pipes, Richard, Robert Conquest, Peter Rutland, Martin Malia, et al. "The Strange Death of Soviet Communism: An Autopsy." *National Interest,* [Special issue], (Spring 1992).

"Propagandu knigi na uroven novykh zadach." [The propagation of books in accordance with the new tasks]. *Bibliotekar'* [Librarian] 6 (1986): 19.

Rabkin, Y.M. "Scientific and Political Freedoms." *Technology in Society,* 13 (1991) 52-68.

Raymond, Boris. "Libraries and Adult Education: The Russian Experience." *The Journal of Library History,* 16 (1981): 396.

————. *Krupskaia and Soviet Russian Librarianship, 1917-1939.* Metuchen, N.J.: The Scarecrow Press, Inc., 1979.

————. Russian Education for Library and Information Service." *Canadian Library Journal,* 48 (December 1991): 399-404.

Rochester, Maxine K. "The Impact of Economic and Social Trends on Education for Librarianship in the USSR." *International Leads,* 5 (Winter 1991): 5-6.

Rogers, Sally A. 'Backlog Management: Estimating Resources Needed to Eliminate Arrearages." *Library Resources & Technical Services,* 35 (January 1991): 25-32.

Rudall, B.H. "Innovative Products and Projects." *Robotica* 8 (July 1990): 182-3.

Ruggles, Melville, J., and Richard C. Swank. *Soviet Libraries and Librarianship: Report of the Visit of the Delegation of U.S. Librarians to the Soviet Union, May-June, 1961, under the U.S.-Soviet Cultural Exchange Agreement,* Chicago: American Library Association, 1962.

"Russian & Ukrainian Archive and Business Research Service." [Advertisement] *AAASS Newsletter,* 33 (January 1993): 45.

Sherbakova, I. "Voina dvum "Sh"". [War against cliche and routine]. *Bibliotekar',* [Librarian] n.s. 3 (1991): 34-6.

Shtohryn, Dmytro, professor of cataloging at the Slavic Library of the University of Illinois. Interview by author, 6 April 1993. Unrecorded telephone interview.

Simsova, S. ed. *Lenin, Krupskaia and Libraries.* Trans. G. Peacock and Lucy Prescott. Hamden, CT: Archon Books, 1968.

"Slavic Librarians' Electronic Mail Forum." *Association of College and Research Libraries Slavic & East European Section Newsletter,* 9 (1993): 48-9.

Slon, Eugene. "History of Open Access to Library Collections in the Soviet Union 1714-1959." Ithaca, NY: n.p., 1974.

_____. *Open Access to Soviet Book Collections,* N.Y.: Ukrainian Library Association of America, 1978.

Stasiuk, Ie. M. ed. *Knyha i biblioteka na sluzhbi nauky: Zbirnyk naukovykh prats',* [The book and library in the service of scholarship: A compilation of scholarly works]. Kyiv: Naukova dumka, 1978.

Studwell, William E. *Library of Congress Subject Headings: Philosophy, Practice, and Prospects,* New York: Haworth Press, 1990.

"Summary Record of the Meetings of the [IFLA] Executive Board held on 16, 20 and 21 August 1991 in Moscow, USSR." *IFLA Journal,* 17 (1991): 424-5.

Turchyn, Andrew. "Needed at the Library of Congress: Classification Changes." *The Ukrainian Quarterly,* 29, no. 2 (1973): 179-94.

_____. "Slavic Publications: Their Cataloging and Classification in American Libraries." In *Cataloging and Classification of Non-Western Material: Concerns, Issues and Practices,* edited by Mahammed M. Aman. Phoenix, Arizona: Oryx Press, 1980: 297-320.

The Ukrainian Herald Issue 7-8. Ethnocide of Ukrainians in the U.S.S.R. Spring 1974. An Underground Journal from Soviet Ukraine. Compiled by Maksym Sahaydak. Trans. and edited by Olena Saciuk and Bohdan Yasen. Baltimore: Smoloskyp, 1976.

"Ukrainska Pravnycha Fundatsia/The Ukrainian Legal Foundation." Proposal Approved by George Soros and the Soros Foundations. April 23, 1992. TMs [photocopy]A. Rutkowski, Government Publications, Cameron Library, University of Alberta, Edmonton, Alberta.

Uporova, V. "Ne prenebregat dostignutym." [Without ignoring our accomplishments]. *Bibliotekar'* [Librarian] 6 (1990): 10-4.

Usdin, S. "Soviet Systems: Much Need, but Few Rubles." *Datamation,* 37 (April 1991): 64-7— 64-8.

Veryha, Wasyl. "Library of Congress Classification and Subject Headings Relating to Slavic and Eastern Europe." *Library Resources and Technical Services,* 16, no. 4 (Fall 1972): 470-87.

Volpe, M. "On the Leading Edge." [Soviet analysis of articles in CLJ; reprinted from *Bibliotekar',* 7 (1989)]. *Canadian Library Journal* 48 (February 1991): 51-4.

Whitby, Thomas J., and Thomas Lorkovic. *Introduction to Soviet National Bibliography,* Littleton, Colorodo: Libraries Unlimited, 1979.

White, Herb S. *Library Personnel Management,* New York: Knowledge Industry Publications, 1985.

Zaychenko, Serguei. "Libraries in Eastern Europe Come in From the Cold." *American Libraries,* 23 (January 1992): 20.

Zhikhareva, N. "Vse, chto mogu lichno ..." [All that I am personally capable of ...]. *Bibliotekar,* [Librarian] 6 (1990): 6-9.

Fourth I. T. Littleton Seminar

Virtual Collections:
Only Keystrokes Away

*Made possible in part
with support from:*

**ADONIS
Apple Computer
Article Express International
CARL Systems
Chemical Abstracts Service
Data Research Associates
Digital Equipment Corporation
EBSCO
Faxon
Heckman Bindery
Hewlett - Packard
Oxford University Press
SOLINET
UMI**

North Carolina State University Libraries

FOURTH I. T. LITTLETON SEMINAR
VIRTUAL COLLECTIONS: ONLY KEYSTROKES AWAY

Tracey M. Casorso

FOREWORD

Increasingly, the information infrastructure for research is characterized by powerful, graphics-capable desktop computers equipped with flexible, sophisticated software and connected to local and national networks for access to a variety of information sources. The growing demand on libraries to provide access to information in electronic form and to integrate library services with other network technologies in academia is forcing libraries to explore information technologies that participate fully in an integrated information infrastructure. The emergence of graphics-based computers and computer networks make possible the establishment of high-speed, high-resolution electronic document delivery services to meet some of those demands.

In a 1983 report entitled "Document Delivery in the United States," commissioned by the council on Library Resources, it stated that "very few people...librarians or their patrons ...have had the experience of rapid document delivery. Almost all of us have learned to work around the limitations of the ILL system. The actual performance of the ILL system has done an excellent job of convincing users to wait." That same report strongly

Advances in Library Administration and Organization, Volume 12, pages 145-148.
Copyright © 1994 by JAI Press Inc.
All rights of reproduction in any form reserved.
ISBN: 1-55938-846-3

recommended investigating the development of an electronic document delivery service, though the authors seemed pessimistic about the possibilities of such a service, and stated that "only when a sufficient body of electronic information has been collected will attention turn to the transfer of it..."

Two pivotal events have brought about precisely the body of electronic information called for in the 1983 report. First, the National Agricultural Library, and many others , have began to create extensive collections of digitized materials by scanning their own materials, building a core collection of electronic documents for an electronic delivery service. Second the development of commercial, high- resolution scanners have made it possible to create digitized documents on demand from existing print copy. The confluence of technological, economic and service factors within the past few years have served as the catalyst in the design and development of high-speed, high-resolution electronic document delivery services such as those described at the Fourth I. T. Littleton Seminar on advances in electronic document delivery entitled "Virtual Collections: Only Key Strokes Away."

"Libraries have a long, rich intellectual history of selecting and making accessible many types of research materials, but that heritage has yet to cope with electronic media", said John E. Ulmschneider, assistant director for Library Systems at NCSU in the opening session. Despite predictions of the worst snowstorm in three years, the day-long seminar drew more than 250 attendees from across campus, the state of North Carolina, and from as far away as Texas and Chicago and proceeded on schedule on February 26, 1993 at the NCSU McKimmon Center. Libraries, of necessity, are investing in the networking infrastructure required to provide network-based delivery of library materials and are rethinking their current service models and professional development as the first steps toward building a "virtual" collection. The morning's program featured the three national and regional library-led efforts that have sought to develop network-based document transmission systems for delivering materials between libraries and directly to the researcher's workstation. The delivery systems-the Ariel Document Transmission System by the Research Libraries Group, the CICnet Network Fax Project by CICnet and The Ohio State University, and the Digitized Document Transmission Project (a collaborative effort by North Carolina State University Libraries, NCSU Academic Computing Center and the National Agricultural Library)" use the Internet and campus networks for transmitting materials but differ significantly in terms of their design, functionality, and flexibility. Marilyn Roche (Research Libraries Group), Robert Kalal (The Ohio State University), and Tracy M. Casorso (NCSU Libraries) each described their respective systems and how these systems have met the document delivery needs of faculty, students, and staff.

Malcolm Getz (associate provost for Information Services and Technology at Vanderbilt University) closed the morning program with a discussion of

"Petyabytes of Information: New Landscapes of Scholarly Discourse." Getz stated, "Rapid technical change in information storage and communication offers new methods for scholars to communicate with one another.... [A]s ... technologies develop, there will be new roles for readers, authors, editors, publishers, and libraries." Getz proposed a number of initiatives in his remarks that would advance these roles.

The afternoon program featured a showcase session and exhibits, a new and welcome addition to this year's seminar. Eighteen applicants were selected to spotlight innovative applications of technology and services for improving access to information. Seminar attendees particularly enjoyed the Geographic Information System (GIS) presentation offered by Lisa Abbott (NCSU Libraries) and Margaret Brill (Duke University). Using a GIS-mapping software package, attendees were able to retrieve instantaneously street maps of their hometowns, schools, and other locations. Fred Heath (library director at Texas Christian University) profiled TCU's "just in time" access for "just in case" subscriptions model for unmediated delivery of research materials to the researcher. "Trinity's Knowledge Network" by Alfred Burfeind and Angela Wolf (Trinity College, Hartford Connecticut) explored the direct access to Trinity's campus-wide computer network that links dorms and faculty offices to information, local library services and libraries, databases, and information servers worldwide via the Internet. In addition to the showcase presentations by librarians, representatives from leading commercial document delivery services also demonstrated their systems and services.

"Users need not come to the collection to use the collection but will be able to access the collection and obtain materials in the format most appropriate for the materials and most useful to the user," said Ulmschneider in his afternoon presentation on "A Model Automated Document Delivery System for Research Libraries." Ulmschneider unveiled and discussed the technical design of the proposed Triangle Research Libraries Network document delivery system. Sheila Creth (university librarian at the University of Iowa) challenged librarians in her dynamic and thought-provoking keynote address "to be everywhere.... [W]e must extend the concept that the technology provides ... beyond the virtual collection ... to the 'virtual librarian.' ... [O]ur challenge is to take the librarian to the researcher's workstation, the classroom, dorm, and lab ... wherever users are located." Creth does not view technology as the real issue but instead targets the need for a fundamental restructuring of library services to take advantage of the power and tools that computers and communications technologies offer.

Marjorie W. Lindsey, retired consultant for the State Library of North Carolina and former editor of Tarheel Libraries, closed the seminar with a tribute to I. T. Littleton. Lindsey worked closely with Littleton on many initiatives when he was director of the NCSU library, including the formation of the Capital Area Library Association in 1979, which is one of the co-hosts of this year's seminar. The I. T. Littleton seminar series, established in 1987 to honor Littleton's achievements, is a reflection of the NCSU Libraries" ongoing commitment to keep researchers and librarians abreast of major library issues shaping the research environment.

The NCSU Libraries wishes to extend a special thank you to this year's seminar supporters: Adonis, Apple Computer, Article Express, CARL Systems, Chemical Abstracts Service, Data Research Associates, Digital Equipment Corporation, EBSCO, Faxon, Heckman Bindery, Hewlett-Packard, Oxford University Press, SOLINET, and UMI. The seminar was partially funded by the Library Services and Construction Act, Title III, administered by the Division of State Library, North Carolina Department of Cultural Resources.

VIRTUAL COLLECTIONS:
THE IMPLICATIONS FOR LIBRARY PROFESSIONALS
AND THE ORGANIZATION

Sheila D. Creth

The theme of this conference, virtual collections, is an exciting and timely one. The reality of virtual collections, or the "new architecture for information delivery," will not evolve in a vacuum but has implications for the role and responsibilities of professionals as well as the organization of library operations and services. The delivery of library materials justifiably is receiving increasing attention as high-speed computer networks offer the potential for a future in which access to scholarly information will be possible in a highly distributed and personalized manner. Computer and telecommunication systems will increasingly provide the means for individuals to retrieve and receive information. The technology that is influencing these changes, though, is a tool without independent power to shape the future. It is individuals—librarians and others—who will design the systems, select and organize information in all formats, and provide the considerable support required by users to navigate the new electronic highways while continuing to learn about the vast resources that are accessible only by wandering the back roads of library stacks. This

Advances in Library Administration and Organization, Volume 12, pages 149-160.
Copyright © 1994 by JAI Press Inc.
All rights of reproduction in any form reserved.
ISBN: 1-55938-846-3

environment presents extraordinary opportunities and challenges for librarians as the full potential of computing and information technology is realized in all aspects of teaching, learning, and research in higher education.

A recent paper on information technology, developed for university presidents by the Higher Education Information Resources Alliance, states that "like it or not, prepared or not, our institutions of higher education are entering the information age. We have experienced more than a decade of proliferation of personal computers on the desks of executives, administrators, faculty, and students; of widely extended access to research resources, teaching techniques, administrative databases, and colleagues across campus and the world. Most institutions report increasing pressure from various constituencies for access to the power they believe to be available through the information technologies: instant answers, process shortcuts, responsiveness to individual needs, cost savings.... This is the time ... to effect the real information technology revolution; adjusting our organizational structures to accommodate and exploit what is valuable in these technological developments" ("What Presidents Need to Know," 1991).

In order to effect this information technology revolution in library services, enormous changes are required of the individual professional and in the operations and organization of the library. If the full potential of information technology is to be realized, library professionals will need to reconceive services in the most fundamental ways and to relinquish mindsets that are rooted in the past but lack currency in today's environment.

LIBRARIES AND LIBRARIANS IN THE 21ST CENTURY

If librarians and libraries are to have a vital role on the campus of the next century, considerable attention needs to be given to two essential components in the equation of quality service: (1) organizational structure and design and (2) professional roles and responsibilities. Technology is exciting, but it is not where the greatest challenge lies. The greatest challenge is in developing the ability of individual librarians to respond in a timely and imaginative way to the opportunities presented by information technology. If academic libraries are to make the transition to virtual collections, then all functions and activities of the university and university library will require reconsideration and will, no doubt, be altered and modified in significant ways during the remainder of this century. The implications of virtual collections and, by extension, the virtual library are profound and profoundly challenging.

The focus of this conference has been on existing and emerging document delivery systems based on technological developments. The implementation of these systems should involve a review of what is desired in a service rather than simply overlaying the technology onto the current construct of service, policy, and procedure. In considering the purpose of document delivery, or interlibrary loan, and how networks will facilitate this traditional library service, librarians should step back and rethink the service from the perspective of the user. Do the powerful computing and network systems suggest a different structure and quality of user service? For example, are librarians prepared to design and administer systems that permit, and indeed encourage, the user to initiate requests for borrowing to another institution via online systems? Computer networks and expert systems make this technically possible, while consortial arrangements among institutions would provide the administrative framework to ensure sufficient control regarding participation. Such a system, however, requires that library staff give up responsibility as gatekeepers for the interlibrary loan program and instead transfer primary responsibility to the user. A system of unmediated interlibrary lending does have a number of administrative implications, including allocation of budget for the cost of borrowing from another institution. The way in which the "book budget" or material funds are distributed may alter substantially as access to materials rather than the purchase of materials becomes more common. Indeed, as a variety of document delivery services emerge, including commercial ones that are likely to dominate the electronic document delivery environment, the use of funds to build collections will be allocated instead to obtaining individual articles or chapters. In addition, these issues that require attention, the possibilities offered by online systems can be fully exploited for timely information delivery only if librarians relinquish the practice of being the intermediary in all interlibrary borrowing.

This realignment of service not only puts the user in the center but supports the development of virtual collections and ultimately the virtual library. The concept of a "virtual library" began to develop over the past several years with discussion focusing on creating shared collections and services among libraries in a consortium. Most recently, the Association of Research Libraries (ARL) issued a SPEC kit on this topic demonstrating the currency this concept is enjoying even if actual application is not yet a reality (The Emerging Virtual Research Library, 1992). The virtual library—as a model—suggests an organization in which a network of people (from various departments within a single library or from multiple libraries) apply their expertise, knowledge, and energy in a collaborative manner to enhance the delivery of information services. The computer systems and international networks provide the foundation on which collaborative efforts will be established and sustained.

Transition to a virtual library—however the concept is defined and refined over time—requires a reconsideration of all functions and activities of the university library and, by extension, those of library staff. Some professionals find the prospect of these changes exciting, while others find disturbing the inevitability of fundamental changes in the organizational structure and in their personal responsibilities and roles. In order for a shift to occur in the roles and responsibilities of professionals, a change in the professional and organizational culture must occur. Flexibility on the part of individual professionals is essential in considering new organizational structures, new working and collegial relationships, and new methods and standards for accomplishing quality work. New ideas need to be considered objectively and not dismissed out of hand even if initially they appear to be unworkable. The very process of considering different approaches to operations and services encourages an assessment of what already exists. The current reality of universities and university libraries requires professionals to re-imagine, to redefine, and to reshape libraries and library services.

This process of considering new organizational structures and professional roles and responsibilities also requires an awareness of the forces that influence universities and their libraries. In a series of meetings involving university provosts and library directors, a number of the critical external forces affecting higher education were identified which includes:

- developing the national research and education network
- strengthening undergraduate education
- increasingly constrained budgets
- proliferating information sources and spiraling costs of materials
- pressing space and facilities maintenance needs
- changing scholarly communication system
- increasing interdependence of library and computer centers
- decreasing prestige of higher education in society
- shifting student demographics
- building relationships with the commercial sector (Dougherty and Hughes, 1991).

While all of the forces affecting higher education have implications for library service and organizational structure, the following are particularly relevant.

CONSTRAINED BUDGETS AND INCREASING DEMANDS

Library staff members have been struggling with runaway inflation for materials while also trying to cope with the proliferation of new print publications and a flood of materials now available in electronic format. During the past three to five years, library budgets have been severely strained, if not outright cut, for materials, staff, computing hardware and software, and other operation needs. These budget pressures have occurred at a time when library users—faculty and students—are clamoring for more timely, easy, and convenient access to information resources (owned locally or obtained elsewhere) and for greater assistance in learning to understand and use the array of complex information resources.

Clearly, library administrators and library professionals need to consider new approaches for allocating funds and providing access to local collections, and they need to determine the most effective use of staff resources in a very different organization and information environment.

The quality of education for the undergraduate has become a national issue at private and public universities. Librarians need to evaluate whether current library services ensure that students, as part of their education experience, are acquiring the knowledge and skills basic for living in a complex world of information.

In 1987 the Carnegie Foundation supported a study of undergraduate education in which 29 four-year colleges or universities were visited (Boyer, 1987). The findings about academic libraries include the following:

- despite idealism regarding the library as the heart of the campus, libraries at most institutions are a neglected resource.
- half of all undergraduates spend "no more than 2 hours" in the library every week.
- over half of the students never use the library to consult specialized bibliographies or to read a basic document.
- about 40 percent never use the library to run down leads or look for further references.
- most undergraduates viewed the library as "simply a quiet place to study."

And one university administrator said that in 25 years, the library will be as obsolete as the unused chapel on campus.

The results of this study are sobering if not alarming. The Carnegie report makes clear that academic librarians are certainly not meeting a goal that each and every undergraduate will develop information knowledge and skills while in a four-year program. In order to reach the campus population, librarians should consider ways to deliver services differently as well as imagining new services that take advantage of electronic resources and telecommunication links. Indeed, the merger of technological developments, constrained budgets, and a large and diverse user population suggests that all operations and services should be re-assessed to ensure the most innovative and effective library services.

LIBRARY ORGANIZATION

The traditional organization of university libraries, structured around public and technical services with a focus on a vertical hierarchical structure, is rapidly becoming dysfunctional. Instead, the library organization should be flexible in design, relying on small groups or teams as the primary way to accomplish that work. Priorities and emerging opportunities should guide the assignment of staff. Professionals should not assume that a current position is permanent either in regard to specific assignments, the duties they perform, or the location of their activities. One author states that the mature organization, with its "long-established norms of stability and security must be replaced with new values such as speed, simplicity, unparalleled customer service, and a self-confident, empowered work force" (Keen, 1991). The pressure on individual library staff to keep up with demands in today's environment, which is often a struggle, means that they deserve and require new ways of accomplishing their work. The redesign of the library organization is imperative, and information technology provides the tools to create a collaborative and virtual organization.

Peter Keen states that "globalization has extended lines of communication and coordination across time zones and locations, affecting breadth of markets, services, customer demands.... This hyperextension of activities is greatly straining the ability of traditional organizations to respond" (Keen, 1991). He goes on to indicate that the pressures are increasing because the stress of "shortened planning development and delivery cycles, and increased environmental volatility have drastically reduced acceptable reaction time." Furthermore, Keen identifies characteristics of organizational complexity as including more managerial layers, elaboration of procedures and controls, administrative overhead, reliance on communication by paper, and the reporting structure. This complexity, he finds, contributes to a sluggish organization in both quality and timeliness of response. While Keen is not referring specifically to libraries, these statements could certainly describe the university library environment. The challenge for library professionals is to examine other organization constructs to determine what is required in today's world.

Peter Drucker concludes that the management of the "new organization" has to draw on three systematic practices: first, a continuing improvement of everything the organization does; second, learning to exploit organization knowledge and developing the next generation of applications from its successes; and, finally, every organization has to learn to innovate—to plan innovation and change in a systematic way. In Drucker's view, a high degree of decentralization is required to achieve this organizational change (Drucker, 1992).

Keen, who sees change as the norm, suggests that the organization should shift "emphasis from organizing by division of labor to organizing by division of knowledge." He considers that the division of knowledge "captures an obvious reality of work in an era of rapid change and uncertainty. Tasks are no longer predictable and experience may no longer be valuable. New inputs of knowledge are needed to define tasks, and multiple skills and experience are needed to complete them" (Keen, 1991).

Charles Martell, in his 1983 book *The Client-Centered Academic Library*, indicated that the "optimal client-centered design would have the following characteristics: most librarians in client-centered work groups and these groups would have high degree of autonomy, all librarians in the work groups would be involved in multi-function roles such as reference, collection development and advisory services to clients, and a high level of interaction with clients would exist" (Martell, 1983). Ten years later, the technology is available to support the dynamic client-centered organization envisioned by Martell.

In the survey conducted by the ARL on the virtual library, library directors ranked the need for new organization structures as critical to creating the virtual library (The Emerging Virtual Research Library, 1992). By exploiting the range of information technologies to create "rich and dense connections," it will be possible for library professionals to maintain, even enhance, their roles and contribution to learning, teaching, and research in higher education.

In order to make the transition from an organizational structure that is hierarchical and segmented to one that is fluid and flexible, library professionals need to experiment and explore, to remain open to considering new approaches, and to keep the user as the central focus.

In 1991 the University of Iowa Libraries began a process of reorganization. The most fundamental change was the establishment of discipline divisions— humanities, social sciences, and sciences—within which every service from cataloging and collection development to reference and user education are incorporated. There are multiple goals in the new organization structure, the primary one is to create an organization that will more nearly reflect the academic model and the way in which faculty and students seek resources to support teaching, research, and independent learning. Secondly, the integrative, horizontal model of the discipline-division structure is intended to bring together librarians with similar responsibilities who are focused on a broad but related group of users in order to address issues such as budget allocations for materials as well as the development of user education programs. It also is intended to encourage and facilitate decisions being made further down in the organization and to discourage an over-reliance on the hierarchical structure.

While the reorganization of the University of Iowa Libraries has been far from smooth, and some number of librarians reject the concept of discipline divisions or working in a team, the structure does meet, to some degree, the goals that were intended. What is important is to explore and test organizational models that move away from the segmented and hierarchical structure of the traditional library to create a more open and flexible structure and to establish structures that have the potential to facilitate greater responsiveness to user needs.

Beyond improvements in the individual library organizational structure and services, options for establishing partnerships among libraries should be explored. Specifically, consideration of shared operations and services among libraries in geographic proximity should be examined to determine costs and benefits. For example, is it feasible for several libraries to share an acquisitions department, or to divide cataloging responsibilities by subject and/or languages, or to contract for preservation activities? Could some number of libraries establish a shared online reference and research consultation service with subject experts from each campus library contributing knowledge and time to the online service? An approach of combining the professional knowledge among a consortium of libraries might well enhance information service for users in certain academic disciplines or fields on multiple campuses.

The library organization structure, staff working relationships, and the communication network among university libraries all need to be examined in order to identify ways to facilitate quality services in a timely manner. In addition, an examination of shared library operations should be analyzed to determine if there are more cost-effective ways to accomplish certain essential services. Finally, we need to accept that re-organization of functions and organizational structure are likely to be a continuous feature of libraries in the future.

The second component in the equation for a viable future encompasses professional changes. It is in this area that the greatest challenge exists—the willingness of individuals to change.

PROFESSIONAL CHANGE

Librarians should be highly visible and well-integrated into the research and teaching activities of their institutions. They should be viewed by faculty as valuable team members in teaching and curriculum design and research endeavors. More broadly, librarians and libraries should be seen as part of the solution (i.e., delivery of quality education and support of research) rather than as part of a problem (i.e., escalating costs in higher education, inadequacy of undergraduate education, and inadequate support for research).

Increasingly, the concept of "library" will be more diffuse and personal for the individual researcher, student, and faculty member. They will think of the library as what they are able to retrieve and store electronically from their individual workstations (even if the retrieval is for print materials). In this context, the location of (and access to) the information professional, who is a critical information resource, should be possible beyond the walls of the library. A definition of the virtual library also could apply to the librarian: in the ultimate virtual library the user has access to universal knowledge without delay at his or her desk. The librarian, transformed into the virtual librarian or information professional, also would be readily accessible to users at their workstations via the telecommunication network. In order to achieve this level and scope of service, librarians need to be bold and imaginative in conceiving of their roles and decisive in acting upon them.

Information technology and communication systems are driving the scope and pace of change in all aspects of library and information service as well as in teaching and research. Though the impact of technology might be felt differently across the spectrum of academic fields and among individual faculty, increased use of information and communication technology in all areas of academic life is the reality for the future. While these technologies offer powerful new means to improve the timely delivery of print and electronic information, they also offer the potential for greater access to the knowledge and skill of the information professional. High-speed and ubiquitous communication networks will make possible not only virtual collections but the virtual librarian!

Existing and emerging technologies make it possible to offer services in new ways and to design new services. For example, provision of basic reference service via electronic mail systems should be standard both in responding to basic questions or requests for in-depth, research-level consultation. Librarians also should teach via the Internet, or the campus network, and should use video or fiber-optic transmission systems available for "distance teaching"—on and off the campus. We should be rapidly transforming the traditional library ("we are in the library available to answer your questions") to the teaching library ("we are everywhere instructing on information sources, search strategies, and the analytical skills necessary to use a vast array of sources"). The availability of information technology and communication systems to teach and to learn is not futuristic, it exists today.

Indeed, librarians use these very systems to expand their own knowledge on an issue or topic through participation in discussion groups on the Internet. A variety of topics are examined by librarians across the country and around the world—including reference, user education, interlibrary loan, rare book cataloging, and copyright, to name just a few of the more than 100 library listservs. The online discussion format allows individuals to share their knowledge and experience and to learn from the views and opinions of their colleagues, all in an inexpensive and convenient manner through the Internet. The individual librarian does not have to wait until he or she attends a conference or meeting, nor rely on contact only with colleagues in the home institution. While this dynamic source for learning is used extensively by librarians for their own development, so far they have failed to tap its potential for instructing library users. Recently, an individual conducted a session over the network to instruct people in how to navigate the Internet—a prerequisite being sufficient knowledge to at least get into the system. The class had a worldwide enrollment in the tens of thousands. This suggests that librarians could provide effective instruction to the undergraduate population via the Internet, informing them about library and information services and resources in all formats and instructing them on the use of the Internet as well.

In addition, librarians should develop computer-assisted instruction (CAI) packages for both general orientation and reference assistance, as well as for instruction in the use of a specific bibliographic tool or electronic text source. CAI programs, or tutorials, could be available in a variety of formats, depending on the nature of the instructional package, including access via the campus network, the library online system, a stand-alone system at a particular location, or on floppy disks. Some librarians have become actively involved recently in assisting, and even encouraging, faculty in the redesign of their courses using multimedia technology and online interactive programs. It is time for the information professionals to use these same technologies in developing instructional programs for library users.

The focus for future reference service should be on taking the reference desk and the knowledge of the reference librarian to the classroom, the dorm, the office, the lab—wherever users are located. This requires exploring new models for reference service. Jerry Campbell, in his article "Shaking the Conceptual Foundations of Reference," states that what is required is a new paradigm in reference services, one that is not a "building-centered ... 'make them come to us' model" (Campbell, 1992).

NEW MODELS FOR REFERENCE

In a discussion on the Visions listserv, Anne Lipow provided a description of a reference construct that is based on a service available at Disney World (Lipow, 1992). Characteristics of this service include remote access by users via the "teledesk," which consists of interactive visual and voice connections between the user and an advisory service consultant rather than a "reference librarian."

The idea of the "teledesk" is to maintain not only a level of personalized service but also a distributed service, one that is greater in efficiency and more responsive than the current library reference or information desk. This is not far-fetched and the technology is available now.

A forerunner to the teledesk concept was initiated by the University of Southern California Library in 1985-86 when two "satellite libraries" were created—one in a dorm and the other in a student activity center. These satellite libraries were supported entirely through computer access to the online catalog and other information sources, with teaching and instruction provided by librarians in these nonlibrary locations. The technology used at USC less than 10 years ago seems almost primitive considering what can be offered today via powerful telecommunication systems and an array of software products. The ability to take library information and services out of the library by use of technology is a reality and should be pursued aggressively by librarians.

Most universities now have computer clusters distributed in multiple sites around the campus—offering the opportunity for librarians to use these as "satellite libraries" or information centers. Librarians could conduct instructional sessions periodically at these sites, teaching access to the online catalog and the Internet as well as providing demonstrations of other electronic products. They also could instruct users remotely via the campus network, with the students distributed at the multiple computer clusters around the campus and the librarian located in the library. HyperCard orientation programs developed by librarians could be made available at each of these sites, and the availability of online reference services via e-mail could be posted at each computer cluster site as well as being part of a menu selection offered at each workstation. In addition, librarians could use conference software to offer instruction throughout the semester to students on information resources related to the specific course. As the course instructor gives assignments to the students requiring use of library and information resources, the librarian is available to provide guidance via the online network. The potential exists at this very moment for librarians—who are a critical information resource— to be available both physically and electronically across the campus, rather than requiring that faculty and students always come to the library.

Librarians need to find ways to transform services through the use of computer technology and telecommunications rather than only offering efficiencies in the delivery of information. Unless education and research are improved, how will the payoff of the millions of dollars that universities have invested in technology and information systems be demonstrated? When electronic systems for delivery of information are created, but there is a failure to teach people how to make full use of these systems, only half of the job is done.

There are numerous ways in which the activities and responsibilities of librarians should change—will need to change—if their roles within the information and scholarly communication process are to continue in a vital way—or at all. The professional staff at the University of Iowa recently developed a document that illustrates their vision of the future. It is an ambitious and exciting statement, but it cannot be achieved without reconsidering services in fundamental ways and relinquishing the security of past practices and activities to venture out on the thin ice of innovation. Librarians occupy a unique position within the academy with strong links to faculty and computing professionals. Librarians have a rare opportunity to forge new alliances and partnerships on the campus. They can provide the leadership that will exploit fully the information technology necessary to ensure that universities have access to the full range of ideas, opinions, historical perspective, and data required for learning and research. This is an awesome responsibility. Virtual collections are useless if individuals in all sectors of the university do not have the knowledge or skill and the financial and intellectual capability to access and use these resources. To accept this challenge as information professionals means we accept the excitement and the discomfort related to creating fundamental change in our organizations and services, roles and responsibilities. This is necessary if we are to provide the leadership required in the information world of the next century.

REFERENCES

Boyer, Ernest L. *College: The Undergraduate Experience in America*, (New York: Harper and Row, 1987), 160.

Campbell, Jerry D. "Shaking the Conceptual Foundations of Reference: A Perspective *Reference Services Review*, 20 (Winter, 1992), 32.

Dougherty, Richard M. and Carol Hughes. *Preferred Futures for Libraries: A Summary of Six Workshops with University Provosts and Library Directors*, (Mountain View, CA.: The Research Libraries Group, Inc., 1991), 10.

Drucker, Peter F. "The New Society of Organizations," *Harvard Business Review*, 70 (Sept-Oct 1992), 97.

The Emerging Virtual Research Library, (Washington, D.C.: Association of Research Libraries/ Office of Management Services, 1992).

Keen, Peter G. W. "Redesigning the Organization Through Information Technology," *Planning Review*, 19 (May/June 1991), 5, 7.

Lipow, Anne. "21st century job description," VISIONS Listserv (August 1991).

Martell, Charles. *The Client-Centered Academic Library: An Organizational Model*, (Westport, Ct.: Greenwood Press, 1983), 73.

"What Presidents Need to Know ... about the Integration of Information Technologies on Campus," *Higher Education Information Resources Alliance (HEIRA)*, (Boulder, Colorado: CAUSE, 1991), 1.

NEW TECHNOLOGIES, INTERLIBRARY LOAN, AND COMMERCIAL SERVICES:
A SYMPOSIUM ON THE DESIGN AND FEATURES OF ELECTRONIC DOCUMENT DELIVERY SYSTEMS

John E. Ulmschneider

I have a short slide show I would like to show you. This slide show and other demonstrations you're going to see are novel technologies for many of us. Novel technologies, as we all know, lead to novel expressions. In works of art, we know that as technological innovations come along, artists make use of them to make new and novel artistic creations. The same thing is happening to us in the more mundane endeavor of communicating information within the scholarly community. First of all, commonplace technologies are available today that make it easy to produce information that exists both on paper and in electronic form. For example, we use word processors and other computer tools to generate information that is in electronic form fundamentally, but comes to its full fruition on paper. There are more sophisticated but still accessible technologies that produce useful documents which only exist in electronic form; I'm going to show you just such a document. Finally, there are advanced technologies that produce "documents" which capture and present

Advances in Library Administration and Organization, Volume 12, pages 161-165.
Copyright © 1994 by JAI Press Inc.
All rights of reproduction in any form reserved.
ISBN: 1-55938-846-3

information in ways quite beyond the reach of our normal concept of a "document." We don't have a vocabulary that can give us a name for these "documents" yet, but they will be an important part of a library's collection and librarians will be responsible for ensuring that users can find and retrieve them.

In point of fact, it's the users, not librarians, who are actively exploring and seeking to find the most useful of these new modes of expression for the work they do. One of the reasons we are here is to learn about these new technologies and to discover a way to help users in storing, organizing and using these new modes of expression. But the eyes and ears of the users are open to the marketplace and alert to the evolving solutions for working with these new modes of expression. Users will not be satisfied with existing solutions from us, but will come to demand more as they find different solutions presented to them by the marketplace, especially in a sophisticated user community such as here at North Carolina State University. Already this community is demanding more than perhaps we're ready to do right now, and there is no reason to expect that demand to fall off; on the contrary, we can expect the pressure to increase. For example, industry people who follow the maturation of the multi-media market believe that it will be driven by entertainment value. They believe it will follow the same market development pattern as home video: start small in a niche market with high demand, such as pornography (which was very important in the beginning days of the video market), and expand from there. But I think the industry may have a surprise, because I feel that multi-media documents are such a new concept that their development will be driven by different things. In fact, I believe it will be driven as much by the utility value of documents to users as their entertainment value in the mass market. And it's users in the academic community who will be most concerned with utility value.

I'm going to show you a little movie, a movie that falls into the category of cheap thrills. It's the kind of thing that's very easy to do on a MacIntosh. Then I'm going to show you how you can take this kind of cheap thrill and make it into a useful document that can server a useful purpose in any kind of research or scholarly communication setup.

Text from movie:

> Male voice: The kitchen today is like a factory in a lot of ways. The product can only be good if the right tools are used. So modern factories use the best machinery that money can buy. As a result, the work is done faster, better and easier. Just as it is in the modern kitchen. See what I mean?
>
> Female voice: Golly, I'm so impressed!

It's a cheap thrill and a cheap effect, but I want to point out a couple of important aspects. First of all, that was a little movie right inside my presentation--it was part of my presentation document. I was able to pull it up and play it, and I didn't have to do anything special, you'll notice. The second thing is that the movie isn't actually inside my document. It actually resides outside of my document, which has a pointer to it. So I can use that movie in other documents if I wish, since it's not an integral part of my original document. I'm going to show you another example of that same movie in a different setting. This is a WordPerfect document generated with WordPerfect for Macintosh, with the same movie embedded within it. Now one of the things scholars like to do is to find convenient ways to express data on paper: innovative graphical presentations, for instance. Let's suppose that you have a dataset that has many variables that change over time and you want to be able to express those in a chart format on a piece of paper. It's difficult because the only available method is to print multiple versions of the chart—each one expressing the time-series change in the data. But here's an example of what you can do with an embedded movie in a document to express lots of data in real time. This is a chart of data on changing liposuction rates in industrial economies. It captures a timeline of data for several countries and several groups of people over about 10 years of time. I can do several things with this chart. Remember that all this is done within a WordPerfect document. If I want to show you each year of data one year at a time, all I have to do is click and show you. You can see it change. Isn't that a convenient and even powerful way to express a dataset? Right within a WordPerfect document. I can make it more dramatic and play it automatically when the page containing the chart is displayed. I can speed it up, I can slow it down, I can make it do all sorts of things to emphasize specific datapoints of interest.

The point I want to make, in these two documents, is that I had a pointer within the documents, a pointer down to where that little movie resided on my hard disk. It was the same movie in both documents. I could have taken that same dataset, that same movie and put them in all kinds of documents. It's a demonstration that even at this immature state of the technology, we—re already reaching for standardized ways to express useful information from within a "normal" document.

These example electronic documents demonstrate that, in a sense, electronic document delivery is not something as far in the future as you might think, and presents a short-term challenge to all of us. First of all, I think it's an immediate marketplace challenge both for suppliers of documents and for librarians. As I said earlier, I think that immediate utility motivates users, and I also think that convenience drives the world. As anything becomes more convenient, users will take advantage of them. The more convenient we make it for users to receive and use electronic documents, the more they will be used.

Second, I think that early success in document delivery will happen to those developers who balance well both technology and users. One of the things you'll see and hear a lot today are experiments, experimental efforts of developers trying to match technology to users. There is little consensus about what works right in the match-up. But the people who will be successful are those who get the best balance and the best match between the two. Thankfully there's no single market, and there's no single supplier. Rather, there is a fruitful ground in which to experiment and a richness in the experiments that are going on.

Third, everyone involved, but particularly the vendor community, senses an exciting market opportunity. I hope they're right and they hope they're right. I wish I could learn if they're actually making money on this stuff or not. The market opportunities will be an important goal in developing and deploying appropriate technologies for document delivery.

Finally, I think this is a fundamental intellectual challenge to all of us. We are right now formulating a new intellectual foundation and heritage for managing this new kind of information, just as we have a long heritage for managing many other kinds of materials in libraries. It's an exciting time to be thinking on these fundamental questions, to be rethinking the roles that authors and libraries and suppliers play in moving information from the author out to the author's intended audience.

This time of critical reflection about current service models is addressing most of all fundamental principles of interlibrary loan that libraries have supported for nearly 100 years. There's a great deal of writing in the literature about what interlibrary loan is. Many people are no longer using the term interlibrary loan because we're rethinking the entire concept, and the phrase now seems inadequate in the phase of an emerging "virtual collection" that wouldn't seem to need interlibrary loan at all. We're going to see what I would call the first steps toward a virtual collection. It is a collection that is more comprehensive than a physical collection in that it has a broader range of materials than a physical collection: it is not limited to physical items, but can access network resources and use electronic documents. The virtual collection will include a vast array of both printed materials in electronic form, printed materials in normal printed form, and electronic materials that can never exist on paper. It will be a collection that can be more accessible than a physical collection, because with electronic materials, users won't have to come to the physical location where materials are housed in order to use them. Ideally the collection will be deliverable in a format that's most appropriate both for the user and for the material—a format that's the right match between the technology and the user. And all this won't seem, on the face of it, to involve interlibrary loan.

But a virtual collection will have another face too: it will be a collection that will join materials into a comprehensive repository of knowledge, because it will have to join the expertise to manage the repository of knowledge as well as the repository of knowledge itself. I think that for libraries there will be a considerable intellectual investment in service, in redefining service that will be fused with new technologies. It's been said that "digital libraries" are a misnomer, because what we think of as a library is a great deal more than the things that are in a library's collection. It will be no different for the new kinds of materials from the way I look at it. Services like interlibrary loan will be redefined and reconceptualized, but the services will remain.

What we're going to see are basic technologies under development that will have an important role in creating virtual collections. These technologies fall in three arenas. First of all, there are technologies that deliver printed materials in electronic form. At the base of these technologies is the creation of full-text databases and scanning and storing full-page images. Second, there are technologies for delivering electronic documents that never appear or cannot appear on paper. And third, there are technologies for locating and requesting both kinds of materials in a convenient manner. Those are the things that we're going to talk about here today and those are the things you are going to see in the exhibit area.

IMAGE-IN THAT! GREAT IMAGES SENT 'OR ERE YOUR PULSE BEAT TWICE

Marilyn Roche

I am going to be speaking about Ariel, the image transmission system for the Internet. What is it? Where did it come from? What is its genesis? How does it support broad demand for information, for quality output, and for timely delivery? Where is it going? How dynamic is Ariel?

What is Ariel? It is software that permits the rapid electronic transmission of high-quality, scanned images over the Internet. What were some of the requirements that public services librarians gave us for Ariel? They wanted nondedicated equipment—equipment that could be used for other purposes in the ILL office, in branch libraries, or in faculty offices. They wanted fast scanning, transmission, and printing. They did not want to have to wait. Nobody wanted to photocopy, and they wanted to use the Internet for transmission to avoid additional costs to the library for the telecommunications. They wanted error-free transmission—no wavy lines, no loss of data, no margin truncation, and high image resolution. What is the value of the document if you cannot read it or the value of a graph if some of the figures are missing? They wanted it to be on plain paper—no recopying of fax paper.

Advances in Library Administration and Organization, Volume 12, pages 167-173.
Copyright © 1994 by JAI Press Inc.
All rights of reproduction in any form reserved.
ISBN: 1-55938-846-3

We will now take a look at what Ariel offers. It consists of a scanner, and, as I said before, you do not have to photocopy first. The software compresses the image down to one-fifteenth of its original size if it is text and down to one-eighth of its original size if it is a photograph. It scans and stores files in TIFF (tag image file format). We use TIFF because it is the standard used for fax and for other scanning, and we felt that we were not being proprietary in choosing it. You can store information temporarily while you are sending and until there is successful receipt of the Ariel image, or you can store it permanently if you think the document is going to be used over again.

The transmission part—what happens? It is error free. If there is any noise added by the telecommunications lines at either the sending or receiving end, the file is sent again. There is a check sum taken so that the receiving end knows exactly what has been sent. Users will not receive the file unless it is being sent error free, and there is guaranteed transmission. Ariel software ensures that if the transmission gets stuck in a node, the Ariel transmitting machine will recognize the problem and retransmit. At the receiving end, the PC takes a check sum and the Ariel image is held in an active file where it can be stored temporarily until it is printed. Printing can be done at night, unmanned or unstaffed. During the daytime, users may want to employ the scanner and PC for other jobs and turn it on for Ariel at night—walking away and letting the images come in and print out. The printed files may then be stored permanently. At the receiving end, there may be other uses for the transmissions. They can be sent to another Ariel machine in the system on campus or sent from the ILL office to a branch library or a faculty member's or student's workstation. A fax machine may be designated as an interim printer so that folks who already own fax machines can use them as printers.

Ariel is a fairly straightforward, simple piece of software. A two- or three-character destination code represents the IP address can be used because Ariel has an alias file; the alias file is built using the addresses of partners within a consortium or resource-sharing group. Users enter two or three letter code which will suffice for the destination. A patron's name is needed and some sort of note. This header is visible to a faculty member at a workstation who is sending a request to an ILL department using this very basic means of conveying the request. There are various defaults that can be selected. Some of these include resolution—high or low. Fax machines used as receivers provide low resolution, while printers have high resolution. The menu choice of "Dither on and off" refers to grayscale or shades of gray. Dither on would be for photographs, dither off for text. There are various degrees of brightness and contrast available depending upon whether the images are colored, on glossy paper, and so forth, but typically, the "zero/zero" setting is best for brightness and contrast. Manipulation of the default section is not usually necessary for the typical kinds of transmissions in interlibrary loan. At the bottom there are options to have transmission and sending off or on, and so forth. The printer does not have to be on when scanning, and users may select letter- or legal-sized paper.

Ariel also provides a series of different assists. There are queues to show what has been stored permanently or temporarily (both found in the send queue, for example), the number of files that are actively being sent, and the number that are on hold (on hold being the permanently stored files and those in the print queue). The hold queue may hold legal-size documents while letter-size documents are printing. Users may also choose "on hold" to print files at a later date. Files on hold also may be sent downstream to other Ariel machines.

What is the technical performance? This is of great concern to ILL departments trying to achieve greater efficiency. Scanning time, based on the type of scanner selected and the amount of grayscale in the photograph, can range from six to eleven seconds. Printing time without Ariel often takes two to four minutes for large image files. With Ariel but without a J laser card, it takes 30 to 60 seconds per page; with an accelerator card, it takes 10 to 20 seconds per page. Sending and receiving time is between two and 60 seconds. Even images sent to Finland or Australia require less than a minute to arrive if the receiving end is on. Summarizing Ariel's benefits, there are no postage or phone bills or copying costs, there is increased productivity, it is mainstream, it is very simple to use, and there is ongoing development.

Next I would like to discuss Ariel's genesis and look at some of the conditions that have been mentioned by Dr. Franklin D. Hart, NCSU Provost, and by other people concerning what is going on in libraries today.

The first conditions that existed were the vast proliferation of journals, budget constraints, staff, shelving maintenance, preservation, and storage constraints. This led to resource sharing, which is up about 1,000 percent since 1980 for many libraries. Ariel was needed for the rapid deployment of these materials. The second set of conditions involved the rising cost of traditional ILL resource sharing, caused by the decreasing percentage of available journals being purchased and increasing patron awareness of ILL. This is the old field of dreams concept—build a field and they will come.

The second set of conditions led the Association of Research Libraries (ARL) and Research Libraries Group (RLG) to develop a cost study, which found that the median cost to lend is $9 and the median cost to borrow is about $18. The range for borrowing, (10 to 90 percent) is from $10 to $30 per item. A look at a scatter diagram of the unit costs for filled-transaction lending reveals clusters around the $9 and $10 range. The unit cost per filled transaction for borrowing shows clusters around the $18 to $20 range.

Books represent 40 to 60 percent of borrowing and lending. Ariel can be of some assistance here. Tables of contents and parts of chapters can be sent, but it is really in the area of photocopying where Ariel can be of the greatest assistance. Consider the unit cost of photocopy activity for lending. Remember that photocopying also represents 40 to 60 percent of ILL transactions, and unit costs cluster around $9 for lending and between $12 and $22 for borrowing.

The third set of conditions—budget inadequacy—leads to new materials and new methods for obtaining these materials. Traditional ILL should be used for books—rare, old, or fleeting—and difficult-to-find articles. Perhaps fee-based services, either among universities or some of the fee-based vendors, should be used for recent, easily-acquired materials. It may be less expensive to buy than to obtain through traditional ILL. Ariel serves both the traditional and the fee-based models well. For RLG members, SHARES is a traditional resource sharing, and the University of Pennsylvania stated that 60 percent of its photocopy requests are now being sent and received via Ariel. Ariel has established a new citation- and article-level service called Citadel, "cita" for citations and "del" for delivery. We found that users want information easily. They want to be able to get into a database, find what is needed, and obtain it very quickly. They do not want to have move to between a lot of files. They want it economically (which means free), and they want it conveniently (which means on their desks yesterday). To accommodate these needs, some files have been placed into Citadel in ways that are not being represented elsewhere. For example, the ABI Inform is the full ABI Inform, not a subset. The periodicals abstracts have 1,650 journals that have been selected specifically for research purposes. Newspaper abstracts are fully abstracted including art reviews, movie reviews, theatrical reviews, and obituaries. It is the newspaper from front to back. There are also dissertation abstracts and Public Affairs Information Service (PAIS). Some of the other files contain citations that appear six to eight weeks earlier than the abstracts. These are scholarly files that probably are not available elsewhere in this form. The Avery Art and Architecture Index, the World Law Index (which is the index to Hispanic legislation), the Index to Foreign Legal Periodicals, the History of Technology, and the Hispanic American Periodical Index (HAPI), all have document delivery available via Ariel, fax, or USPS.

Upcoming is the ISIS index, the Emmian?? files from the former Soviet Union. These are the economic, social science, and legal journals obtained from Russia's Academy of Sciences. These are in cyrillic as well as romanized. Also coming is per-search pricing—offering the option of subscription or per-search pricing for both these commercial files and for scholarly files—document deliveries for more titles than are currently available, and Z39.50 client access. Users with Innovative Interfaces or NOTIS systems can get client-server software for Z39.50 access, which means they can search the Citadel files using their own search engines and OPAC commands. This makes searching very comfortable because it uses the commands they already employ.

Ariel is a dynamic system whose benefits include the addition of new files and document suppliers, the fact that no special training is required, the new Eureka interface, no-connect time charges, no charges for downloading, and file-specific searching to limit the size of a search result. Indeed, even if a large search result is obtained, it can be shortened by sorting by date, form and genre, language, and so forth.

The Eureka interface, mentioned above, evolved because folks said they wanted a common command language interface. This is a wonderful match to the Z39.50, permitting the use of your own interface or the common command language. It has extensive online help, new indexes, labeled displays, result-set sorting, and various ways to create a bibliography and download it using the Citadel and Eureka search service. It provides easy, efficient searching, enhanced access to the Citadel files, reviewing and combining of result sets, printing and downloading, and document ordering through Ariel.

The screens are straightforward and there is lots of help onscreen showing what to do, or type for the various commands. For example, suppose someone decided to select a long display of 85 records, but there are only 68 records available. When the number 85 is entered, an error message appears because it is impossible to carry out that command. If the user then chooses record 11, he or she will get the long record for 11.

What are the advantages? Competitive pricing, patron-initiated document request either through OPAC commands or through Eureka, staff-initiated document request, and quick Ariel delivery. The articles are copyright cleared and are single-point invoiced from multiple suppliers. Why might you want to do it? It can be accessed through your local area network (LAN), and the costs are predictable because subscription pricing allows unlimited searching for the one subscription price. It is less expensive than CD-ROM or tape leasing, and existing hardware already owned is maximized. Ariel can link a campus LAN to researchers, to the ILL department, and to available files through RLG, OCLC, your local OPAC, CD-ROM, and so forth.

Future steps for Ariel will be the importation of foreign TIFF files—files produced outside of the Ariel scanning mechanism. These may be files that are produced by Carl UnCover, by UMI, by Engineering Information (EI), and others. We will be pulling those files into the Ariel arena so that they can be transmitted via Ariel to the end user. Transmissions over non-Internet lines will occur using SprintNet and SprintLink. Those use the same TCP/IP protocols employed by Ariel. Downloading and uploading to diskette will emerge so that if Ariel is in a remote location lacking Internet connectivity or fast telecommunications lines, a patron can download to a diskette, take it over to the ILL department, upload it, and send it out. Combining the TIFF, ASCII, and foreign TIFF files, this is kind of like multimedia, only at a much lower level. This is taking the foreign TIFF files, pulling them in, mapping them with something that is scanned using Ariel, and bringing in some electronic information and merging it together for faculty use at a student workstation. There is also a "store" and "forward" capability. Most people who have Ariel do not realize they have this capability because we have not provided the documentation. However, a user can pull or push material from an Ariel server to an end user. Therefore a faculty member could query a server that has documents on it and have those pulled or have the server push the document to his or her workstation. This is very convenient, because the end user does not have to have Ariel on regularly to capture an image as it comes shooting over the Internet. Some of the users on the Ariel list serve have asked for additional assistance. They would like to have high-speed scanners used. When the Ariel developers first selected scanners, they decided to try to maximize the speed at a minimal price. Scanners are, in a sense, bi-modal. There are very expensive scanners that scan very quickly, and there are scanners that are affordable but scan more slowly. There are folks out there that want to use high-speed scanners and are willing pay the price to have that speed available. Ariel is now researching high-speed scanners. A TIFF file reader has been requested. Many people would like to see the image on the screen. At first everybody wanted this because they wanted to check to make sure they were sending the piece accurately. They found that that is not a problem. Very rarely does anything have to be re-sent. Faculty members said, however, that they would like to be able to read a file and not have to download it. We are researching the different TIFF file readers available. Another concern is A4 paper. Outside of the United States, A4 paper is used, which is longer and narrower. Ariel has the facility, although somewhat primitive, for handling A4 paper by pretending it is 14-inch paper. We want to have this fully integrated so that Ariel knows when it is receiving A4 and can slightly reduce the image, so that it prints as it has been sent.

Duplex printing—all of us are aware of paper costs and of the advantages of having duplex laser printers that print on both sides of the paper. Then there are windows in OS2 environment, which everybody would like to have. ILL software—OCLC ILL software to RLIN ILL software—would allow a staff member to take the information from a request automatically and put it into the header of the Ariel transmission without having to key in any kind of address or patron name or some sort of ID number. Custom-header pages are considered desirable, mostly by foreign countries that would like to have their own languages on the header page and their own copyright indications. Needless to say, it is not available right now.

Ariel has now shipped over 500 units and in addition two large consortia will be coming online within the month. There will be over 600 institutions or libraries that have Ariel software. It is mainly being used in ILL departments, but branch libraries at Dartmouth, University of Pennsylvania, Penn State, Princeton, and Duke have Ariel installed. Some of the schools and department libraries also have it in faculty offices. California State University and University of Pennsylvania are using Ariel in their storage facilities as a scan and send device. No printing is done there, just scanning and sending. There are a fair number of local consortia using Ariel—many Health Sciences libraries consortia, the Greater Boston consortium, Oregon, and so forth— and a large number of international consortia in Finland, Sweden, Norway, Apeka, the Jeti, European consortium, Kaval, Australia, and NECA in the maritime provinces in Canada. Document suppliers are using it as well—EI, UMI, and Bolt for the Index to Foreign Legal Periodicals.

I would like to mention Ariel's output. Non-roman comes across very well. Brightly colored, glossy paper and shades of gray scan well. Health Sciences libraries have found that Ariel is a very effective device for sending illustrations from textbooks, even full-color images on glossy paper. However, you still have to turn the pages manually as you scan. Having said that, there is a sheet feeder on the scanner so that if you do have photocopied material, you can put them in the sheetfeeder to feed automatically. In conclusion, we think that Ariel does what the character in *The Tempest* said, "I drink the air before me and return "or ere your pulse beat twice."

THE OHIO STATE/CICNET NETWORK FAX PROJECT:

A COOPERATIVE LIBRARY PROJECT

Robert J. Kalal

INTRODUCTION

As an introduction, let me state that I am the associate director of Academic Computing Services (ACS) at the Ohio State University. My areas include Distributed Computing, Campus UNIX Support, and liaison with OSU Libraries. Among the projects we have worked on with the libraries is development of image transmission and, more specifically, Internet delivery of fax images. With this project, ACS developed Internet/fax gateway workstations to send documents in fax format over the Internet using TCP/ IP protocols. ACS then worked with the CIC Libraries to integrate these workstations into a CIC Interlibrary Loan Delivery System. [As you may know, CIC (the Committee on Institutional Cooperation) is a consortium of the Big Ten schools and the University of Chicago.] I take care of overall project coordination, budget management, and library liaison for the project and serve as general technical gadfly and critic. In addition to me, the core project team includes Bob Dixon, director of ACS and principal investigator for the project

Advances in Library Administration and Organization, Volume 12, pages 175-188.
Copyright © 1994 by JAI Press Inc.
All rights of reproduction in any form reserved.
ISBN: 1-55938-846-3

grants; Bob DeBula, leader of the ACS UNIX system support group; Doug Karl, ACS senior network engineer; and Jim Skon, our graduate research associate. Skon was preceded by Khalid Mirza, who graduated with a doctorate in engineering last year and now works in robotics research for a firm in the auto industry.

This project is an example of how effectively libraries can get together to support a cooperative endeavor. It also illustrates how well technology can be employed at minimal cost when campus librarians work closely with their computing counterparts and build on existing public software. The project team members devote only a small fraction of time to the project. The core team was assisted by the Interlibrary loan librarians and staffs at CIC institution libraries and several Ohio libraries, especially the OSU Libraries which coordinated CIC participation.

NETWORK FAX BEGINNINGS

First I will tell you a bit about the project, its goals, and development and then I'll describe the operation of the system and workstations. We began the project some time ago to explore general image transmission and network issues. Our network engineers had been using some inexpensive PC clones with software based on the KA9Q networking software for various campus networking utility projects such as packet filters to isolate public student labs from the Internet, network monitoring stations, network statistics gathering tools, and so forth. We had even been recycling some obsolete original IBM PCs from public labs to do this work.

The KA9Q software is a TCP/IP networking package. It was developed originally for packet-switched, amateur radio use by Phil Karn, then of Bellcore. The package runs on many computers including PCs and UNIX systems. It can serve as a general network foundation and network router, and it even provides PPP and SLIP serial TCP/IP connectivity. When used on IBM and clone PCs, it provides TCP/IP functions, network interface drivers, a limited pseudo-multitasking capability, and a programmer's tool kit and interface. Karn allows free use and distribution by educational institutions and most true nonprofit groups.

Since ACS had a great deal of experience with the KA9Q software in other network applications, the team decided to use it as a base for image transmission testing with XT-class personal computers.

The team put together a demonstration where a programmer sat at a PC, fed a document into a low-resolution Group 3 fax machine, transmitted the document to a PC equipped with a fax interface card, and then stored the resultant file on the PCs hard disk. He then used the TCP/IP File Transfer Protocol or FTP function in the KA9Q software to send the file over an ethernet to a PC across the room, where it was printed out on another fax machine.

In essence, the fax machines were simply inexpensive scanners and printers. They were connected directly to the demonstration units and dedicated to the task. This connection was made with a commercially available "null telephone company" box. This adapter dealt with phone concerns such as dialing and ringing. The demonstration units could also serve as general purpose Internet/fax gateways, reformatting the synchronous fax image transmissions into discrete files for transmission on a packet-based TCP/IP network. The ethernet strung across the room could have well been any TCP/IP network, including the wider Internet.

CICNET, OARNET, AND LIBRARY VISION AND SUPPORT

CIC has had a continuing interest in network issues and formed CICNet, which connects the CIC schools and, as the midwestern regional NSFNet affiliate, provides Internet TCP/IP connectivity to the region. In 1990, our people took the demonstration setup to a CIC meeting in Chicago where it caught the eye of CIC networking and library people. CICNet was looking for new and innovative ways to use the network. The CIC libraries were looking for new ways to deal with interlibrary loan.

It is well known that traditional interlibrary loan is typically very labor-intensive and is an expensive proposition. This has been especially true for libraries with large or unique collections. They usually become net lenders and absorb most costs of ILL. One problem in assessing these costs has been the lack of hard data. Research Libraries Group and the Association of Research Libraries have addressed this problem with a nationwide study of ILL costs. The state schools in Wisconsin have also addressed it with a detailed study of costs in the Wisconsin system. Early reports confirm that ILL is a costly enterprise. It is also a slow process. These problems inhibit the widespread flow of information and make the researcher's job harder.

The CIC library people had been working to address the cost and speed issues. Because they were regular ILL partners, they had equipped CIC libraries with hopper-feed, plain-paper, auto-dialing Group 3 fax machines. This accelerated the delivery of the many documents that could be copied. Technically unsophisticated, and thus low-paid, student employees would copy a document, check the copy quality, feed the copies into the hopper on a fax machine, and auto dial the requesting CIC library. With this approach, documents could be sent over phone lines by fax from library to library rather than mailed with attendant delays or sent by overnight messenger at high cost. However, costs were still substantial and telephone toll charges grew. Network technology itself contributed to the growth in this area. As campus network access to information and off-campus library catalogs increased, it became easier for scholars to find and request documents from distant libraries.

With a vision of the implications of combining network technology and their needs, the CICNet and CIC library people provided grant funding and asked us to use our basic gateway mechanism to develop a system of Internet/fax workstations linking their libraries' interlibrary loan fax machines. This would reduce communications costs and speed delivery. We agreed to develop this system. The goal of the project was to develop a low-cost Internet/fax workstation integrating inexpensive, off-the-shelf microcomputer and fax components with readily available software. The resulting workstation was to be operable by nontechnical people and serve as an economical adjunct to CIC's existing fax machines.

OARNet is the statewide Ohio Academic Resources Network. It provides Internet connectivity in Ohio and serves Ohio's universities and colleges as well as commercial interests. The Ohio schools are vitally interested in networking potential. OhioLINK is bringing statewide networking to Ohio's academic libraries and is a key component of OARNet's traffic and future. OARNet also shares many of the goals and concerns of CICNet. Therefore, OARNet joined the project with a joint grant to ACS, OSU Libraries, and the University of Cincinnati Library and Computer Center. This allowed us to include the University of Cincinnati Library in our development testing and resulting production system. The State Library of Ohio, also an OARNet client, also joined in the production system.

PROTOTYPE UNITS

With the concept already proven, the team's job was to develop an easy-to-use user interface and the control software needed to integrate the various fax and network tasks so we would not need a programmer sitting at each PC as in the original demonstration.

The team built several prototype units at a cost of less than $2,000 each. They were built using inexpensive, name-brand PC/XT clones and Hayes/Quadram fax cards. The clones were selected for their reliability, low cost, and compatibility. The Hayes/Quadram fax card was selected because of its reliability and its publicly available programmer's tool kit for use in developing the custom control software. We had a great deal of experience with the Western Digital Ethernet Cards in local networking jobs, and were comfortable with their use. We selected a standard EGA as the most economical display for a flexible interface design at that time.

The relatively slow speed of the XT clone PC did not affect operations as the speed of the fax card was the limiting factor. The PC platform and DOS operating system were not ideal because they did not support multitasking and pre-emptive interruption. However, they were economical, and the KA9Q software provided most of the multitasking support needed.

The team then worked out software to automate the process and connect the various tasks of receiving a fax, storing it as a file, sending it to the remote system, and so forth. Using KA9Q as a monitor under DOS, we designed the various components to operate asynchronously. With that approach, sending and receiving fax documents locally is independent of remote network activities. This allows scanning or printing and operation to overlap and improves the operator's productivity.

The team then used the prototype units to develop a windowed, menu-driven user interface with on-screen user help and on-screen system status reports. We met with interlibrary loan (ILL) librarians from the CIC schools, and they helped us to design the interface and to deal with typical interlibrary loan work flow issues. Some of the input was a surprise. We frankly expected a great deal of interest in high resolution, on-screen document preview and in scanner and laser printer input and output. However, the ILL librarians told us that low cost, ease of operation, and the ability to work with their existing Group 3 fax machines were the most important immediate considerations.

The ILL librarians told us that Group 3 resolution, at 200 dots-per-inch was acceptable for most documents. They told us not to consider Group 4 or scanners and laser printers for the initial systems. We moved consideration of those issues to a later project phase.

They also told us that they preferred to preview documents by first copying them. This allowed lightly trained student employees to establish quickly image quality while copying and then return the originals to the stacks. On-screen preview would be a slower process and would keep the student employee and the original tied to the workstation. We deferred on-screen preview to a later phase.

The ILL offices also needed to keep using their existing fax for normal telephone use with libraries outside the CIC document delivery system. We made the "null telephone company" optional and redesigned the hardware and software to support connection of both the gateway and fax machine through campus phone lines. This also allowed one gateway in the ILL office to route documents to fax machines in other libraries around campus. We then added software to deal with busy fax machines and retries.

Finally, they wanted the user interface as easy to use and foolproof as possible. A centrally administered database and menu was developed for ILL fax locations at CIC schools. The operator simply selects the university and then the location at the university from on-screen menus.

To enhance reliability and simplify disk management, we developed a "notify and retrieve" operational model. In this model, the local unit notifies the remote unit that an image is available. The remote unit then determines if it can accept the image at that point and either retrieves it or schedules later retrieval. After the remote unit retrieves and successfully prints the image, it deletes the original from the local unit's disk. The fax and network processes are completely independent. This helps with work flow problems by freeing both the operator and the fax machine for other work.

We then set up the prototypes with the new software and conducted an intensive, multisystem local test. There were thinnet and ethernet cables, PCs, fax machines, and telephone lines strung about the room. The machines had little signs, "University of Cincinnati," "Ohio State," and so forth. They were busy constantly interchanging images to prove that the system could handle a continuous load.

BETA TESTING

After the local testing, we sent beta test workstations to the interlibrary loan units at Ohio State University, the University of Cincinnati, and Indiana University. After initial testing, these workstations were in regular service delivering documents for over six months. The beta testing included use of thinnet, thicknet, and 10baseT ethernet connections for Internet access in the test libraries.

The beta test results were good. To quote Scott Seaman, then Interlibrary Loan Librarian at Ohio State Libraries, "The system is impressive and wonderfully simple to use...." We did find a few surprises. In one case, the OSU library interlibrary loan clerk called to tell us that there must be something wrong with the gateway workstation. The on-screen status reports showed that it was very busy but nothing was printing out on the fax machine. When we investigated, we found that another university had discovered that the unit was truly a general purpose Internet/fax gateway. We had left a blank spot in the user menu of destination fax machines at Ohio State. This was so that we could keep testing in the event one of the usual phone lines was out. The remote site could simply enter the phone number of a temporary machine. Well, they noticed that "feature" and were using the OSU library's gateway workstation to send interlibrary loan documents to the State Library of Ohio in downtown Columbus. We have decided to leave the "wild card" phone number slot in the menu as a useful tool for any campus that wants it, but we have recommended that the gateway phone line be restricted from long distance calls. With their need proven, the State Library of Ohio eventually joined the project and installed their own gateway workstation.

PRODUCTION UNIT DEPLOYMENT

After the beta test, we shipped production units to the CIC libraries. The production units cost $2,500, as we had to move to a 286 PC/AT-clone for the workstation. While we did not need the performance of the 286, we could no longer find a low-cost PC/XT clone that we considered widely serviceable, available, and reliable enough to support a multistate system with both urban and rural locations. We evaluated a number of low-cost AT-class PCs, and settled on the AST bravo 286 for the production units. Because the bravo included an on-board VGA adapter, we switched to a VGA monitor.

The AST units did give us several new advantages. The first is that they are plug upgradeable to 386 machines, thus providing a flexible upgrade potential. Also, the ASTs support a hardware password feature to enhance keyboard security. The on-board VGA gave flexibility for future interface enhancements.

We purchased the CIC production units through a local vendor who handled much of the hardware integration and setup. The vendor unpacked the computers, installed the fax and network cards and basic software, tested and repacked the assembled units, and provided an extended warranty. We shipped the units in two boxes, computer and monitor, with only network software installed. They came with two pages of setup instructions, pretty much just "plug this into power, a phone line, and the Internet, and then turn it on." When the unit came online, it notified us over the Internet. We then tested the network configuration and downloaded the fax control and interface software. Finally, we sent the seven-page user document to the library's fax machine through the gateway as the first transmission.

Using a small but reliable local PC vendor as a system integrator and tester allowed us to produce the units with minimal staffing while maintaining a low unit cost.

NETWORK FAX SYSTEM OPERATION

Moving now to the system in operation, Figure 1 shows typical setups at two universities. The actual system is made up of 16 campuses including the Big Ten schools, which are Penn State, the University of Chicago, the University of Cincinnati, and the State Library of Ohio. There are also branch or satellite campus locations and a unit in the ACS development laboratory.

The fax gateways are connected to the Internet and to telephone lines. Fax machines in university libraries are connected to local telephone lines and listed on the system menus. One fax machine is located adjacent to the gateway and used for all sending.

Figure 2 is an operational overview. Starting at #1, to send an article, the operator feeds the document into the local fax machine and autodials the gateway workstation. Second, at #2, the fax machine sends the document to the gateway workstation, which receives the document and stores it as a series of files. Then, at #3, the gateway workstation prompts the operator to select a destination from a menu.

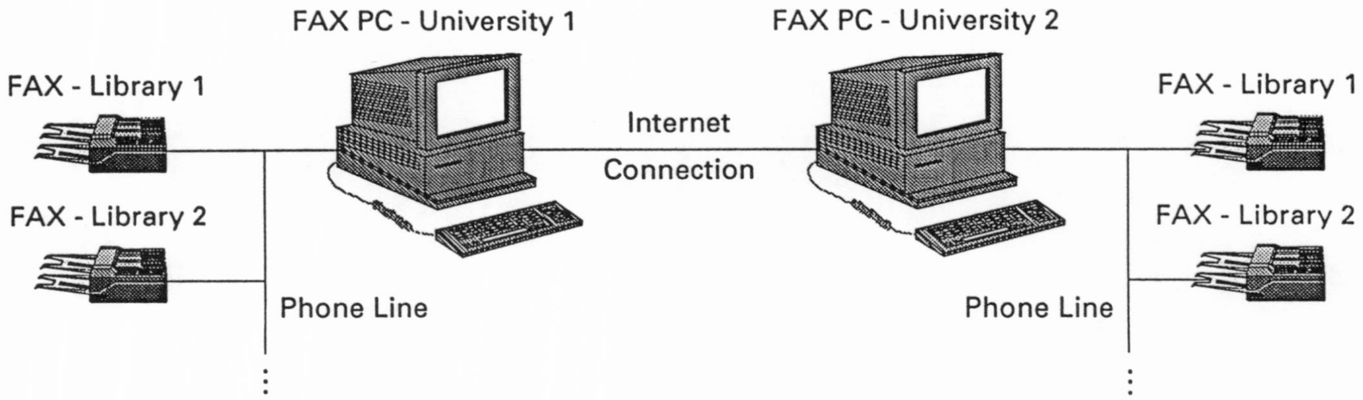

Figure 1. Typical Setups at Two Universities

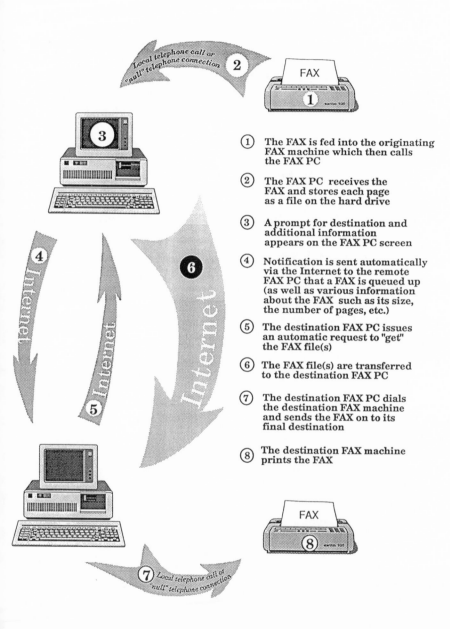

① The FAX is fed into the originating FAX machine which then calls the FAX PC

② The FAX PC receives the FAX and stores each page as a file on the hard drive

③ A prompt for destination and additional information appears on the FAX PC screen

④ Notification is sent automatically via the Internet to the remote FAX PC that a FAX is queued up (as well as various information about the FAX such as its size, the number of pages, etc.)

⑤ The destination FAX PC issues an automatic request to "get" the FAX file(s)

⑥ The FAX file(s) are transferred to the destination FAX PC

⑦ The destination FAX PC dials the destination FAX machine and sends the FAX on to its final destination

⑧ The destination FAX machine prints the FAX

Figure 2. Operational Overview

At #4, the sending gateway then notifies the destination gateway over the Internet that a document is ready. At #5 and #6, the destination gateway retrieves the document. At #7, the destination gateway automatically dials the appropriate local fax machine that, at #8, prints out the document.

The software automatically deals with disk full, fax busy, and other concerns. It schedules later transmissions and retries, automatically sends a confirmation message, deletes the original files after the document has been successfully printed out, and keeps the operator informed with simple English status displays. These displays stay on screen at all times and cover error conditions, disk storage situation, local fax link status, and network status.

Figure 3 is an example of the status screen as shown in the user document. Notice the local and network status at #1 and #2 on top and the disk status at #3 and #4 at the bottom. Error messages show up in windows at the center of the screen. An incoming fax from another library requires no local operator action, so the fax status lines simply change to show that the gateway is processing a document. When a fax is sent from the local gateway, destination information windows cascade down from the information window at #6.

Finally, Figure 4 shows an example of the destination windows. They first allow you to enter the recipient's name. A user then simply picks the university and library. If users want the gateway to deliver to a fax machine at a location not on the list, they may enter the local telephone number at the destination school and then select "Send FAX."

PROJECT EXPERIENCE

We found that the major operational problems were not technical ones. In a year and a half of production, we have had only a handful of software problems. All of these were fixed quickly. There have been only two hardware problems, one was a bad monitor replaced under warranty, and another was a bad disk on our test system.

We did experience problem after problem with network connectivity to the libraries and within the libraries, as well as network coordination on the campuses. While dogged work by campus librarians got most of the libraries up and running in the first few months, the final two did not come online until December of last year and January of this year.

Traffic through the system ranges from 500 to about 1,000 documents each month. The average document is 12 pages long and uses about 60 kilobytes per page. From this, the load the system places on CICNet is up to about a gigabyte per month. The largest users are Indiana University, Purdue University, Northwestern University, the University of Minnesota, and the University of Iowa.

Most of the feedback received shows that the CIC institutions feel that the CIC Network Fax Document Delivery System has either reduced or cut the

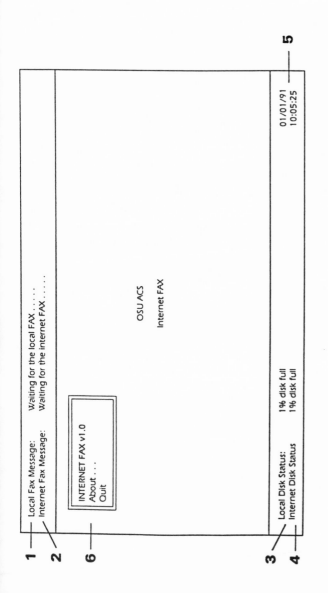

Local Fax Message: Waiting for the local FAX......
Internet Fax Message: Waiting for the internet FAX......

INTERNET FAX v1.0
About....
Quit

OSU ACS

Internet FAX

Local Disk Status: 1% disk full
Internet Disk Status   1% disk full

01/01/91
10:05:25

1 — Message line for local FAX activity.   4 — Status line for local FAX storage on disk.
2 — Message line for Internet FAX activity.   5 — Current time and date.
3 — Status line for local FAX storage on   6 — Menus for Internet FAX.
disk.

Figure 3. Status Screen

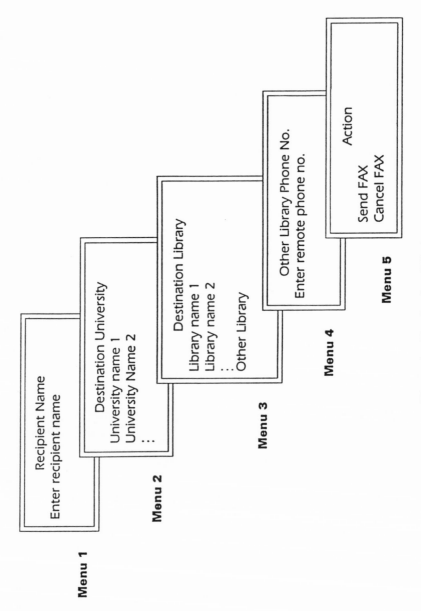

Figure 4. Destination Window

rate of increase in direct ILL costs. Because of staffing constraints, we do not have hard data yet but are hoping to begin a study of communications costs with help from several schools. The expected savings would come by cutting long distance telephone charges and, in some cases, by improving workflow. Of course, the traffic diverted from the telephone lines moves to the institution's Internet connection. This connection, while not free to the institution, has usually been subsidized by the institution and provided at no charge to the using departments.

NETWORK STANDARDS, CURRENT WORK, AND FUTURES

We began this work when no standards for Internet image transmission were available or even under development. While we believe strongly in the importance of standards, the CIC libraries needed the capability quickly, and we responded with the tools we had. In the meantime, however, an IETF Working Group has developed a standard approved as RFC 1314. While we did not have the resources to work actively with the group, we monitored their progress and fully supported their work. We are now implementing their work as our image transmission base. The use of standards-based open systems will encourage the free flow of information and will allow diverse document delivery systems to interoperate.

We have now run test systems running 386 and 486 PCs as we explore other image techniques. We are also exploring a UNIX base, using the LINUX public (AT&T-free) version, to keep costs low and help with multitasking concerns in a more demanding environment as we move toward more intensive image-conversion processing. If we were to build new units today, we would doubtless use a 486-based PC. The cost would be much lower than the original CIC production units because of the current demand-based, commodity-style PC market.

On the image side, we now support output on laser printers, on-screen image preview, and are implementing scanner input. Laser printer output was a priority enhancement as some CIC libraries needed to free up their fax machines for input.

Scanners and laser printers complement our implementation of RFC 1314. While implementing the standard we are changing the design to transmit the highest resolution possible. Software in the receiving machine will scale the image to whatever output device is chosen. We also use one unit outside the CIC system as a general e-mail-to-fax gateway for the OSU campus.

While it is now possible for the sending gateway to specify any fax machine or fax-equipped PC on the receiving campus, we need to explore supporting more flexible delivery options—such as delivery to the scholar's desk—as a standard displayable-image file and the rerouting of image files at the receiving library. We also need to develop a distributed database of system participants. This will allow us to add features that support local tailoring and administration of the menus. Then local campus librarians could add their own destinations. These could include direct delivery destinations for heavy and regular users.

CONCLUSION

Finally, I want to mention two things. The first is a problem, or perhaps an opportunity, we on the technical team see. The second is a future direction to explore.

From the technician's viewpoint, we are struck by the waste of time and energy caused by deleting the scanned documents after they are transmitted. While we understand that the reasons are legal and cultural rather than technical, the waste is still there. If we could resolve the legal and cultural issues, we could today be building a cooperative database of commonly requested documents from existing print collections. Instead, we are retrieving and scanning the same documents over and over again.

Secondly, since we began work in this area, there have been exciting and interesting developments in multimedia electronic mail. MIME (multimedia extensions to e-mail), provides a way to attach encoded documents to Internet e-mail in a standard way. Many user e-mail programs such as ELM, PINE, and POPMail clients already support MIME extensions and can decode and display MIME attachments on the user's desktop computer. MIME can provide a way to build document delivery direct to the scholar. The delivery mechanism can be built on existing public software and can use existing mail routing and delivery techniques.

NCSU DIGITIZED DOCUMENT
TRANSMISSION PROJECT:
A SUMMARY

Tracy M. Casorso

It occurred to me as I was preparing for my presentation that in keeping with the spirit of the conference it was time for me to graduate from the overhead projector and use a more sophisticated means of presentation. As you well know, there are any number of tools available to enhance one's presentation— video clips, multimedia, networked computer applications to take one's audience zipping around the Internet. Yes, it was time to take that step forward. After reflecting on this issue for quite sometime, I decided I did not want to advance too quickly—alas, I discovered I am not the risk taker I so pride myself on being—overheads it will be.

INTRODUCTION

Research libraries are undergoing a fundamental restructuring and repositioning of interlibrary loan and document delivery services within their organizations and are looking to the application of electronic delivery as a means of reducing overhead costs, improving turnaround time/service, and

Advances in Library Administration and Organization, Volume 12, pages 189-202.

as a mechanism for delivering documents originating in electronic form. There are three components that go into making up an integrated electronic document delivery system: collections, a requesting mechanism and a delivery mechanism.

The NCSU Digitized Document Transmission Project, an experiment and research initiative in electronic document delivery, is investigating the third of these three components, the delivery mechanism. The project was designed to identify and investigate issues systematically in the network-based delivery of library materials.

There are five parts to my presentation. I will begin by providing background information on the NCSU Digitized Document Transmission Project (DDTP), why and how it started, and what we hoped to accomplish. I will then describe the project system, both the platform and software, and how the software evolved over the course of the project. Third, I will explain how the system functions within an interlibrary loan unit as a means for transmitting documents between libraries. Fourth, and most exciting, we also investigated electronic document delivery via a campus network to the researcher's computer; I will report on this initiative. Last, I will provide an overview of our findings and the current status of the NCSU DDTP system. (For a more in-depth treatment of the NCSU DDTP, I refer readers to various papers and reports cited in the bibliography.)

BACKGROUND

The NCSU DDTP began as part of the larger National Agricultural Text Digitizing Project (NATDP) conducted by the National Agricultural Library (NAL) with funding from the U.S. Department of Agriculture (Andre and Eaton, 1988). In 1987, the NAL initiated a three-phase investigation into the use of digitizing and networking technologies for improving access to agricultural literature. The first two phases of the NATDP, involving the NAL and 42 land-grant libraries, were devoted to the development of CD-ROM prototypes using optical disc technology and to the evaluation of different indexing and retrieval software packages in order to identify the most appropriate package for retrieving both text and image data (Eaton and Andre, 1986). The third phase of the NATDP mandated the investigation of alternative delivery methods given the limitations of CD-ROM technology.

STAGE ONE: NCSU-NAL JOINT PROJECT ON THE TRANSMISSION OF DIGITIZED TEST

In early 1988, the NCSU Libraries together with the NCSU Computing Center entered into discussions with the National Agriculture Library. These discussions led to the design of a pilot study to test the transmission of images over the Internet following the recommendations of Clifford A. Lynch in a white paper commissioned by the NAL. (In his paper, Lynch surveyed state-of-the-art telecommunications options for the transmission of full text and detailed the advantages to the scientific community of the establishment of an electronic document delivery system [Lynch, 1988].) With a grant from the U.S.D.A., the NAL, already equipped with a DOS graphics-capable workstation, installed network connections; and the NCSU Libraries, already connected to the network, purchased a Macintosh graphics-capable workstation. The NAL and NCSU successfully transmitted digitized TIFF images between the NAL's NATDP proprietary, DOS-based scanning workstation and NCSU's unmodified Macintosh computer. Remember this was 1989. The results of the study demonstrated that network-transmitted images were superior to telefacsimile transmissions. (A computer-based scanner electronically scans a document at a resolution of 300 dpi—a 50 percent difference in resolution produces a far more accurate replica of the original document, better preserving the level of detail in terms of graphs and illustrations so critical in scientific publications. Other key achievements included the ability to operate in dissimilar computing environments; the identification and resolution of most key technical issues concerned with compressing, previewing, manipulating, and printing; and using local networks linked to national networks. The project management also identified the administrative and procedural issues involved in carrying out computer-based document delivery within the existing support matrix for ILL activities (Casorso, 1991).

Based on the findings of the pilot study, the NCSU Libraries prepared and submitted a proposal to the U.S. Department of Education to expand the investigation to explore further the issues involved in bringing digitized document delivery to a substantial community of researchers. The proposal, funded in 1990 by a U.S. Department of Education Title II-D Research and Demonstration grant, called for installing off-the-shelf, graphics-capable, networked hardware platforms, along with off-the-shelf software, at up to 12 land-grant campuses to test and evaluate a full-scale, digitized delivery system among a representative subset of the land-grant library community.[1] Stage I of the two-stage expanded initiative investigated the digitization and transmission of library materials between remote libraries. Each participating library was equipped with a non-proprietary, graphics-capable, networked hardware platform, located in the library interlibrary loan office for the electronic receipt, display, distribution, and output of digitized interlibrary loan materials requested by the project participants. Stage II was implemented when the investigation was expanded in 1991 to test direct delivery of digitized library materials to the researcher's workstation via campus networks.

The goals of the NCSU DDTP were four-fold:

1. To investigate the technical, procedural, and user-response issues involved in bringing digitized document delivery to a substantial community of researchers
2. To establish further libraries as players in the development of a national research information network
3. To expand the use of networking technologies by the agricultural research community
4. To examine issues related to selecting hardware platforms for delivering graphics-based materials over established networks.

In addition to NCSU and the NAL, 12 land-grant institutions, representing most of the regional telecommunications networks, were selected to participate in the project. The key prerequisites for participating in the project included high-speed network connectivity from the interlibrary loan processing area and library systems support for troubleshooting network problems and operating graphics and network-oriented desktop computers (Casorso, 1992a).

SYSTEM DESIGN

The technical design, as stated, specified the use of nonproprietary, readily available technologies and widely supported standards, as well as established national and local networking infrastructures. (See Figure 1: DDTP Transmission Schematic.) There are five components that make up the system:

1. Hardware: A Macintosh computer, Abaton scanner, and Apple LaserWriter Postscript-compatible printer were installed at each site. The Project team selected the Macintosh platform because of its consistent and easy-to-use environment, connectivity architecture (high-speed networking hardware and software are standard components of the Macintosh), and its open environment that connects to most any network configuration supporting DOS and Unix.

2. Standard image format: During the joint project in 1989, the project team examined several options and agreed upon the Tagged Image File Format (TIFF) as the file format standard. TIFF is widely supported by scanning, digitizing, and image-editing software, as well as optical character recognition software. During the first two phases of the NATDP, the NAL had established a high-throughput, production operation for scanning and producing CD-ROMs containing images of the scanned materials. Although capable of high speed and exceptional quality, the NAL equipment and software were proprietary and did not support the standard TIFF selected for the third phase and the expanded initiative. The primary contractor for the equipment provided software to translate the proprietary format of scanned images into TIFF.

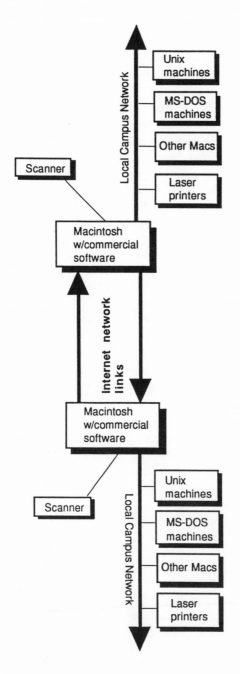

Figure 1. DDTP Transmission Schematic

3. High-speed data communications link: High-bandwidth connections (defined as the ability to perform Telnet/FTP operations directly from the project workstation—preferably Ethernet bandwidth available in the interlibrary loan area, and T-1 links from the campus to the Internet) from the libraries to their local Internet nodes were required to accomplish transfer of scanned image files .

4. A host computer at the recipient site: To ensure round-the-clock availability, sufficient disk storage, and access from other locations on campus. At NCSU the NCSU Computing Center established one of its VAX computers, as the receiving node; from that node, computers in the NCSU Libraries could pick up incoming images at any time, from any location on the campus network. Approximately half of the 12 project participants elected to use a local host computer; the remaining participants used their ILL DDTP computer as the host computer.

5. Compression: During the pilot project uncompressed images files were transmitted between libraries to test the time required to transmit uncompressed scanned images of entire journal articles. Since each journal article consisted on average of 8 megabytes of scanned data, even high-speed transmission of the files took an unacceptable length of time. Because of the large amount of white space in textual materials, archiving and compression commonly achieved 80-90 percent compression; on average, compressed journal articles required about 800k of storage space.

SOFTWARE DESIGN

The project design proposed two approaches to software for the project. During the initial phases of the project, participants used existing, unmodified applications programs for the Macintosh computers to scan images, compress them, transmit and receive them, then print and/or view them:

- Scanning: Abaton scanner desk accessory
- Compression: StuffIt Deluxe
- Transmission/Receipt: NCSA Telnet
- Printing: SuperPaint 2.0

The use of independent software components permitted participants to carry out project operations, but required considerable knowledge of each individual application and an unacceptable amount of operating time. The time required to activate each program for each step of scanning, compressing, transmitting, receiving, uncompressing, and printing compromised productivity levels. Approximately eight months into the project, the project team designed and implemented a HyperCard application that streamlined and simplified the

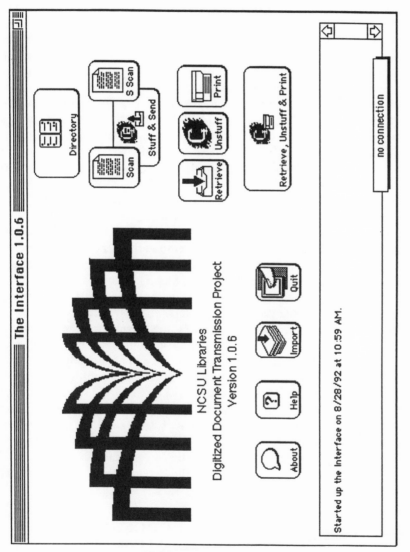

Figure 2. The Interface Opening Screen

entire process (Casorso, 1992a). The first release of the application allowed participants to perform operations with a single click of a mouse button. It included a directory of sites participating in the project, including their IP addresses, and other information for performing FTP operations and controlling the receipt of image files (Casorso, 1992b). (See Figure 2: The Interface Opening Screen.)

At this point, I would like to walk through the ILL process using the NCSU DDTP system. Once the borrowing library verified the ILL request, the ILL request is transmitted via OCLC ILL Subsystem to a project lending library. The phrase "NATDP" in the *maxcost* field of the OCLC record flagged incoming requests to indicate that the request was to be delivered electronically. Upon receiving the OCLC request, the lending library retrieved the document from their collection, electronically scanned the material and a copy of the OCLC workform into a electronic folder. The folder was identified using the OCLC ILL Subsystem request number. This naming convention allowed the borrowing library to readily identify the incoming documents. Once scanned, the document was automatically compressed and transmitted to the designated intermediate host machine at the borrowing site.

Staff at the borrowing site periodically checked their host machine by activating the retrieve function of the system interface. Files were retrieved individually or in batch; the auto-feature of the HyperCard interface automatically decompressed and printed the files. The system deleted the file(s) both on the host machine and the workstation once a file was printed, downloaded, or delivered via campus networks to the researcher.

The DDTP software has two features that significantly enhance the functionality of the system and distinguish it from other delivery system designs. One, the system allows for ownership of and access to the TIFF file, thus allowing the operator/recipient to import the file or portions of the file into a wordproccessing package or a graphics program. And two, the "import button" allows libraries to fill requests for materials that already exist in electronic form that is multimedia materials such as the clip John Ulmschneider demonstrated this morning, data sets, and digital video. Any file that exists in electronic form can be transmitted via the system interface. I could send you a copy of the system interface using the system interface! (Morgan and Casorso, 1992).

STAGE TWO: ELECTRONIC DOCUMENT DELIVERY VIA CAMPUS NETWORKS

Stage one of the NCSU DDTP involved the transmission of digitized library materials between the NAL, NCSU and the twelve participating libraries. Stage two was designed to investigate the technical and management issues related

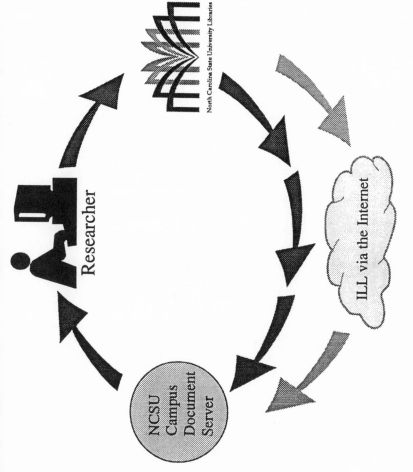

Figure 3. Electronic Document Delivery via Campus Networks

to the direct delivery of the digitized materials to the researcher via campus telecommunications networks. The non-proprietary and open technical design of the DDTP system allowed the project team to implement the second phase of the project: direct links to faculty and student users of research materials via computers located in branch libraries and direct delivery via a campus-wide accessible server. Although direct delivery was originally a component of the Title II-D grant request, it was later eliminated due to cost restraints. Fortunately, the project team was able to resurrect it as a result of equipment support from Apple Computer, Inc. In February 1991, the NCSU Libraries received two complete desktop computer systems from the Apple Library of Tomorrow (ALOT) grant program to investigate issues related to the direct delivery of digitized research materials to researchers via campus networks. (See Figure 3: Electronic Document Delivery via Campus Networks.)

The project team developed a document server model entitled the Electronic Document Delivery Service (EDDS) that allowed researchers on a campus network to retrieve their requested library materials electronically. Using the EDDS, researchers submit their document requests via the campus electronic mail system to the libraries" interlibrary loan department.

EDDS supported multiple platforms, including Macintosh, DOS and UNIX. Requests were filled either from in-house collections or through DDTP sites, by obtaining a scanned electronic version of the article. The electronic file was then stored on the NCSU server.

Staff at the NCSU Computing Center developed and mounted on the campus server a UNIX program called, "Loan Shark" that upon receiving an image file performed three functions: (1) placed the incoming image file into an individual user account, (2) issued an e-mail notification complete with instructions for retrieving the file, including a unique log-in and password, to the researcher informing him/her that the requested file has arrived; and (3) issued an e-mail notification to the ILL department that the file was placed on the server by the lending library. (See Figure 4: EDDS Logical Schematic.)

Upon receiving notification that a requested document has arrived the researcher retrieves the file from the server via FTP, decompresses the large image file, and either views it on screen, prints it, or runs it through an optical character recognition program to create an ASCII file. The research also had the option of picking up a printed copy of the requested article at his/her branch library where branch library staff using a project computer workstation retrieved the file from the server and provided a print copy. Researchers using the Macintosh platform were provided with a *HyperCard* application called *Document Assistant*. This *HyperCard* application, an abridged version of the system application, streamlines for the researcher the process of unarchiving and printing the requested library materials. It was not necessary for the researcher to have *Document Assistant* to use the EDDS. It merely functioned as a user-friendly interface that the researcher had the option of using to

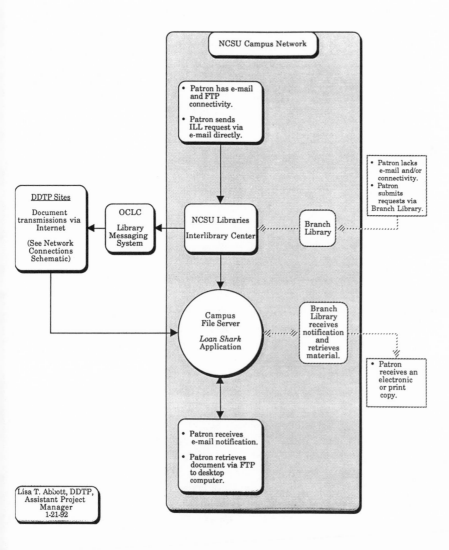

Figure 4. EDDS Logical Schematic

unarchive and print the TIFF images. It eliminated the need for importing the digitized document into a graphics program before obtaining a print copy. The service is not limited solely to the delivery of journal articles; any type of library information that can be captured in digital form or that already exists in digital form can be delivered over the Internet and across campus networks to the researcher.

The project team demonstrated in stage two that it was possible to deliver digitized library materials across platforms and via campus networks to the researcher's office workstation; end-user response was positive. "EDDS is the best thing since sliced bread," said College of Textiles faculty member Carol Carrere after receiving the first seven requests she had submitted via EDDS. Not surprisingly, the most popular aspect of EDDS was the requesting component. Of the 219 requests submitted in the four month period, 73 percent were submitted directly by the researcher via an unmodified e-mail request. Of the 149 requests filled, either by interlibrary loan (scanned at a DDTP site) or scanned from NCSU collections, 27 percent were retrieved via FTP to the research's office desktop computer. Key factors contributing to the use of EDDS include access to high-speed connectivity, printing speeds, and computer skills (Abbott, 1992).

FINDINGS AND ILL WORKFLOW IMPLICATIONS

Implementing an electronic document delivery service between libraries and/ or for researchers requires a solid and ubiquitous network infrastructure: broad-based, high-speed network connectivity; trained staff to operate networked, graphics-capable desktop computers; local systems staff to install and maintain networked services; and ultimately savvy users. The successful design and implementation of an electronic document delivery system demands fundamental changes to current ILL operations in order to integrate and fully utilize a electronic document delivery system's capabilities. The ideal being a system entirely unmediated by library staff allowing the enduser a means to easily identify, request and receive a document(s) regardless of format, and via a means deemed most appropriate, electronically, via fax, or in print form.

The DDTP system represents, as stated in the introduction, but one of three components that comprise a thoroughly integrated system. From a day-to-day-operations perspective, the DDTP interface system does not impact on the ordering/ requesting mechanisms in place within ILL. The delivery and receipt of digitized files does require fundamental changes workflow: shifting from processing physical packages to creating and delivering electronic files (Ulmschneider and Casorso, 1993). The experiences, knowledge and expertise gained in this project will form part of the basis of an integrated system currently under design.

ACKNOWLEDGMENTS

I would like to recognize and thank the DDTP participants. The DDTP could not have been done without the tremendous efforts of staffs and local participants at the 13 participating libraries. Particular thanks go to the staffs of the two lead institutions: North Carolina State University and the National Agricultural Library. The principal investigator (Susan K. Nutter) and project director (John E. Ulmschneider) could not have succeeded in carrying out this investigation without the support and dedication of these individuals. I would also like to thank the directors of the land-grant libraries who provided such strong support and matching funds throughout out the project. Special thanks goes to former Associate Provost for Academic Computing Dr. Henry Schaffer and the staff at the NCSU Computing Center for their advice on technical platforms and assistance with software development. At NCSU Libraries, Eric Lease Morgan was chief architect of the DDTP interface software, Lisa T. Abbott served as Assistant Project Manager for the EDD Service and Carolyn Argentati coordinated branch library participation. Special thanks to Marti A. Minor DDTP Production Coordinator and Administrative Assistant.

NOTES

1. The project team is made up of Susan K. Nutter, Director of NCSU Libraries and Principal Investigator; John E. Ulmschneider, Assistant Director for Library Systems; Tracy M. Casorso, Project Manager; Lisa T. Abbott, Assistant Project Manager; Eric L. Morgan, Technical Consultant; and Marti A. Minor, Production Coordinator. The twelve land-grant institutions participating with NCSU and NAL in stage one of the project are: Clemson University, University of Delaware, Iowa State University, University of Maryland at College Park, Michigan State University, University of Minnesota, North Carolina Agricultural and Technical State University, The Ohio State University, Pennsylvania State University, Utah State University, Virginia Polytechnic Institute and State University and Washington State University.

REFERENCES

Abbott, L. (1992). "Electronic Document Delivery via Campus Networks," The NCSU Libraries *FOCUS*, 13 (3), 3-11.

Andre, P.Q.J. and N.L. Eaton (1988). "National Agricultural Text Digitizing Project," *Library Hi Tech*, 6 (3),61-65.

Casorso, T. (1991). "The North Carolina State University Libraries and the National Agricultural Library joint project on transmission of digitized text: improving access to agricultural information," RSR: *Reference Services Review*, 19,15-22.

Casorso, T. (14 September 1992a). "Electronic Document Delivery Transmission: The North Carolina State University Libraries Initiative." *Proceedings of the LITA Third National Conference*, Denver, CO.

Casorso, T. (1992b). "NCSU Digitized Document Transmission Project: Improving Access to Agricultural Libraries," *The Electronic Library*, 10, (5), 271-273.

Eaton, N. L. and Pamela Q. J. Andre (15 November 1992). "The National Agricultural Text Digitizing Project: Toward the Electronic Library: Report of the Pilot Project, Phases 1-2, 1986-1992."

Lynch, C. A. (1 December 1988). "Roles for Telecommunications and Computer Networking in the National Agricultural Library Text Digitizing Project." National Agricultural Library White Paper.

Morgan, E. and T.M. Casorso (1992). "Digitized document transmission using HyperCard," *Macintoshed Libraries*, 5,47-53.

Ulmschneider, J. and T. M. Casorso (1993). "Electronic Document Delivery: An Overview With a Report on Experimental Agricultural Project," *Advances is Library Automation and Networking*, vol. 4, edited by Joe A. Hewitt, Greenwich, CT: JAI Press.

PETABYTES OF INFORMATION:
FROM AUTHORS TO LIBRARIES TO READERS

Malcolm Getz

The rapid expansion of the use of electronic tools for creating, storing, transmitting, and using information creates opportunities for scholars to express their ideas in new ways. Compared to conventional methods, using powerful computers to create texts, algorithms, databases, sound, and images, will enable scholars to work more quickly, to craft investigations of greater sophistication, and to express their ideas in forms that are more useful to others. Compared to printed materials, scholarly works in digital formats can be stored so much less expensively that more information will be stored. High-speed data-communications networks will turn each workstation[1] into a sophisticated information appliance, providing rapid access on demand to vast numbers of texts and other information sources. The electronic information products fetched to the workstation can be useful in various ways in instruction, in research, and in the creation of new intellectual products. This is the promise of the electronic era: a global virtual library of unsurpassed richness, ease of use, and availability. If realized, such an electronic environment will transform the nature of scholarship and its influence on society.

Advances in Library Administration and Organization, Volume 12, pages 203-237.
Copyright © 1994 by JAI Press Inc.
All rights of reproduction in any form reserved.
ISBN: 1-55938-846-3

Indeed, the value of these developments for scholarship is but one of the many benefits we will realize because of the rapid improvement and wide application of electronic tools. The use of high-capacity, high-speed information systems is transforming retailing and manufacturing, health care, and finance at least as rapidly as it is transforming higher education. The advance of information systems will affect every part of our society, mostly for the better. With greater numbers of, and better quality, information products, more readily accessible everywhere by electronic networks, more people will use more knowledge, more effectively, for more purposes than has previously been possible. The promise is enormous.

The challenge before us is both technical and institutional. How can we encourage the advance of this environment in such a way as to ensure cost effective results and maximum social benefit? This essay sketches the changes coming with emerging technologies and identifies the institutional arrangements that may evolve as a consequence. It identifies problems that may occur and suggests some initiatives that may both encourage the advance of an electronic scholarly environment and promote the emergence of cost-effective and broadly beneficial institutions for scholarly communication. Although this discussion focuses on scholarly endeavors, many of the issues relate to the larger world as well.

A first concern will be with the logistics for information, that is, the implications of changing technologies for the placement of production, storage, and delivery of information products. Design of the electronic environment involves many decisions about location. Will a large electronic storage depository hold all the information relevant to a given discipline and be accessible from everywhere through networks? Such a facility would take advantage of large economies of scale in storage but would incur the cost of large volumes of communication. Alternatively, decentralized information storage would minimize communication requirements. The balance to be struck between centralized and decentralized storage arrangements will evolve as the technologies change, but this balance is one of the most important issues in emerging markets for electronic information products. This essay suggests directions markets will likely take.

Given optimal balance in patterns of storage, how will readers "navigate" the network to find information products suitable to their needs? The electronic environment excels at enabling users to locate relevant information easily; however, designers of information systems face a number of choices about investments that will aid navigation through electronic information services.

How will the electronic distribution of information products affect authors, readers, editors, publishers, and libraries, given the logistics of the information environment and the tools for navigating it?

Finally, what will be the nature of the markets for electronic-information products. What will the products be? What kind of price structures and payment mechanisms might develop? Will competitive markets establish an efficient level of production of information products, or will unfettered markets fail to achieve efficiency? If we can anticipate the possible failure of the markets, what steps might we propose now to make failure less likely?

THE PRESENT SCENE

At present, print products dominate publishing and libraries. Research libraries generally commit 30 to 35 percent of their budgets to materials. Less than half of the materials expenditures buys books; more than half of the materials budgets buys serials (serials requiring an even greater proportion in smaller libraries and in scientific and technical libraries) (Cummings et al., 1992). Much less than 5 percent of materials budgets goes to the acquisition of electronic information products. Currently, libraries use computer systems chiefly for managing their inventories.

Academic libraries took about 20 years to adopt computer-based bibliographic utilities and online circulation systems. Academic libraries adopted online catalogs and optical disk systems within 15 years. By the mid-1990s, well over 90 percent of the college and university libraries in the United States will be using electronic circulation systems, catalogs, and optical-disc-based systems with indexes to citations to articles.[2] Some publishers are distributing journals electronically, with some titles being electronic versions of printed publications and others being new titles that exist only electronically. An example of the former is *The Journal of Biological Chemistry*, distributed by the American Society of Biological Chemists and Rockefeller University. *The Online Journal of Current Clinical Trials* distributed by OCLC is an example of the latter.

Software vendors are creating new products that will affect scholarly communication and libraries. First, several vendors have announced that their products will incorporate a client-server architecture so that client software on individual users' computers will be able to search databases on disparate servers available on campus and international networks. The International Standards Organization is defining a suite of protocols for the interaction of bibliographic clients and servers; the protocol Z39.50 defines the client-server linkage for searching. Readers using a Z39.50-compliant client can search remote library catalogs and databases as easily, and with the same interface, as they can search their local library's catalog. With suitable contractual relationships among libraries, a reader in one library may place a request for delivery of materials from another library without the intervention of the user's local library.[3] With these arrangements, the costs of lending items among libraries should fall sharply.

Second, several vendors are distributing the page images of journal articles in electronic format. UMI calls its product ProQuest. Within a year, the

ProQuest system will have a jukebox of compact discs linked to the campus network and to the local library catalog and databases so that readers using their computers will be able to search an index file in the library, identify a citation, and if willing to be billed suitable fees, have articles delivered to their work sites, either in print by messenger, or as fax by telephone, or as an electronic file via network directly to the workstation. The ProQuest system currently has over 300 journal titles, and UMI expects the number of titles to grow into the thousands.

Third, several libraries are scanning older materials to create electronic, digital image files of the pages scanned. For example, the Columbia Law Library launched Project Janus in January,1993. Within two years, the law library plans to be scanning, annually, 10,000 old volumes whose copyrights are in the public domain. The library will discard the print volumes after scanning them. Columbia expects that the scanning program will be less expensive than building additional space to hold an equivalent volume of texts in print. Other libraries will scan materials to preserve their contents when the acid paper on which they are printed threatens to disintegrate. Digital scanning may replace the microfilming of decaying materials.

Fourth, the Internet is growing in both the number of users and the amount of information it provides. OCLC, RLG (Research Library Group), and CARL (Colorado Association of Research Libraries) individually offer large databases linked to delivery services. Dozens of other entities offer services via the Internet. Tens of thousands of scholars routinely share mail and manuscripts via the Internet. In some fields of science, communication via the network is becoming a primary vehicle by which scholars gain reputation.

The world of scholarly communication is changing. The following discussion explains the pattern of change and anticipates changing roles for the participants.

TECHNOLOGIES FOR SCHOLARLY COMMUNICATION

The impetus for change comes from rapid developments in electronic methods of storing, retrieving, and distributing information. Because systems with significantly lower costs are likely to replace more expensive methods, it is essential to understand the patterns of costs made possible by new technologies.

Storage

Storage of information in digital format has substantial economies of scale. Megabytes measure storage capacity. The text of a book occupies approximately one megabyte of electronic storage space.[4] Put the cost of storing information as a printed book at \$12.[5] A thousand megabytes is a gigabyte, and the cost of storing a gigabyte of text in book format is, then, $12,000. The thousand floppy disks needed to hold a gigabyte of information (off-line) would cost about $1,400. Imperial Chemical Industries' Digital Paper holds a gigabyte (off-line) at a cost of about $10.[6] At present, the economies of scale in digital information storage are exhausted at about 1,000 gigabytes (a terabyte). However, technical progress in storage systems is rapid, so we might expect even greater economies of scale for storage in the future. A system might evolve which holds a thousand terabytes (a petabyte) in a jukebox and can fetch any megabyte in a minute or two. A petabyte would be roughly the equivalent of a billion books. The cost of the medium (tape, compact disc) for storing the content of a book might be much less than a dime. The printing and storage costs for a book come to about $12, so the cost advantage of large-scale electronic storage is at least 100 times that of print. Electronic files may often be "compressed" to achieve even larger economies. With network access, a single electronic copy may serve many more users than can a print volume, yielding still larger economies of scale.

The compact disc offers compelling storage advantages as well. A CD holds 500 megabytes of formatted information, the equivalent of 500 books. A device costing less than $5,000 puts information on a blank disk that costs about $40. A single CD then stores information for about $100 per gigabyte off-line. However, when a manufacturing process creates a master that enables inexpensive replication of multiple copies, the cost per compact disc drops sharply. A quantity of 1,000 identical discs might cost $6 per disc. That puts the cost of storage at $12 per gigabyte off-line when information is to be widely distributed and stored at many sites. The cost advantage of various digital storage technologies is very large compared to print.

If our society continues to spend what it spends now on information storage, we will be able to store at least one hundred times as much. If new information products are more valuable because of their color, animation, and photographic and algorithmic content, perhaps the amount spent on storage will increase. The amount of information available for widespread use could increase by several orders of magnitude. We might then measure information resources in petabytes, a new dimension of national wealth.

Communication

There are also economies of scale in data communication systems now generally available. An ordinary telephone line can move data at 9,600 bits per second via a modem that costs about $250. There are eight bits to the byte and a million bytes in a book. The text of a book would move at such a rate in about 15 minutes. TCP/IP is a communication protocol that relies on electronics separate from telephone lines. For short distances, data can flow over telephone-like wiring at 10 megabits per second. Coaxial cable systems

(Ethernet, for example), offer the same service over longer distances. A book would move at such a rate in about a second.[7] When buildings contain workstations at reasonably high densities (that is, when buildings contain several dozen computers, such as on university campuses), the costs of wiring and electronics seem to be comparable to telephone wiring. Some computers have Ethernet communications built-in. Ethernet boards can be retrofit for about $200 each. Thus, where wiring dedicated to data communication is installed, data can flow about one thousand times faster than through telephone lines, for costs comparable to a dedicated telephone line. Current optical fiber systems move data at about 100 megabits per second, a 10-fold increase over Ethernet. Such fiber systems may be about four times more expensive than copper cabling and electronics, so where the volume of data traffic demand it, communication by fiber is less expensive than copper systems, per bit moved.

Data communication systems have two components. The "long distance" component uses trunk lines to move large volumes of information between cities or between major nodes within cities. Trunk lines take advantage of the economies of scale in high-capacity transmission systems. "Local loops" connect individual computers to each other and bring them together to connect to the long-distance service. The local elements may include premises distribution systems within buildings and network links among buildings. Somewhat different issues are important in each of the two components.

The High Performance Computing Act of 1991[8] established as a national priority the creation of a high-capacity National Research and Education Network (NREN). While a senator, Vice President Albert Gore introduced the bill, and he and President Clinton advocated the development of "information highways" during their campaign in 1992. Development of gigabit-per-second capacity devices for use in trunk lines seems possible later in this decade. Such a service could move data at a burst rate of 1,000 books per second, presumably at a much lower unit cost (that is, much lower cost per book moved) than telephone lines.[9] The primary focus of the NREN has been on the development of higher-capacity technologies, primarily for use in trunk lines. Of course, the trunk lines derive their value from their ability to support local services.

The capacity of communication systems will continue to improve and the cost per gigabit moved will continue to fall. The Asynchronous Transfer Mode (ATM) now being developed in the telephone industry will move data at up to 2.5 billion bits per second.[10] AT&T has successfully tested in a laboratory a communications system based on soliton waves over optical fiber, which moves information at twenty gigabits per second over long distances (Keller, 1993). It will be some time before such systems are deployed. In part, AT&T achieved this capacity by transmitting a signal on each of two wavelengths or colors of light, a technique called wave division multiplexing (WDM). With various improvements, including using many more wavelengths of light simultaneously, more advanced optical fiber technologies may approach 1,000 gigabits per second (that is, terabits-per-second) capacities (Vetter and Du, 1993). Communication systems with WDM optical trunk lines will be enhanced with photonic switches, allowing signals to move optically from origin to networked destinations.

Continued technical change in trunk line services will enable larger volumes of information to move greater distances at lower costs. Indeed, the cost of long-distance service, for practical purposes, is unrelated to distance. As a consequence, information providers who use the long-distance service may be located at any node and enjoy the same communication costs. Similarly, users of services delivered by the trunk lines will incur the same long-distance communication costs regardless of the node at which they connect. Enterprises for whom access to data communication is a significant concern will be able to choose locations at nodes where other costs are low, typically smaller cities. Institutes of higher education of lesser size and more remote location should be relatively better off.

The local loop is the source of the greatest expense in building a communication system. The few hundred to few thousand yards needed to link each communication terminus to the trunk lines imposes great costs because these systems must serve the computers individuals use for their work, and therefore must be deployed in quantity. Low costs will be very important if network access is to be widespread. In the long run, whether copper wiring (like that used for telephones), coaxial cable (like that used by the cable television industry), or fiber lines will be the medium of choice for the local loop remains unclear.[11] Given the expense involved in reaching millions of individuals, deployment may take decades, during which time technological options will continue to evolve. Many observers expect that ultimately, the very high capacity of a fiber link will be justified for the connection to each computer.

The services people want to use will be a main determinant of the choice of system for local connection. The most demanding service is probably full-motion video with sound. To send the rough digital equivalent of existing television signals will require about 28-million bits per second of flow. If the video information is compressed before being sent and then decompressed locally before use, a flow of much less than 10 million bits per second might support video with sound. On the other hand, high-definition television (HDTV) will likely impose much greater demands on communication systems. Moreover, if the video information is to yield moving images to be viewed as the signal arrives (rather than the bits being stored locally for viewing later), then the bits must arrive on time and in order. Many data communication systems use asynchronous methods that cannot guarantee timely and sequential transmission, particularly when communication lines experience congestion. Isochronous data communication with sufficient capacities to support high-definition television with high-quality stereo sound, delivered like telephone service from any point to any other point on the network on demand, will probably require fiber through the local loop to the terminus.

When moderate data communications (say, 10 million bits per second capacity to individual computers) are available on every college campus, in every school, and—in all likelihood—in many homes, a considerable suite of information resources will be available everywhere. Workstations on the network will have the resources of the network, so the relative advantage of location enjoyed by campuses or cities with libraries holding large print collections will diminish. We can imagine, then, every scholar, every school, and many homes and businesses having online access to petabyte libraries.[12]

Logistics

Large economies of scale in storage combined with economies of scale in communication will affect the logistics of information similar to how interstate highways and air freight—combined with mechanized warehouses—affect the distribution of goods for retail sale. Even grocery chains depend on rapid delivery from a few central warehouses to dispersed retail sites. Because computer cash registers at the point of sale track transactions in detail, retailers may easily restock store shelves from quite remote warehouses with daily (or more frequent) shipments. Thus, retail chains achieve much lower costs by operating fewer warehouses. Indeed, for clothing and other nonperishable goods, one warehouse might serve the whole United States.

To continue the analogy, national electronic warehouses may gather information products and distribute them by data network to customers across the country or around the world. The economies of scale in storage mean that larger storage facilities house information at much lower cost per unit than smaller ones. Moreover, if the same warehouse serves all, there need be only one warehouse. This analogy breaks down in two ways. First, an electronic warehouse need contain only one of each item (not counting security back-ups probably kept off-site) because copies can be made on demand. Second, over the network, the reader can identify information products, then order and receive them automatically on demand. Retailing does not yet routinely offer this capability. However, shopping at home—using Prodigy or CompuServe online electronic catalogs with pictures (perhaps even video) and order forms— is possible.

In retailing, there may be further economies from a central repository. Managers may place production orders with more precision and in a more timely manner because events in a single warehouse cue action (for example, when the size 12 in green is selling well). The manager can observe what is moving and follow trends more quickly. In an information repository, a manager may be able to coordinate disparate information products by use of common numbering systems and integrated retrieval software. However, electronic networks may enable such coordination among dispersed sites, rather than requiring a central facility.[13]

At the same time that technical changes seem to favor large database servers on the network, the costs of local storage are falling as well. Individuals will likely have more storage at their local workstations—storage for information products used frequently, for products that demand high-speed communication, or for products that are unique to individuals' tasks. In particular, compact discs hold 500 megabytes of data and can come from a master mold at a cost of less than $6 each in quantities of 1,000 or more. The cost of storing information on a compact disc approaches the cost per gigabyte of the largest storage systems when the CDs are produced in quantity for distribution. Of course, with network access, information need be stored only once whereas with distribution by compact disc, the same information will be stored at many redundant locations. Until high-speed network access is common, however, the compact disc (or a similar device) seems likely to have a significant role. Indeed, for people such as accountants and engineers who use large volumes of relatively static information, optical discs may be suitable for an extended period of time.

The demands on storage and communication systems will grow, in part, as sound and video become embedded in documents. Authors may express their ideas not only in text and graphics but also with animation, video, and sound in "compound documents" or "multimedia." Video of the level of quality that has been the standard in the United States for the last 40 years, requires more than 28-million bytes of storage for each second of video. With compression, by limiting the size of the video image, cutting the number of frames displayed per second in half, and by lowering the quality of the sound, an emerging standard for video in multimedia documents requires 150,000 bits per second. At this rate, a CD can hold nearly an hour of video and the CD can transfer the video information to the display device fast enough to be displayed on the fly. The resulting image, however, is of lesser quality than standard television.

If authors and readers are to share within documents the kind of video sequences that are of higher quality than that just described, they must either use storage devices that are both more commodious and faster in the transfer of information than CDs, or they must subscribe to communication networks that provide very high performance. Because such networks are likely to be expensive and require decades for deployment, the CD-quality of video for multimedia will likely find a market for some time to come. Many personal computers will have on-board compact disc drives, in addition to internal drives and floppy magnetic disks, as standard storage devices.

Between the small-scale personal storage systems and the large-scale storage services on the national network will be the campus storage services. Campuses (or enterprises) will have storage services linked to campus networks, which take advantage of the economies of scale available in storage technologies. Campus storage has two justifications. First, individuals may use campus storage to maintain personal files. Individuals will elect to use the more economical, local network services for back-up and archival storage and for files larger than they retain at their workstations. For example, the campus service may include tape and optical systems that may not be economic for individuals. Second, campus facilities will store information that several individuals on the campus will share. The campus store of shared material is, of course, an electronic library. It will include books, journals, and essays, as well as visual, auditory, numerical, and algorithmic information. Personal and campus storage will reduce the load on national network communications systems.

For research universities, the campus storage system is likely to require the largest-scale storage devices, thereby realizing large economies of scale. The campus facility seems likely to hold most of the core of texts and tools routinely used by undergraduates to minimize demands on the national network. In addition, campuses with research missions are likely to store unique materials, the products of their own faculties, that the campus shares with the world.

The electronic information environment will handle larger amounts of information, just as modern grocery stores handle many times more products than grocery shops did before 1940. For texts, the distribution service might handle working papers with the same ease as polished, final works. During the 1980s, electronic innovations in printing gradually reduced the minimum optimal press run for a book from a thousand to just a few hundred copies.[14] In the 1990s, high-quality photocopy machines printing at 600 dots per inch can operate as network print-servers, printing books from electronic files and applying soft bindings. The minimum optimal press run will become one copy. With conventional printing, a publisher made a judgment that a title was of sufficient interest that sale of the minimum press run was a reasonable probability. Although review, editing, and promotional costs remain fixed elements of the total cost, the printing process no longer represents a fixed cost per title. As a consequence, publishers can produce many more titles. The fact of academic "publication" will have a weaker link to "quality."

With the cost of storage being, at most, one hundredth of the cost of printing and with communication costs falling dramatically as well, authors will be able to share much larger amounts of information. They might distribute the numerical data used in their empirical work as an ancillary to their report of empirical results. They may distribute mathematical models as algorithms in computer-manipulatable form. Graphics, sound, and video sequences may move over the network in the same way as text. More varieties of research will be electronically publishable as the cost of distribution falls. Scholars may share their work at earlier stages in its development, with working papers being available on the network. Of course, with so much available, readers may expend extra effort and require extra help to find material of interest.

"Navigation"

Petabyte files of information will require new methods of organization, which will then provide new ways for users to find relevant information. In a networked environment, there are two strategies for providing "navigation"; one is hierarchical. The hierarchical arrangement consists of a series of menus. Each menu invites a reader to make a selection that results in a move to a lower, more detailed menu. If a hierarchical structure is the norm, the publisher will profit from more favorable placement in the hierarchy. If one publisher's materials appear higher in the hierarchy or at the top of menus, it's products will have an advantage because readers come to them first. The Sabre reservation service developed by American Airlines offers an analogy. Sabre is a computer service licensed to travel agents. Competing airlines contended that Sabre listed American's flights first, putting competitors at a disadvantage. If such bias were proven, it might be grounds for anti-trust action. Monopoly of navigation tools for information sources might justify anti-trust action.

Nonhierarchical navigation relies on an exhaustive search for specific terms or tags. A search of an electronic library catalog enables one to find a specific work or group of works based on a single search string. (A search string in this context is a group of characters, usually a word or phrase.) Generally, one does not step down through the hierarchical structure of, say, the Dewey Decimal System. Nonhierarchical searching usually requires more computer cycles than hierarchical systems. Nonhierarchical systems are more effective ,with well-structured information and with particular components (authors, titles, subjects) put into tagged fields (for example, the title is tagged 245 in the MARC standard used in libraries) to enable the reader to define searches and reduce the probability of error. (Errors involve both the omission of valued items and the inclusion of unvalued items in the search result.) The use of open-vendor standards for tags makes nonhierarchical searching easier. The MARC format adopted by the Library of Congress and widely used among libraries specifies tags related to library catalog information. The notion of standardized tags can be extended in the manner of the Standard Generalized Mark-up Language (SGML) to full-text files, and beyond to graphics, algorithms, and the other components of compound documents.[15] The file systems associated with computer-operating systems might also include more information about the files in their headers. Apple's Macintosh operating system includes an identification of the associated application software, date of creation, and size. Information about SGML tagging, graphics, and indexing could be included in file headers in a modern computer file system to aid search and retrieval. With standard tags, readers may search rich files of diverse information with reasonable economy in a nonhierarchical manner.

Online library catalogs work efficiently, in part, because an electronic index to catalog information points to particular items. Full-text files could be similarly indexed, but indexing requires computational resources, and indexes may occupy as much storage space as the original text. Although some works (perhaps top-quality works) will justify full-text indexing, many will not. Searching quantities of un-indexed text requires a considerable amount of computational resources. If the documents do not have standard tags embedded, nonhierarchical searching may have too many errors to be useful for ordinary purposes.

Network navigation, then, will almost certainly include hierarchical elements. For the most part, readers are likely to depend on packages of information products supplied by publishers and on reading lists published by editors to benefit from the guidance of informed "navigators" and trusted colleagues. Of course, searching citation indexes will be easy and inexpensive. Scanning full-text files of documents will be routine for certain well structured, pre-indexed files. Large amounts of information, however, will likely be stored without indexes and will be found by citation in a relatively hierarchical manner.

Authors may aid navigation. They might supply tags, key words, and abstracts. Publishers might include citations for index entries and might include complete indexes to the full-text in some instances, to enhance the value of their products. Database distributors, libraries, and indexers may build navigation tools and offer them on various terms over electronic networks. There will be new markets for these navigational instruments.[16]

Navigation of networks for information will probably involve software on the reader's computer that provides a personal "front-end." With such client software, diverse information resources on the network will look as though they were stored locally. The local client software will present a screen that invites a user to make a request, perhaps by means of menus and icons. The software will translate the request into a standard, compact form and send it over the network to a remote server. The server will respond with an appropriate package of information. The local client software will receive the information package and display it. Compression of information packages will economize on storage and communication costs. The local client software will then decompress the package for use. The information package might be character information with tags identifying authors, titles, headings, and other components. The client might use the tags and map the components into design software that presents information in a typeset format. The information package might contain graphics, sound, animation, and other data structures that the client software could interpret and make available for local use. This client software, then, will turn a general-purpose computer workstation into an information appliance, able to fetch from the network and display for local use, a wide variety of information products. Of course, an online information vendor whose servers work best, who provides the most valuable kinds of information economically, and who provides easy navigation, will have market advantages over less-capable information providers.

Existing online information services such as Prodigy and CompuServe offer examples of client software interacting over the network with large, online repositories of information. These systems are proprietary so that the client software works only with a given repository's files. The Wide Area Information Service (WAIS) and Gopher are two software products in the public domain, that provide client software for searching remote databases.[17] In the next generation of client software, we might expect generic programs that conform to standard protocols and interact with a variety of networked information vendors. In the library world, the Z39.50 and related standards define protocols for vending queries receiving response from software clients of one vendor to networked information providers using software of other vendors. There will be a number of software vendors providing client software just as there may be many vendors offering server software.

AGENTS IN SCHOLARLY COMMUNICATION

The emergence of more information products in electronic format together with suitable navigation tools creates significant opportunities for much larger amounts of information to be made available economically. What are the implications for authors, readers, editors, publishers, and libraries?

The Author

Authors will consider measures to retain control of their works in the inherently volatile electronic environment. They will also face the challenge of creating compound documents.

Authors look for recognition. A distribution service must assure authors that readers cannot easily misappropriate their works. For many kinds of work, an author also expects compensation. If a jingle in a national advertising campaign contains a line from a play, the playwright will expect financial compensation. Of course, an author's recognition and compensation will be greater when more readers can readily find and use the author's work, even over an extended time.

Ensuring that authors receive recognition for their ideas may require that the electronic distribution channel include mechanisms for establishing the ownership and authenticity of a document. With printed works, authors affix "© 1994" to establish their claims, and, if they wish, submit a copy to the Library of Congress.

Information products distributed electronically are inherently more volatile and therefore more difficult to control. As a first step before distribution, an author might seek to register the document to establish ownership. Posting a copy of the document to a third party and receiving a coded authentication stamp in return would enable the author to prove ownership at a specific point in time. The author will have established his or her identity with the registry in advance, perhaps receiving a personal identification number for use in registering documents. When an author posts an essay, the registry will return an individual date stamp, with time to the second and with an encrypted string of characters unique to the author. When registered in this way, an author could prove that he or she had posted the essay at a given time. If someone else retrieved a copy and posted it with another registry and claimed original or even simultaneous authorship, his or her claim could be disproven. The designation of year in the conventional copyright notice is no longer a sufficiently detailed time claim. The registry could authenticate the electronic document at any time in the future. The document authentication authority might also retain an archival copy of the work at the lower expense of off-line storage to make possible incontrovertible verification for an indefinite period. Such registration for authenticity will typically be a by-product of posting a work with a service agent when the author wishes to share it on the network. For books, deposit with the Library of Congress plays this role; for journals, a receipt from the editor on the event of the original submission plays this role in an informal way; for electronic materials, the registration for authenticity could be decentralized and yet be made more formal. Software vendors might market packages to create the encrypted string to all those interested in offering registry services.

For compensation, one might imagine a mechanism embedded in the electronic distribution service that makes use of electronic accounts and payments. In the telephone industry, a 900 number service will charge fees electronically to the caller's telephone account. Bank credit cards are in wide use and enable transactions by mail, telephone, and fax. In an electronic-information distribution environment, one might imagine an account number system similar to telephone and credit card numbers. Encryption of account numbers with public and private keys might make theft of accounts more difficult.[18] With the use of secure accounts, the transaction cost of soliciting payment should be very low, so it might be economical to charge and collect fees as low as a few cents per transaction. An author's recognition depends on readership, so readers' interests will also be important. For authors, editors play the role of reader's advocate, soliciting materials to increase the value of their publication, offering advice to authors about how to shape the product, and establishing a reputation for the publication that attracts readership, adding value to the authors' work. Authors will continue to value the services of good editors, and the electronic distribution service should enhance the work of editors.

A second issue for authors is the prospect of creating compound documents. On the one hand, the creation of sophisticated compound documents may be more expensive than creating text alone. On the other, documents with significant multimedia components may be more valuable than text documents.

The creation of conventional text is largely a cottage industry. An author or authors write the text. When a publisher agrees to publication, authors may engage an artist to render a few diagrams and, perhaps, an editor to put a final polish on the language. Even a college textbook will typically involve only a year's worth of effort, perhaps spread over several calendar years interspersed with other activities. In extreme contrast, the creation of video materials with high production values (usually the result of employing professional actors, directors, sound engineers, and videotape editors) may cost $100,000 per hour of video, perhaps much more. Double that cost if one contemplates an interactive computer interface that enables the user to read text, see graphics, and navigate through the video and other materials at will,and in a fashion that reflects meaningful connections in the content. A series of five hours of interactive material designed to match the topics in a textbook might cost $1 million to produce. The author, then, may be more akin to a television producer than to a scriptwriter. With such high stakes, the products must achieve a large audience and the production process must be well managed. Like the entertainment movie industry, the prospect of a few "blockbusters" may lead many to try to create such products. The paradox is that the mass market for information products linked to the national network may give very high rewards to the very best and leave little reward to the second best. The phenomenon may parallel the effect of recorded music on vaudeville entertainers. Live, but second best, singing lost out to the best, delivered electronically.

Of course, electronic tools should make creation of compound documents easier. Software and hardware for handling sound and video are becoming less expensive and more common. Software such as *Authorware* provides tools that enable an author to script an instructional session, issue questions, and allow the software to respond intelligently to a range of responses, including "fuzzy" spelling. Even so, the graphics design talents needed to produce high-quality multimedia presentations are rare enough to lead one to believe that many multimedia products will come from teams of practitioners with significant budgets.

The value of compound documents has several roots. On one level, some scientific ideas are only understandable in a three-dimensional animated representation. Text, alone, describes the folds in proteins in a very limited way; a 3-D, animated graphic representation makes the ideas plain. On another level, foreign languages have the most meaning when spoken by native speakers in the context of interpersonal exchanges that have meaning in a particular culture. Even a video "talking head" can carry an energy and authority not equaled by text alone. On another level, interactive instructional tools give instant corrections on drills. Interactive tests can choose which question to ask next based on the test-taker's success on previous questions.[19] Instant, adaptive responses embedded in context-rich associative sights and sounds may be more cost-effective learning systems than lecturers armed only with chalk boards, texts, and paper exams.

Authors, then, face a riskier environment with opportunities to have substantially greater effect by producing rich, compound documents, but at the cost of much larger investments of time and funds than have been required for success in print.

The Reader

Readers have a number of interests in the distribution of information; electronic methods will advance many of them. The quality of images used, the timeliness of access, and cost are all important. Perhaps most important is the method by which a reader decides what to read. The scarcity of a reader's time may be the most influential element in the process of distributing information.

Readers respond to the quality of information displays. For print publications, publishers hire designers and create attractive displays of text and graphics. Accurate typography, careful proofing, and pleasing designs yield products readers enjoy using. Because most designing and proofing now involve electronic tools, one can assume that electronic information products can be attractively displayed. Text products, for example, may have embedded codes for layout and page design so that they display attractive page-images. The reader decides what kind of display device to use for intellectual work and will also decide whether to print a given page or simply use it on the screen. Although many older computer screens provide relatively poor images, screen technologies continue to improve. Nevertheless, there may be a physical limit to how well affordable screens can display information.[20] Therefore, readers may print some documents routinely for careful study. On the other hand, readers consult many sources quickly for reference, to check a citation or fact, or for brief textual comparison. Such use of tools on-screen is quick and will probably not justify the delay and cost of printing.

Readers care about timeliness in two ways. In many settings, information is most valuable when it is new. The time lags involved in producing conventional printed publications can amount to many months and sometimes years. When an information product reaches readers, its content may be out of date. For this reason, many investors rely on electronic access to stock market information instead of waiting for its publication in a newspaper the following day. In scientific circles, getting successful reviews of grant applications is essential to survival. Proposal writers highly value having bibliographies that are comprehensive and current to give assurance that their proposed work is original and takes advantage of the latest methods. If electronic formats shorten distribution times and ensure comprehensiveness and accuracy, readers in many fields will value the electronic sources.

Retrieval also involves time. Once a document has been distributed and someone has decided to read it, how long will retrieval take? For conventional printed documents, if the local library holds the document, the reader faces the time required to travel to the library and locate the item. If the document is not in the collection, the reader may request its loan from elsewhere with delays typically measured in days or weeks. Ultimately, some scholars must schedule trips to remote libraries to use their holdings. Scheduling such trips may take years.

With electronic delivery, readers may have documents come to their workstation (or fax) in a matter of seconds or minutes. One might imagine electronic storage of items in a local electronic library. Local storage might be appropriate for frequently used items. Local storage reduces demands on long-distance communication. If documents arrive electronically within a minute or two, readers might regularly consult more documents. Because electronic documents may include numerical data sets, sound, and moving images, for many purposes readers may ultimately value electronic documents more than they value print documents.

Readers also care about cost. In a conventional setting, readers may subscribe to frequently used documents and buy relevant books. They depend on their library to acquire a second tier of useful materials. Because students and people from different disciplines will buy different things for themselves, libraries buy all the primary materials as well. However, print remains an expensive choice, especially for libraries. If libraries are viewed as agents for readers, then the rising costs of collection programs in libraries is of significant concern to readers. The methods of distributing information electronically appear to be much less expensive than those for print, especially if storage costs are included. Electronic distribution holds the promise of lowering costs, allowing libraries and their readers access to more information products for a given budget. If the cost per use, on average, is lower, we would expect readers to consult more information products routinely.

Most importantly, the reader's time is scarce. They value being able to identify relevant material and to use it with as little time delay and cost as possible. Relevance has many dimensions and the essential problem for the reader is to be able to anticipate what may be most helpful. Readers can afford to examine only a small portion of all that authors write, even within a discipline. Selectivity, if measured as the proportion that an individual reads of all that is available, will increase as electronic distribution makes more information products available at lower cost. When petabytes of information are readily available to all by network, readers will highly value elements that enhance selection and navigation.

Readers depend on at least four methods for deciding what to examine. First, they value the selections of editors. In book publishing, the name of the publisher carries a history that may influence readers; for example, Yale

University Press implies a certain distinction. For a journal, the character of recent articles enables readers to predict the character of future articles. Hence, a journal title develops a reputation, enhanced by the reputations of the scholars on the editorial board. If an essay appears in a top journal, one can depend on the review process for establishing relevance to the discipline, quality of scholarship, and a degree of originality.

Second, readers depend on works being cited by others. Thus, one relevant essay may lead backward in time to other relevant sources. In this way, the pattern of citations produces a general indication of the influence of a particular work and its author. Published citation indexes facilitate this activity. Readers follow these trails too. Although this is not a method for identifying new material, it is particularly useful when one is investigating a focused topic.

Third, readers browse. They may depend on the cataloging in a library to place similar items together so that one interesting title leads to others nearby on the shelf. Some readers also browse the tables of contents of journals, looking for works by known authors, topics of interest, or allowing themselves to be drawn to essays with provocative titles.

Fourth, readers use pre-prints or working papers. Essays in some disciplines appear first as working papers, perhaps several years before being published in journals. Authors often present working papers at conferences or symposia so that personal interaction may generate ideas that improve the final work or lead to the identification of substantial errors or to the realization that similar work has already appeared elsewhere. For some conferences, publishers distribute the papers presented as proceedings with varying amounts of editorial attention. Readers understand *caveat lector* when they use material they know is unedited.

Readers also learn about relevant material in other, less-formal ways— friends mention a work, they hear about a work at a conference, an editor asks for a review. Electronic distribution might provide a number of advances that will enable readers to choose what to examine more carefully. These advances encompass many of the functions we now associate with editors.

The Editor

Editors are agents for both readers and authors. They solicit manuscripts, review them, make suggestions for changes, and decide what to publish. They shape what they present to readers who depend on the reputations of editors in deciding what to read. Each editor may have a specific audience in mind and knows that tastes differ between audiences. For example, work that is too technical for one audience may find approval with another. Authors often write with a specific editor in mind, casting particular ideas in ways that will appeal to a specific editor and to that editor's intended audience.

Ultimately, editors are arbiters of quality and originality. The best scholarship appears in journals with excellent reputations for sophistication, originality, and relevance to the scholars in a given discipline. Readers are more likely to read and cite an essay appearing in a journal of excellent reputation. Moreover, as a good journal succeeds in attracting excellent work, it builds its reputation and its readership. In this way the editor's publisher prospers by selling more subscriptions and sustaining higher prices, and the editor's reputation advances as well.

The influence of editors will likely increase with electronic distribution. There will be more information available. Readers will use more of it, so the scope for editorial review will be broader, encompassing compound documents and possibly information products for different purposes.

Although portions of the editorial process will continue unchanged, new procedures also may appear. At present, authors generally keep manuscripts private and submit them to one editor or journal at a time. An editor typically may solicit comments from two referees. The editor then makes a judgment about publication in light of the referees' reviews. This process is accelerating with electronic exchanges. Authors may submit manuscripts electronically; indeed, some editors require it. Referees comment via the network and the editor can correspond electronically with the author. The electronic manuscript feeds the printing process, reducing the time to production as well as costs. In truth, however, little of the delay in the editorial evaluation process is caused by the post office; editors and referees spend most of the time considering the manuscript.

A description of a more radical departure from present modes illustrates the potential forms of editorship that might be possible with electronic distribution. Some of these ideas are in use in the "high energy physics-theory" (hep-th) bulletin boards developed by Paul Ginsparg at the Los Alamos National Laboratories.[21] Physicists post their working papers in a fashion that makes them available via electronic mail to anyone on the Internet.

An author might post an essay, on an electronic bulletin-board fashion (getting a registration string as a receipt that proves ownership) as version D (for draft) and invite a circle of acquaintances interested in the topic to comment on the draft. The author might use a standard method of labeling the essay, such as SGML tags. In addition, the author might rate the work on several scales: originality, theoretical sophistication, empirical content, its relevance to specific sub-disciplines, and its relevance to the larger world. Indeed, professional societies might standardize rating scales for this purpose. By means of self-rating and tagging, authors can enable any interested person to see version D, much as authors now share working papers or present works-in-progress at conferences. Alternatively, some authors might choose to limit such postings for "members" or subscribers only.

Editors might scan the electronic "bulletin board" for drafts to solicit promising essays for their publications, much as editors may solicit essays from works presented at conferences. The editor and colleagues might make private comments to the author, suggesting how to improve the work or make it relevant to a particular audience.

Some comments might also be public. Colleagues or editors might draft comments for attachment to version D, which are then accessible to the author and to anyone reading version D on the network. The online evaluators might offer their own ratings of version D using the same scoring scheme as the author's. With tagged ratings usable in network search-strings, readers could search for essays by subject and by ratings of attributes or quality.

The author might ultimately replace version D with version C (for complete) and actively solicit evaluation by the best editors. Editors could assign ratings, suggest revisions, and ultimately identify a revision as version A (for the best works) or B (good and interesting) in their reading list. Indeed, one might imagine editors posting reading lists because all the essays are available on the network as version D or above. Moreover, to become an editor, one need simply post a reading list. Perhaps any reader might be able to render a rating, a little like the movie review system in *Consumer Reports*. Readers send cards to *Consumer Reports*, rating the movies they have seen. *Consumer Reports* then issues a rating that reflects a statistical summary of all the ratings sent in by its readers. The problem with such a system is that a given viewer may not have the same tastes as the set of people who review for *Consumer Reports*. To allow for differences in tastes, a system could categorize reviewers in various ways. For scholarly work, one could consider reviews by any of the following groups: faculty at research universities, other faculty, graduate students, undergraduates, nonacademic professionals, and others.

Of course, editors need reward for the quality of their editorial efforts; otherwise, there will be too few editors. In addition, readers want to depend on the best editorial advice in deciding what to read. Thus, we might expect editors to sell their reading lists using a network payment mechanism. Editors could claim exclusive listing for the first few months for works on their A lists. Moreover, the listing could be richer than simply "yes, I accept this" or "no, I do not." The editor might well provide ratings on multiple criteria. An author's works will then have public ratings on multiple criteria, and a reader should be able to select items for reading using subject and multiple-rating criteria.

It is conceivable that authors will retain ownership of their documents and retain control of versions on network servers. The author might receive royalties related to use. Indeed, the electronic distribution service might require a payment from the author to post D works, much as authors bear the cost of sharing working papers. Some authors have successfully launched presses; Professor Edward R. Tufte and the Graphics Press is a good example. Starting a "press" should be easier as the cost of electronic distribution falls.

In short, authors would post articles on databases, to be enmeshed in a broader literature with many online editors. The electronic system would then support the four formal methods readers use to decide what material to consult. The editors' reading lists act as quasi, online journals. Editors could offer readers much more information about what to read, and what other information products might be useful than when their work leads to the creation of a printed product.[22] Readers may easily track citations over the network. They can browse using many criteria, including subject (the author's self-identified key words and perhaps discipline categories defined by a professional association). They might also take advantage of the multidimensional ratings to acquire empirical work, theoretical sophistication, and the like. The electronic system should also support ready access to works in progress, conference-style essays, numerical data sets, and compound documents having more varied purposes than conventional texts.

Of course, printed products will continue to be important, and electronic analogs of printed products will be valuable in the electronic world. The more radical possibility sketched here illustrates the potential offered by electronic tools.

The Publisher

Publishers are the entrepreneurs of the information marketplace whether they are universities, nonprofit professional societies, or for-profit ventures. Publishers bear the risks of launching new products, make judgments about whom to engage as editors, design promotional efforts, and ensure quality control. When a product fails to find a market, the publisher incurs the financial loss. In recent decades, many successful publishers have added new journal titles, suggesting that there are economies of scope (i.e. a publisher who already has a number of titles may bear a lower cost to add a new title than a new publisher faces to initiate one). Many professional societies have created stables of journals, each focused on somewhat different audiences in their disciplines. Publishing houses also identify new audiences and launch journals to suit them, much as breakfast cereal manufacturers try to create products with different combinations of flavor and crunch. Not all new products are successful, but launching several at once, the publisher has an improved chance of having a winner. This makes it more difficult for a new publisher wishing to enter the marketplace.[23]

Electronic distribution adds a third market to the two markets conventionally pursued by publishers. First, publishers offer projects (such as software for workstations, conpact discs, or other devices) directly to individuals who will continue to buy them for frequently consulted information or multimedia documents. Publishers may sell products directly to individuals over the network as well. Second, publishers offer products to libraries. These may be the same products offered to individuals or products created especially for libraries. For example, libraries may acquire large databases of top-quality material in disciplines relevant to their campuses. A publisher might package prime material with associated indexing and make the package available for storage on campus library systems. Indeed, such a service could include daily, online updates.

Third, publishers place information on the national network where they permanently reside accessible over the network. Enterprises like OCLC, Dialog, and Meade Data maintain large databases online. Publishers could use the database agencies or could mount their own file servers on the network. Information offered over the network would be available on different financial terms than those offered to libraries for local storage. Such information would be useful to campuses that chose not to store a particular product locally. Publishers might also market over the network products that would not be economical for libraries or individuals to store locally.

A critical task for publishers is to attract readers to their products. Rawlins suggests that sales of information products by subscription may become even more important in an electronic environment (Rawlins, 1992). With the significantly lower costs of electronic information, the publisher may sell a subscription to an information service like *Prodigy* or *CompuServe*. The subscriber might download this month's new books or any title in a backfile and have access to this week's magazines, or today's newspapers. Subscriptions give publishers a revenue stream that will support a wide variety of information products. Individuals may choose to subscribe to several such services, selecting those that meet various needs. Of course, the quality of navigation tools, the breadth and depth of coverage, the quality of presentation (especially of compound documents), and price, will differentiate the services of publishers.

If subscription becomes a dominant mode for access to electronic information, then publishers—network service providers—will have less difficulty in enforcing ownership rights. What individuals choose to do privately with information products should not affect publisher revenue, indeed, the more useful the products, the higher the demand. Publishers need to impose ownership-discipline primarily on other network service providers. Such providers may be easier to police.

Use of subscriptions lowers the transaction cost to buyers (that is, readers and users of information). They can easily make payment for large quantities of materials in a single transaction. If the standard way to obtain materials is to subscribe to a service—much as news distributors subscribe to the Associated Press (AP)—then all who use information should pay through their subscriptions. Those enforcing ownership then need only to identify individuals or agencies reselling information who are not subscribers. (AP can more easily identify a newspaper that does not subscribe to AP but that reprints an AP story than it can tie an individual payment to the use of each story.)

Major software companies now employ people to scan electronic bulletin boards looking for people offering their software for resale. If they can easily check their records to verify and the relevant rights assigned, they can more easily know when someone is reselling software without authorization. If every individual electronic information product requires a transaction to occur, then documenting and tracking ownership and enforcing rights will be more difficult. If subscription contracts establish blanket rights, then it may be easier to distinguish the authorized from the unauthorized. When an information product is being made readily available on the Internet by unauthorized users, the owner can search the Internet and find people who are reusing their materials. If the owner can easily identify those not authorized to use it, the costs of enforcement are lower conversely, those who have subscribed to a blanket service can be more easily identified and can more easily prove their authorization and legitimacy. As a result, owners will have a lower cost of enforcing rights with subscriptions than when materials are sold by the piece.

The important boundary here is the one between relatively public access and privately controlled access. Suppose an authorized user downloads an information product from a service and then mounts it without permission and in violation of the license agreement on a server to allow use by everyone within a department in a university. In short, the department has not subscribed to the data. In this case, the owner of the data might have federal marshals go to the campus and inspect each server on the campus to determine whether unlicensed copies of the relevant database are in use. When the marshals find copies of unlicensed software, the university pays a large settlement. Other campuses read about the settlement and police themselves more effectively. Enforcement methods are easier if licenses apply to relatively large sets of materials rather than to individual components, such as "titles" or even "essays." The campus that fails to buy the broad license is most vulnerable to a visit by the marshals, hence the notion that subscriptions to large "databases" may be a more effective pricing structure than selling individual titles. Where databases are relatively large, have effective navigation tools built-in, and will be shared among a significant community—even within the ivy walls of a campus—an owner of a subscription service will likely enjoy success in enforcing property rights at a relatively modest cost. The larger the database and the wider the likely circle of users, the lower the cost of enforcing the rights. Where collaborators want to share small pieces of data, say individual essays, in an essentially private way, the cost of forcing payment will be prohibitive. Moreover, such private sharing has been the traditional domain of fair use copies under the copyright law.

The Congress enacts laws governing intellectual property to discharge its responsibility under Article I Section 8 of the Constitution, namely, "To promote the Progress of Science and useful Arts, by securing for limited Times to Authors and Inventors the exclusive Right to their respective Writings and Discoveries." The Constitution has two purposes here. First, it seeks to encourage authors and inventors to produce new intellectual products.

Therefore, it invites the Congress to enact statutes that make it easier for authors and inventors to receive income from their intellectual works. Second, it encourages authors and inventors to make their intellectual products public so that they may have wide effect. It is the copying of an author's work that receives protection under the copyright law, and to receive a patent an inventor must describe the original ideas in detail in a form that becomes public record.[24] In addition, at the expiration of the "limited Times," the works and ideas that are protected by law move into the public domain and may be freely copied and used by all. In effect, then, the Constitution provides for laws that make it easier for authors and inventors to earn income from their intellectual works in exchange for those works being publicly announced immediately and moving to the public domain in the future. The Constitution then avoids two alternatives. First, it avoids exclusive reliance on licenses and contracts where the burden of enforcement falls wholly on creators of intellectual property. Second, it does not provide for perpetual rights to intellectual property; instead, it broadens the scope of the public domain. As it does on many subjects, the Constitution strikes a balance among competing interests.

To understand the role of the public domain in promoting "the Progress of Science and useful Arts," one might imagine that individual words were "copyrightable." In such a case, any neologism could be used only by permission of the copyright holder. Words and phrases used in this essay like "computer," "byte," and "optical disk" would, then, likely be controlled by copyright. Authors would seek to avoid standard words. Writing restricted to words over 50 years old would be hard to comprehend. Because a robust public domain is valuable for the advance of science and culture, copyright law generally holds that individual words are not copyrightable; indeed, only copies of whole works are copyrightable, not the words and ideas themselves. Given the apparent acceleration in the pace of development of intellectual property, perhaps the balance to be struck between protecting, on the one hand, copyrights and, on the other, the public domain might shift somewhat toward extending the public domain.

As the costs of electronic storage and distribution decline, publishers will be able to charge less and earn more profit. If sale by subscription over public networks grows in importance as suggested here, then publishing—defined as those entrepreneurs who make significant information products available for sale—may become a more highly concentrated business.[25] Broader definitions of fair use and shorter periods of copyright protection might be desirable countervailing forces.

Advertising plays a role in financing some publications. Certainly, advertisers will want to subsidize access to certain information. As electronic information products become important, advertising will find a place. Just how advertising might be appended to electronic products is unclear. In Prodigy, for example, ads appear at the bottom of the screen as information one has requested appears at the top. Presumably the price to the reader of services that include ads will be less than the price of services that exclude ads. In short, advertising will likely play a role similar to that which it has played in print.

The Library

The emergence of an extensive set of electronic information products will dramatically affect the three main functions of libraries. First, libraries acquire new information to make it available to the library's clients on demand. Electronic products will accelerate the timeliness with which new information becomes available and will enable producers of information to distribute information directly to readers. Readers will value their library's ability to negotiate site licenses for large information packages and their ability to store information locally, and thereby to economize on long-distance communication. Of course, libraries will continue to provide service to those who do not have personal workstations with network connections.

The library's second function is to organize what it acquires so that users can find what they need. The cataloging of books has consumed a considerable part of most libraries' budgets, but the appearance of electronically shared catalog information has significantly reduced the cost of building a library's catalog. Electronic tools used for finding are more valuable than printed ones, and most libraries now make extensive use of purchased electronic indexes. As markets for electronic information products continue to evolve, we may expect libraries to depend more on purchased "finding" tools and services, and less on locally developed catalogs and guides.

The library's third function is to store the information acquired for future use. Although most of the use of information products occurs when they are new, some use continues, so libraries generally contemplate sustaining at least a core of their collections in perpetuity. Of course, publishers reprint works of continuing interest, so a library might meet its perpetual horizon by buying anew each generation. Alternatively, a library might seek to sustain its stock. Electronic storage will be of such low cost, that reformatting older materials to an electronic format may enable preservation of larger amounts of such materials.[26] At the same time, the rapid increase in the number of information products will cause libraries to become increasingly selective. That is to say, the proportion of all that is available that a library chooses to keep for long periods will become steadily smaller.

A local library may choose to subsidize some information sources for its primary clients. That is to say, the library may choose not to pass along all the use-based charges its users incur. The library may buy or license a number of core materials for campus use and provide them to readers without incremental charge. Some collections may have subscription fees that are not use sensitive; for example, files stored locally on the campus may have flat fees that the libraries absorb as overhead. Collections might come in larger units, such as, the "literature of psychology" rather than individual book or journal titles, because publishers can make large packages available as economically as they can a subset of modest size. Publishers will offer navigational tools built-in, and local adaptation will be uneconomic. Of course, in some fields, fully developed electronic packages may not be available, and conventional library operations will continue. Collections from other regions of the world are examples of such fields.

Libraries may also offer assistance in navigating external sources. Such assistance may include expertise in finding documents not in the mainstream of scholarly literature and in automated accounting and billing systems. For example, the document delivery services developing now may value local libraries as agents. As agents, libraries may promote the use of delivery services, train users, resolve problems, automate billing, and perhaps merit discount prices (Getz, 1991-92).

Libraries, then, may be active agents for readers, offering training in the use of the local and international networks. They will maintain local electronic collections and provide subsidized access to basic materials. The preservation of older information materials may become both less expensive and more selective. The character of libraries will, then, be quite different from the familiar institutions shaped by print technologies.

MARKET FAILURES

The opportunity to distribute information products electronically has many intriguing dimensions. It is difficult to anticipate exactly how the technologies will evolve and what product types will be successful. We depend on competitive market forces to direct developments. Those entrepreneurs who anticipate the technologies well, should be able to benefit markedly from successful innovation. Those who misread will fail. Competitive forces and the profit motive should provide cost effective production of information that readers value highly. In general, consumers rule competitive forces so markets produce results that are socially beneficial.

However, in some instances markets fail to provide the best possible results. Two sources of market failure are possible here: excessive market power and poorly defined and enforced property rights.

Market Power

When a single agent controls a significant part of the supply of a commodity with few close substitutes, we say the agent has significant market power. A market with only one supplier is a monopoly. The firm with market power will earn higher profits than if supply comes from many competing agents; the profit comes from restricting production in order to increase price. The firm with market power will earn revenues over and above the opportunity costs of the resources used in production. These excess revenues or rents would not exist in a competitive market. If firms with significant market power dominate the electronic distribution of information, we might not see the full benefit of the technology because firms with market power tend to charge higher prices and restrict use.[27]

Similarly, when there are few buyers, the buyers may exercise market power by restricting the quantity purchased to hold down price. A market with only one buyer is a monopsony. If only one agent accepted contributions to the literature of a discipline, say chemistry, that agency could exploit authors by reducing royalties, perhaps even requiring payments by authors.

Large economies of scale in production tend to create market power. Information storage seems to have substantial economies of scale. As a consequence, a few firms might dominate the supply of certain kinds of information products. The economies of scope in the introduction of new journals might become even more significant as journals become text databases and articles become additions to the database. Could a single agent control the medical database such that authors must submit to the single entity and readers must buy from the single source of supply? Authors would get less because they face a buyer with monopsony power. Readers would pay more because they buy from a firm with significant market power. In such a system, there would be less information than in a system where market power were inconsequential.

A high level of market power poses not only an economic burden but also an intellectual one. If a single agency controlled the supply of information products, it could manipulate the flow of information for various purposes. Censorship would be easy for political purposes, to discourage scientific adversaries, and to define artistic merit .

Significant participants in the market, public-policy makers, and philanthropic interests might wish to promote the development of institutions that are more likely to be competitive. A critical factor is the ease with which new publishers can enter a market. The development of standard methods for posting essays on public bulletin-boards, the creation of inexpensive methods of registering documents, and the encouragement of the development of open-vendor standards for tagging and labeling documents should increase the ease with which authors can retain control of their information products and lower the cost of new publishers entering any information market. It may be desirable to maintain a distinction between owners of navigation tools and ownership of other information products to prevent the hegemony of navigational tools. Domination of navigation tools should not lead to domination of information products in the way that competitors alleged that American Airlines' Sabre reservation system helped American dominate air travel in some markets.

The degree of market power a firm enjoys relates to the price elasticity of the demand curve for its products. The more it differentiates its products from those of its rivals, the less response its buyers will show to price changes, that is, the less elastic is its demand: the less price-elastic the demand, the higher the percentage mark-up that will maximize profit, and the higher the degree of market power. Some information products appear to be well-differentiated from others, especially when they have reputations for high quality. Libraries, especially, have responded only modestly to price increases and so exhibit relatively price-inelastic demands. As a consequence, the mark-ups and the prices have been high in some cases. For electronic materials, the price structure could change to a fee per use for each article. In such a case, the user will likely face an individual fee per use. Users may then have an opportunity to reflect on the value of seeing a particular information source when deciding to use and pay for it. As a consequence, the demand may be more sensitive to prices than libraries have been. Fees based on usage may then produce demands that are more price elastic, so the market power of individual sellers may be much less.

Of course, a pay-per-look price structure is the antithesis of a prepaid subscription price structure. Yet the two price structures may co-exist. The pay-per-look offering may be necessary for sales to individuals with limited or occasional interest in a set of publications. It may provide a ceiling for subscription fees. Subscription offerings may be valuable for sellers to guarantee markets, to reduce transactions cost accounting, and to encourage campuses and other intermediaries to help enforce licenses and copyrights. Subscription offerings may also enable the seller to take advantage of the economies of scope in bundling a large number of information products together. It is not clear that the market power of sellers of information products will be lower in an electronic arena than it is in the present print arena.

Property Rights

A second source of market failure results from inadequately defined property rights. When laws inadequately define property rights or when property rights are expensive to enforce, then prices do not carry full information about social values,and resources may be misallocated. When pasture land without fences is available without charge to everyone with livestock, overgrazing is likely because no individual has an incentive to husband the land's use. When ocean fishing is unregulated, trawlers may fish species to extinction because the fish bear no price. No individual fisherman has an incentive to leave breeding stock in the ocean. If authors and publishers cannot easily establish and enforce ownership rights to electronic information products, then the allocation of information resources will not be optimal.

For example, if posting an essay on an electronic bulletin board would allow anyone who reads it to use the ideas without recognizing the author and—where appropriate—offering compensation, authors will not post their ideas on bulletin boards. Bulletin boards may, then, be vehicles for conversation, but authors are unlikely to use them for ideas valuable enough to be marketed.

Publishers will invest in the creation of information products only if they expect to be able to generate a revenue stream. If a distribution channel does not ensure that ownership rights will be enforced—and that owners will be compensated—then publishers will not commit valuable products to that channel.

If the electronic mode is to succeed, it must include mechanisms that help establish and enforce ownership rights. The availability of inexpensive registration of documents should make it easy to prove ownership. The development of low-cost ways of collecting fees is relevant. Publishers may wish to offer license agreements that allow broader use, including campus site licenses, because in this way they can more easily enforce licenses and make collections. There may be advantages to selling licenses for larger packages of information products, rather than individual parts, because the transaction costs will be lower. The optimal unit may have more than a hundred times the content of a typical print journal now, and perhaps many orders of magnitude more.[28]

The problem of software piracy extends to all information products distributed over the network. Once a user has a copy, the cost of making copies is very low, so informal sharing is likely. Enforcement of ownership rights has more chance of success when one is dealing with institutions and formal resale of software. Perhaps this is an important role for libraries, namely as agents for institutional purchasers of information products with campus-use site licenses.

SUMMARY

Delineated below are the significant features of scholarly communication in a world where petabytes measure quantities of information.

1. Vastly greater amounts of information will be readily available to more people.
2. Rich compound documents will enable scholars to express their ideas in more useful ways.
3. Workstations will be everywhere, linked to high-speed networks, making them information appliances.
4. Optimal balance in patterns of storage will be between large depositories that readers may search via networks and local storage.

5. Scholars will share working papers via bulletin boards creating effective online conferences for sharing works in progress.

6. Scholarly societies and publishers will require standard methods of tagging documents, including SGML and other identifiers, so that they can embed new works more easily into the database of existing literature.

7. Better information products will have navigational aids built-in, including full-text indexes and standard tags. As a result, information products may be hundreds of times larger than "books" or "journals," becoming then "databases."

8. Authors will adopt systems for labeling their new work including abstracts, subject descriptions, and indications of the sophistication of the intended audience.

9. Authors will deposit copies with third parties to register their works and establish authenticity.

10. Authors and editors will invite online discussions of manuscripts and reviews, with new labels emerging from the discussion. Editors will moderate such discussions.

11. Authors, readers, and universities will be concerned to avoid market power in information markets by allowing relatively easy development of new publishers.

12. All concerned will wish to find low-cost ways of maintaining property rights.

Initiatives

We might view the above summary as an agenda, a set of desirable results that we wish to promote. A number of initiatives might advance the cause.

First among these will be the encouragement of electronic journals, especially those that set important precedents for the electronic format. In particular, electronic journals should include support for compound documents, means to assure author's property rights, and industry-standard tagging systems for navigation.

Second, more scholarly societies or others might create online conferences for sharing working papers similar to the process currently underway at Los Alamos. Such conferences would be readily available on the Internet so that interested parties could participate. Creators might establish rules for registering submissions to establish ownership and for tagging original works to navigation. Moderators will want to maintain sufficient oversight to encourage appropriate submissions and discourage inappropriate ones.

Third, there is room for development of some common tools—developments that might best occur in the context of efforts to launch new information products. Among the necessary infrastructure will be systems for tagging the components of compound documents, systems for registering and archiving documents to assure authenticity, systems for accounting and billing for services, and systems to enhance the process of review and critique. If participants in the information marketplace can develop these tools in ways that are broadly useful and not dependent on specific vendors, such developments can facilitate decentralized ownership and control of information production, enhancing the prospect that competitive markets will produce efficient, socially useful results.

ACKNOWLEDGMENT

I appreciate the helpful comments of Martin Runkle on an earlier draft of this essay.

NOTES

1. A workstation is a personal computer linked to networks and file servers. It is much more useful than a simple terminal linked to a mainframe computer, and has more uses than a stand-alone personal computer. The sophistication of workstations will continue to increase. File servers may be thought of as powerful computers designed to support workstations.

2. Malcolm Getz, John J. Siegfried, and Kathryn H. Anderson, "Diffusion of Innovations in Higher Education" work in progress based on the authors' survey of 239 institutions.

3. The Research Library Group/Association of Research Libraries' study of interlibrary loan costs suggests that the library requesting the loan of an item incurs an average of $18.62 per transaction and the library lending the book incurs a cost of about $10.93 primarily in staff time. With Z39.50 remote searching and associated borrowing arrangements, readers should be able to borrow books from other libraries at a cost of about $10.93, saving the $18.62 of costs associated with the local library participating in the transaction.

4. Storing an image of each page instead of a code for each character in the text requires about 20 times more storage. Applying compression algorithms may reduce storage requirements by about four times.

5. Perhaps a third or more of the cost of producing a book is in editing and manuscript development, costs that will be incurred regardless of how the resulting content is stored. At present, final preparation typically involves representation of the book in an electronic file, coded for typesetting. This file can be used to drive a printer. Electronic laser printers which attach soft binding can produce a printed book of intermediate quality for, say, $2, for a single copy. Higher quality printing devices can approach this cost per unit with long press runs.

The bulk of the cost of storing information in book form is the cost of the shelving. Ordinary open-stack library space with shelving has a typical cost of $150 per square foot and holds about 15 volumes per square foot at capacity. That puts the cost of space to hold the book at about $10 per volume. The cost of the printing plus the cost of the space to hold the book comes, then, to about $12, exclusive of authoring, editing, design, and promotional costs.

6. Getz (1993), provides a full discussion of storage technologies and measures the economies of scale in storage. Creo's Digital Paper tape-drive maintains a terabyte of data on-line for $260 per gigabyte, that is, about $0.26 per book in capital costs.

7. The capacity of data communication systems are typically rated at peak-burst rates, an ideal engineering capacity. In production use, some systems yield a third or less of the design capacity. For example, Ethernet puts the information into packets and attaches origin and

destination labels that move with each packet. Ethernet traffic often flows on shared cables, so there may be congestion. In addition, devices that connect one link to another may operate more slowly than the design capacity of the links themselves. The maximum flow of data through a system will be limited by its slowest element. Of course, total flow can be increased by operating links in parallel.

8.   PL 102-194 High Performance Computing Act of 1991 (An act to provide for a coordinated Federal program to ensure continued United States leadership in high-performance computing, approved 12/9/91). (Note: This citation was copied on-line from Legi-Slate, an electronic information-service, to which the Vanderbilt library system subscribes over the Internet.)

9.   The idea of a data network originated in the 1960s in the Department of Defense Advanced Research Projects Agency (DARPA) with the goal of high-performance links of the computer sites connecting to research labs across the country. The NSFNet began in the mid-1980s as a subsidized operation in order to link the NSF supercomputer sites for research. Many supporters of the 1991 legislation envision data network services coming to every home with widespread educational and commercial purposes. An issue is whether regulators will allow telephone companies to distribute video and other information services through their network in competition with cable television firms and other information providers.

10.   ATM moves packets of a standard length of 53, 8-bit bytes over a variety of communication lines, from ordinary telephone lines at low speeds, to very high speeds over fiber. Each packet may follow a somewhat different route to its destination depending on traffic flow and congestion at the instant of its transmission, so packets may arrive out of order, to be reordered at the destination before use. This asynchronous flow is suitable for electronic mail and text, but may have limited suitability for sending video for display as it arrives, unless the flow is at substantially higher speeds than required by a single user's application (Ramirez, 1993).

11. Wireless communications systems will fill some roles. Infrared systems will be useful within individual rooms, as in a classroom, perhaps. Radio systems will be useful in portable systems suitable for brief messages. The radio frequency spectrum is finite, however, and has many claimants. The bandwidth, that is, the needed communication capacity, required for sending large documents, graphics, images, sound, and video will justify physical connection (see, "Wireless Communications, Special Report," 1993).

12.   McGarty (1992), suggests that the economies of scale relevant to the market for communication service providers is modest. Indeed, because economies of scale in service provision are negligible, the market need not be regulated and will likely not be dominated by a monopoly, in contrast to the state of the telephone industry over most of the last century.

13.   Indeed, one can imagine customers placing orders electronically that trigger the production of a specific device, tailored to the customer's needs. Dell Computer manufactures personal computers after customers place orders (85 percent by telephone), with production within four business days of receipt of the order. McGraw-Hill offers the publication of economics texts on demand for as few as fifty copies. The professor who adopts the text may select essays for inclusion in the text from a large file of essays. Each teacher can tailor the text to an individual class (see, "Duel," 1993).

14.   The minimum optimal press run is the minimum number of copies of a book that a publisher can afford to print given the fixed costs of setting up the press and the price at which books sell. As the fixed costs of set-up have fallen, shorter press runs have become economic. With tagging by a Standard Generalized Mark-up Language, adoption of a common design fixed in electronic code, and use of an electronic printer and binder, the cost of printing a single copy of a title is the same per unit as the per-unit cost of printing hundreds of copies.

15.   Perhaps leading software packages for text processing like Microsoft Word and Word Perfect will include tools for SGML. Such tools might work as follows. An author would highlight the title, then scroll down a menu of SGML tools and choose "title." The software then inserts the appropriate tags as hidden text. After completing the tagging, one can save the document

in "SGML format" that would store the file without formatting but with the SGML tags. The software should also read files saved in the "SGML format" and allow the reader to format the document with a standard style sheet. In this way, documents could move from one environment to another without formatting, but be displayed locally with formatting. In disciplines with accepted subject classification systems such as the one established in economics by the Journal of Economic Literature, subject designation should have reasonable order and be tagged using SGML-like tags. More software now supports SGML (see Said and McManus, 1993).

16.   One can imagine software that would read the full text of a document with SGML tags, including keywords identifying subjects, and automatically create a MARC-tagged bibliographic record for use in a citation index.

17.   For an overview of Gopher and WAIS see Krol (1992).

18.   The Kerberos authentication protocol developed at MIT as a part of its Project Athena gives an example of a system for assuring the identity of individual users and their authority to use particular services. Passing of authentication keys among Kerberos servers across the network may be needed to establish identities on remote servers.

19.   The Educational Testing Service has announced that their Graduate Record Examination will be administered electronically within a few years.

20.   Because of the capital costs of quality workstations with good monitors, and of the associated high-speed network that turns a workstation into an information appliance, we may be concerned that the development of electronic communication may increase the distance between the well-endowed "haves," and the low-budget "have nots," within academia and beyond. The possibility of printing documents on demand for delivery offers an alternative. Institutions that have not been able to afford to accumulate major library collections may be able to search databases on-line using relatively inexpensive tools and have documents printed remotely and delivered within a day or two. The emergence of electronic information products may lower barriers to information by providing lower cost access than is feasible with print collections alone.

21.   The hep-th service has authors submit essays in the T$_E$X format-tagging language that is commonly used among mathematicians and physicists, so that the service can handle equations and graphics. The Internet address of the physics bulletin board at Los Alamos is: hep-thαxxx.lanl.gov (Taubes, 1993).

22.   One can imagine readers creating electronic filters for their mail and for the databases to which they subscribe. The filters would allow material of greatest interest to come to the top of a queue on the user's workstation. The user defines interest in a variety of ways that are relevant to the tags found in the electronic environment. In effect, then, items posted for public access might be broadcast to a select audience, and pass through to those who have set their filters to allow access. In an active stance, the criteria in the filter might be applied to databases to identify and retrieve items of interest. The richer the cues built into the database, the more powerful the filters can be.

23.   Noll and Steinmueller (1992) suggests that the cost of subscriptions to print journals is inversely proportional to their circulation as one might expect of products that have high fixed costs. In this view, the proliferation of low circulation journals focused on narrow subdisciplines is an important source of the high cost of journals. Electronic distribution should have much lower fixed costs, so the inverse association of cost with circulation should be much less. Even quite small communities of scholars should be able to share works electronically with little overhead, much as the physicists share working papers as discussed by Taubes (1993).

24.   With respect to copyright, the U.S. Constitution has its roots in the statute of Anne, adopted by the English Parliament in March, 1710 (see, R.R. Bowker, 1886).

25.   Perhaps publishers will be more likely to subscribe to the Copyright Clearance Center and similar service agencies. Such agencies license the use of copyrighted materials, collect fees for use, and police those who use copyrighted materials illicitly.

26. The life of specific electronic storage devices remains a subject of study. The primary difficulty may not be the preservation of the media (although that is a concern), but rather maintaining the devices to read them. Perpetual storage using electronic means probably involves rewriting the information to new media every decade or so.

27. The efficiency of market results might be considered dynamically. Are firms with market power more likely to invest in research and development, discovering ways of reducing costs or introducing new products? The history of industry does not give a clear answer. Consider two competitive industries. Agriculture is a highly competitive industry that is quite innovative, thanks in part to government supported land grant universities and agricultural extension services. Textiles is a competitive industry marked by low research and development efforts and little technical change. On the other hand, consider a firm in an industry with little competition. When Gillette enjoyed high levels of market power in selling safety razors, it suppressed introduction of long-lasting stainless steel blades for decades. Stainless steel razor blades were finally introduced by a small firm, Wilkenson Sword. More recently—and probably as a consequence—Gillette has invested heavily in research and development and introduced new products with considerable frequency. Successful firms with significant market power may use part of their revenues to invest in research and development and be on-going innovators. However, such action cannot be assumed.

28. Jenson (1993) reviews the mechanisms used by the music and other industries to collect royalties and suggests that the copyright law include a compulsory license fee as a default that encourages rightholders and users to negotiate more flexible and appropriate payment formulae tailored to specific circumstances.

REFERENCES

Cummings, Anthony M., Marcia L. Witte, William G. Bowen, Laura O. Lazarus, and Richard H. Ekman. *University Libraries and Scholarly Communication.* Washington, DC: The Association of Research Libraries, (1992), pp. 53-81.

"Duel." *The Economist,* (January 30, 1993), pp. 57-58.

Getz, Malcolm. "Information Storage." In *Encyclopedia of Library and Information Science,* 1993 (forthcoming).

Getz, Malcolm. "Document Delivery." *The Bottom Line,* Winter, 1991-92, 5(4, Winter, 1991-92): 40-44.

Jenson, Mary Brandt. "Making Copyright Work in Electronic Publishing Models." *Serials Review,* XVIII(1-2, 1993): 62-65.

Keller, John J. "Researchers at AT&T Unit Boost Capacity of Fiber-Optic Systems." *Wall Street Journal,* (March 1, 1993), p. B8.

Krol, Ed. *The Whole Internet.* Sebastopol, CA: O'Reilly & Associates, 1992, Chaps. 11 and 12, pp. 189-226.

McGarty, Terrence P. "Alternative Networking Architectures: Pricing, Policy, and Competition." In *Building Information Infrastructure* edited by Brian Kahin. New York: McGraw-Hill, Inc., (1992), pp. 218-270.

Noll, Roger and W. Edward Steinmueller. "An Economic Analysis of Scientific Journal Prices: Preliminary Results." *Serials Review,* XVIII(1-2, 1992), pp. 32-37.

Ramirez, Anthony. "Data Can Move 45,000 Times Faster, For a Price." *New York Times,* (March 10, 1993), p. C4.

Rawlins, Gregory J.E. "The New Publishing: Technology's Impact on the Publishing Industry Over the Next Decade." *The Public Access Computer Systems Review,* III(8, 1992): 5-63. (For Internet access to this article send to LISTSERV@UHUPVM1.UH.EDU the command to GET RAWLINS1 PRV3N8 F=MAIL and GET RAWLINS2 PRV3N8 F=MAIL.)

R.R. Bowker. *Copyright Its Law and Its Literature*. New York: The Publishers' Weekly, (1986), pp. 1-20.

Said, Carolyn and Neil McManus. "SGML Standard Will Star in Boston Seybold Show." *MacWeek*, (April 12, 1993), pp. 1, 124.

Taubes, Gary. "Publication by E-mail takes Physics by Storm." *Science*, (February 26, 1993), pp. 1246-1248.

Vetter, Ronald J. and David H.C. Du. "Distributed Computing with High-Speed Optical Networks." *Computer*, (February 1993), pp. 8-18.

"Wireless Communications, Special Report." *MacWeek*, (February 8, 1993), pp. 20-27.

A MODEL AUTOMATED DOCUMENT DELIVERY SYSTEM FOR RESEARCH LIBRARIES

John E. Ulmschneider

I'm going to talk about a project that the Triangle Research Libraries Network, TRLN, is undertaking to construct a model document delivery system for research libraries in an electronic environment. First I want to give an overview in the context of what we've been talking about which I hope will help you understand the motivation behind this project. Then I want to talk in specifics about how we've structured the project to answer essential questions, and describe the technical architectures and options libraries have for creating an integrated document delivery system.

You've certainly noticed in looking through the exhibits that are a great many experiments in document delivery going on. Most of these experiments right now are addressing what I would call fundamental technical issues, not service or marketing issues. They're addressing standards we should have for capturing electronic documents, standards we should use for communicating those documents, and standards we need for the interfaces that users will employ

Advances in Library Administration and Organization, Volume 12, pages 239-252.
Copyright © 1994 by JAI Press Inc.
All rights of reproduction in any form reserved.
ISBN: 1-55938-846-3

to retrieve those documents. In a sense, as well, they address the library agenda at a very fundamental level. They're forcing librarians to consider the proper role of libraries in the matrix of document delivery options. When users already have the option to go directly to third-party suppliers rather than publishers, and eventually will be able to go directly to authors for materials, what is the appropriate and proper place of libraries? Finally, many of these experiments are amusing at some level because everyone is searching for the user's soft spot. Every commercial provider wants to press the right button. If one of these companies hits that soft spot, it will have a product that's really going to take off.

All of this is being done in the atmosphere in a kind of intellectual free-for-all, as far as librarians are concerned. There is a fundamental reformulation of the publishing engine and enterprise, of the role of technology in publishing and delivery, and of what users demand of the services, but in libraries, there's a whole lot of, "let's sit back and watch." A lot of you are here today because you're sitting back and watching. Unfortunately there's little commitment in libraries to invest actively in addressing these issues right now. But Triangle Research Libraries Network recognizes this issue as fundamental to the work of libraries, and has made a commitment to invest rather than sit back and watch.

There are bottom-line motivations for doing electronic document delivery in libraries as well as intellectual ones. These motivations take several forms.

- First, of course, is the economic motivation. Malcolm Getz talked a good deal about the economic models that govern document delivery; the high cost of materials mandate research into improved document delivery and resource sharing.
- Second is our evolving understanding of access versus ownership. I think that new technologies will change the way we talk about access versus ownership because most of the access versus ownership discussion has been concentrated on the hows. How do we do this? What are the mechanisms—the technical mechanisms for access? We are on the way to solving some of those issues, technically. Getting solutions will help us concentrate on what the users want out of access vs. ownership, rather than how it will be implemented—that is, what access versus ownership means for our clients.
- Third, document delivery technology represents a source of strong commercial competition for libraries. Commercial competition are setting high standards in terms of speed and convenience, standards that libraries will have to meet or exceed. In turn, libraries have set high standards with their level of service and the comprehensiveness of their collections, standards that commercial services will strive to meet. Coupled with that is a service motivation as I said earlier—technology seeds its own kind of demand as users become more accustomed to employing it, user expectations rise, and service needs to meet those expectations.

- Fourth, there is a clear requirement in every setting, but especially in library-operated document delivery, for increased productivity. We are all having to work in this economy where we have to be more productive. The economic reality, a bottom-line reality, is that there is constant pressure to do things faster and better.
- Finally, there is a strong motivation for electronic document delivery coming from the materials themselves. Right now, linear electronic documents, plain unorganized ASCII text, are commonplace. Many of us subscribe to listservs, which are distribution mechanisms for ASCII text. Some of us have electronic text centers in our libraries or elsewhere on campus, which focus on ASCII text. We have electronic text on CD ROM, once again ASCII text. Libraries already must have mechanisms for dealing with ASCII full-text documents, because they're not a future problem they're a current problem. Now there is not substantial innovation in formulating or dealing with linear electronic documents, but we're also beginning now to see the appearance of compound documents, documents similar to what I showed you this morning, a WordPerfect document with an embedded movie and graphs of data. Importantly, such documents are becoming important all out of proportion of their presence in our collections. They're a vanishingly small portion of the collections that libraries have and yet they have a prominence that attracts technological innovation and even professionals to conferences. This prominence stems from the perception of their utility; their functionality, or at least the promise of their functionality, is very important to users. We will see a steady evolution and growth in compound documents, and we need a mechanism, not only just to generate and store them, but to access them and deliver them as well.

Many observers don't believe that libraries are responding well to these motivations right now. Fundamental infrastructure problems contribute to the muted response. Research libraries talk a good talk regarding networking, but the investment structure doesn't reflect the talk. If you attend EDUCOM or other computing oriented conferences, you will see that the tenor of discussion is moving away from, "how do we build an infrastructure" and more to "now what do we do with it." But here in early 1993, a lot of libraries have not even finished building a fundamental networking infrastructure. Unfortunately that leaves us in the position of still needing to do things that we probably should have already achieved.

In part, too, the slowness of response in libraries is because there is a complete reconceptualization that's in process. There's substantial activity in the literature about different models for interlibrary loan. I'm not very conversant with that literature but it's clear there is great deal of thinking going on, though not necessarily a lot of action. In the midst of this reconceptualization there exists considerable enthusiasm for commercial services, which are sometimes seen as holding out the answers to many problems. The presence of commercial solutions in many instances has kept librarians from dealing with the fundamental issues that must be addressed, but it's considered that answers have been found or will be found by commercial suppliers. But with all due respect to the vendors, I think we ought to be cautious in embracing those services because we don't yet have a framework into which they should be placed. Finally, the slow response of the library community is being guided by not just internal management needs but also client and institutional priorities and resources. Often libraries respond positively to commercial options because they appear to be a cost-effective, that is, cheaper solution. For document delivery, it's very easy just to call up a supplier and get what you want—it's absolute minimal infrastructure investment to get that. In serious professional settings now, it is argued that it is cheaper to let someone buy it from a CARL or Faxon rather than supply it from libraries. But in point of fact, the jury is still out on the economics of buying materials on demand, both for suppliers and for consumers. Arguments that support that approach can't yet be set within a framework that would make me believe them.

Research libraries have a special class of problems in crafting a response to underlying motivations for document delivery. At a special library, such as the library run by my colleagues at Burroughs Wellcome, it's possible to craft a wonderful and targeted service environment that optimizes for document delivery. But it is very difficult to scale that up to a large research library with many diverse calls on its resources. Inertia is expensive, and research libraries have inertia in spades—and not in a pejorative sense either. It's simply that changing the direction of a large organization takes a lot of energy. A large institution, a large group of people require sound management and sound political solutions in order to move something forward. The technical solutions can sometimes be much easier than the energy and investment necessary to challenge inertia. Consequently there isn't a concerted attempt to deal with issues. Instead, research libraries tend to change services piecemeal, with the consequent coordination problems, and perceptions of slow movement, which that approach brings.

As Malcolm said, all these issues are not problems—they're opportunities. So TRLN decided to conduct a project that might capitalize on some of these opportunities. We also felt that if TRLN were to set up a project that addressed such fundamental questions, it was also TRLN's responsibility to ensure that the answers would not just apply to TRLN's parochial needs, but would be informative for the profession at large. In the retooling of libraries and publishing for the resource sharing architecture of the future, no library or group of libraries can afford to ignore the larger environment.

The project is conducted by the Triangle Research Libraries Network, which is a consortium of the three university library systems at Duke University, UNC at Chapel Hill, and N.C. State University. We timed our project to take maximum advantage of the evolving management and technical models that we might use in implementing an automated document delivery service. So, we wrote our grant proposal last year and submitted it. The grant was awarded this fall and we'll conclude the project in two years. As it turns out, the timing has been almost exactly paced by the maturation of the technology and standards we'll need to deploy.

We think the TRLN has some special strengths for carrying out the development of a model document delivery system that will inform our profession as well as help us locally. We have an exceptional technical foundation here in the Triangle. TRLN can draw on a very sophisticated research and development community in disciplines crucial to advanced document delivery systems, such as network engineering, computation, copyright law and other legal issues, and library research. TRLN itself boasts of a long record of achievements in development and services; for example, the BIS catalog developed by TRLN was unique in providing joint retrieval sets from three libraries in response to a single search. It was the first and the only truly network catalog of its kind. The network linking together many of the universities in the state is one of the highest and bandwidth, most advanced and most capable networks of its kind in the world. And the history of this collective resource reaches way back; TRLN began cooperative collection development in the 1930s, and Usenet was invented here in the early 1980s. Several current initiatives will contribute importantly to the development of document delivery systems. For instance, TRLN's Council on Library Resources-funded project is examining how libraries should build electronic collections through a client- and discipline-centered approach, and in the process is addressing the issue of intellectual property rights in innovative ways. From this study has emerged the draft university policy statement on copyright. It's an interesting and stimulating document that has generated much healthy discussion and debate in national as well as regional and local forums. TRLN also provides a powerful mechanism for examining and resolving policy issues that arise in developing document delivery systems, bringing to bear the resources of three research libraries to address them in a collaborative fashion. TRLN's ability to focus the efforts of its very different members on specific issues often leads to findings that are generalizable, or at least useful to other research libraries.

TRLN's grant proposal targeted some very specific objectives. First of all, the grant will develop a system that assumes the use of network information resources as much as possible; that means the system is set up such that all TRLN users will locate materials through the TRLN catalogs or other TRLN resources, without regard to the institution they're affiliated with. In addition, users will be able to order materials at the point that they discover them, using electronic ordering, without having to visit their library. Ordering at the point of discovery is a major and necessary convenience, something that users expect to have, and it must be implemented without regard to the physical location of the user.

Second, we want to implement a model system. "Model" means something that just not meet just local contingencies but derives generalized results useful in other settings as well. In order to do that, we're going to study not just the technical models but also procedures and policies, copyright management and administrative mechanisms in a way that will inform other libraries.

Finally, we want to do a real system. "Real" means something that really works, something that TRLN can fully implement and scale up for widespread and full deployment if we decide to do so. We don't want to do a "toy system" or produce only a research platform. We want at the end to have a practical, useable system.

To begin I'd like to talk about how TRLN is structuring this project and then I'll discuss some of the issues involved in developing an architecture for an automated document delivery system. We've designed the project around two teams. One team is the technical group that will design and implement the software for the system. That team is headed by a project manager, and includes technical staff from the libraries and possibly computing organizations at three participating libraries. The team is supported by two programming staff and computing resources funded by the project.

The second team will study policies, procedures, and resources issues. This team is headed by the Associate University Librarian for Public Services at UNC Chapel Hill and includes the Associate University Librarians for Public Services at each of the three libraries, along with other support staff as necessary. Finally there is a principal investigator who acts as the overall project director; that's me.

In carrying out this project, we think it's important to take advantage of the considerable work and development in this field that's already been done— as you saw on the other side of this wall, there's a substantial body of research findings from which we can draw, including actual code and systems that are in the public domain. We don't intend to reinvent the wheel and we will use already developed systems as much as possible. The project will be especially alert to standards development. There exists a body of important standards applicable to this project which we need to take advantage of as well as a group of evolving standards that bear watching closely.

In addition to this principal, underlying, guiding philosophy to use existing resources as much as possible, we also intend to use the most advanced software development environment that we can afford. We don't have an acre of programmers and we certainly don't have an acre of programming expertise. We need to have the best tools that we can use that will help us to move through the development cycle as quickly as possible. So we intend to use object-oriented programming tools and powerful hardware platforms that will help us to develop and test system components as quickly as possible. We will want to use a fast prototyping or rapid development approach. We don't have time to spend a year deciding what we want and to do a careful structured design of what we want, along with functional specifications for what we want, voluminous documentation, and the like. So we intend to develop prototypes and then have a review mechanism using the policies and procedures team to look at prototypes and help develop them functionally. Rapid applications development is a legitimate software engineering approach in this kind of environment, I think. And it's the only way that we'll be able to do this on any reasonable schedule.

Part of quick development and deployment of a system is articulating a clear architecture for the system that lends itself to a rapid development methodology. Now I want to underscore, particularly for the people here who are involved in the project, that we haven't made decisions about the final design of the system. But it's clear that the functionality required in a document delivery system falls naturally into a client server model. "Client/server" is a buzz word in the computing business now, from the technical implementation environment, but more broadly it's a useful concept to organize how we think about a problem. When we talk about document ordering and document delivery, the part involved with ordering a document is intuitively a client function. You ought to be able to interact with a piece of software which will find out from you information such as how do you want to pay for a document, where should it be sent, what format do you want it in, where do you want it to come from. The program ought to be able to interrogate you about those ordering parameters, and then pass that information on to a supplier of the documents. The supplier end of the system we can conceive of as a server. The server finds the document you want, where it is, arranges to have it sent to you, makes the billing decisions, and all the rest. In other words, the server serves up an order that a client has made. Such a natural, intuitive conceptualization of a problem into client/server vocabulary translates easily into a technical architecture that is client/server based.

Part of this architecture is my conviction that the supply of a document is something that ought to be vendor independent. Commercial suppliers will form a legitimate source for documents that we will want to supply to users. In our current service matrix commercial sources are a legitimate part of the process and they will continue to be so. But libraries are also a very important source for documents. Document ordering software ought to determine or decide the source for a document from among a constellation of sources, commercial and non-commercial, based on factors like availability, user profile, user requirements, and the like, and not simply use commercial sources by default. One of the developments in the marketplace that should be a little disturbing to librarians is that contemporary document ordering systems are created by contractual alliances with specific vendors. Libraries can buy online catalog or other document finding software that allows users to order documents from the suppliers of the document finding software, such as CARL or OCLC, but not order documents from other suppliers. If a library owns the desired material, it is very difficult or impossible for the user to order the material from the libraries' collection through the document finding/ordering software. On the one hand it is encouraging to see these products in that it gives shows users the potential for ordering materials at the point of discovery. But on the other hand it is discouraging in that these systems don't provide our users the flexibility that they deserve. To address this issue, we want the architecture for our application to permit vendor independent ordering. We want the server to find the document from the right source, the best source, and not just use a default commercial supplier.

A fundamental part of the system architecture is that its design will have to reduce labor costs. With a system that encourages and generates document orders, it will be prohibitively expensive to have our staff running around verifying requests, making sure the user typed in correct information, and the like. None of the TRLN institutions have staff to implement such a large scale custom-crafted document delivery system. Such a system would, in effect, be like scaling up the customer-attentive services that a special library provides to research library volume, and a research library can't do that. By implementing a client/server environment, we hope to build enough intelligence into a serve so that a server can actually locate documents, doing much of the intellectual and labor-intensive work that a human must perform now. There's conceptually no reason that a server can't, for example, go out on a network and use Z39.50 protocol to find a document that isn't located in the library itself.

This is a schematic of the proposed system functions. (See Figure 1: Integrated Electronic Document Delivery Architecture Logical Schematic.) On the left-hand side at the top is what we think of in the design as the client system. A user can use an on-line catalog or library database, or any other kind of remote service, as a springboard from which to generate an order. The user is free to search throughout the Internet to find things, and then order it at the point of finding it. The user generates an order with a client program, which elicits from the user or collects from the system, or both, detailed information about what the user wants. The document ordering program then passes off the order to a document server, and the document server carries out a series of tasks related to the order: determining whether the person issuing the order is an authentic user of the system and is allowed to use it, what kind of accounting process that person should be subjected to, various sources for the document and options for its delivery, whether the lending charging and copyright policies that apply to this particular item, and the like. Conceptually, the document delivery server should resolve all of these issues and do so in a way that is compliant with protocols used by networks and applications on

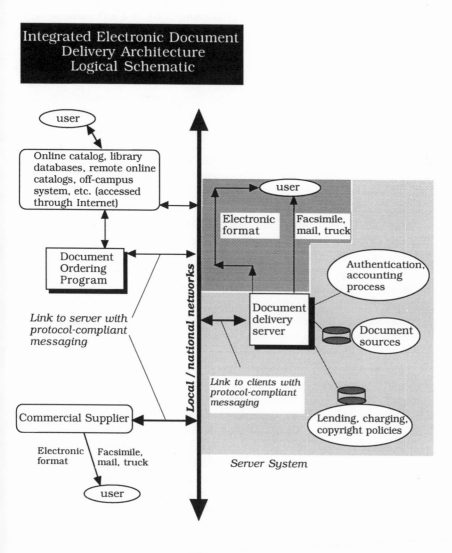

Figure 1.   Integrated Electronic Document Delivery
Architecture Logical Schematic

the network. That means that the communication between the document ordering program and the server, and the server and the rest of the world, is in the form of protocol-compliant messaging.

Once the document server assesses the order and determines the sources for documents, it will pick a source for a document, which can be a commercial supplier library or other source. At that point the order to that supplier will be sent over a network in a protocol complaint message, if possible. The final delivery to the user can occur in two way. For a document that is not available in electronic form, it will be delivered through facsimile, regular mail, or truck. But the system will fully integrate and use, whenever possible, electronic formats. The system will make sure that documents which exist in electronic form can be delivered to the user if it's appropriate for the user. Right now libraries don't have a good mechanism for delivering materials from their fledgling electronic repositories of text and graphics to a user unless the user can bring to the library three or four boxes of floppy disks or something like that. It's important that as we build repositories of electronic text, we also build a facility to deliver to materials from them to users more easily.

Along with the technical architecture, this project will have to closely examine the management side of document delivery. The hard part of a project like this isn't the technology; it's the policies and procedures and the resources to make it happen. The project's policies/procedures group will be articulating issues in this area that are related to document delivery. That means, for example, we will have to talk about issues such as who has access to the ordering system and the conditions under which they have access. For instance, there has already been discussion about whether an undergraduate should have access. We will have to have agreements between us about the source of documents, and agreements about where we go outside of these sources for documents not available there. We will need operational guidelines for running the service so that our clientele within TRLN don't encounter vastly different ways of doing things if, for instance, they're working out of Duke but they find themselves at N.C. State and need to order a document.

Perhaps most of all, we have to resolve the question for this kind of service. We can talk a good talk about technical development, but the real costs are going to be in the personnel and other resources that we need to scale up into a production environment. This policies/procedures group has to arrive at some sense of the possible about this before we actually decide to bring the service on-line in a full scale environment. It involves the bugaboo question of the times: do we charge for the service or not, and if so, how much? The policies/procedures group has to make that decision. It seems that most librarians intuitively believe that we will charge for these new services, because new services in general are not funded or subsidized by our parent agencies. But I don't think that in the course of developing electronic document delivery systems the library community or individual libraries ought to make basic assumptions that it will be a fee service. It's possible to reallocate to cover a new service or it's possible to charge. It's possible even to go out and beg for more money, particularly if you can show how useful or important a service is. TRLN has not yet taken the decision about charging.

There are other issues that fall into the bailiwick of the policies/procedures committee in addition to these basic issues. For instance, there are important and difficult intellectual property issues. Does a document delivery system fall into the arena of fair use, or does it really fall under the model that commercial systems use? When Malcolm Getz was speaking to use earlier today, a colleague leaned over to me and reminded me that the copyright law was designed not just to protect authors, but also to promote the dissemination of information. Right now libraries use the most conservative model possible in addressing copyright, principally out of fear of being involved in a lawsuit. Librarians need to rethink that approach. We need to consider what is an appropriate model and we need to consider that in terms of the economic consequence of the model we're using now. There is a cost associated with the copyright principles that we choose to follow, particularly over the next few years as we develop and mature electronic document delivery systems, and we need to both articulate what the costs are for the different options and to see just what options are most appropriate for us. I am not personally convinced that the copyright models which commercial suppliers use necessarily apply to libraries.

In addition to intellectual property, TRLN and libraries in general have to look at the role of inter-library loan. We have to consider the role of human inter-library loan operations in a highly automated environment where much of the verification and finding of requests is done by a machine. We have to consider the relationship of the growing automated systems with the so-called "traditional" ILL structure. I'm encouraged that people are leaving behind the term "inter-library loan," that librarians are broadening its concept and strengthening the inter-institutional borrowing structure to accommodate electronic documents.

Finally, our project, through the policies/procedures group, will attempt to develop models that are instructive for the profession. TRLN can't develop solutions for libraries, but TRLN both can develop its own solution in a way that is instructive to the profession, and develop policy changes with an eye to their broader instructional role, such as a model policy for charging, a model policy for copyright, model guidelines for access to service, and the like. In addition, we want to build an instructive technical model that is vendor neutral. For instance, our first implementation of a client will be a something that works with our DRA catalog system and supply documents discovered through the DRA software, because that's our local mandate; but the design of that client will be such that it will be able to generate a protocol-complaint to a server from another, entirely different environment. TRLN will distribute its findings through national forums and publications as part of its goal to provide instructive models to the profession.

My last slide is just to let you know where we are with the project right now. We are now in the process of hiring our project manager and we're beginning to examine the technical options and to look at parallel research findings. We're doing lots of housekeeping details. But we've been delayed somewhat in starting the project because we've been distracted by our local priority of implementing the DRA system.

Questions

The question is why did we take the risk of doing this kind of system development? Why did our institution decide to undertake this project, and who got us off the starting line? I think that the institutions in TRLN feel strongly about the motivations that I talked about at the beginning. All of us are seeing strong growth in electronic documents and service demands, and we simply decided within TRLN that it was a high priority for us to address this, and that our clients seem to want us to address this. We felt that the popularity of document ordering services told us that we ought to address this. And finally I think that the lack of development within the field told us that we ought to look at this. We are not going to be the only group developing such capabilities; we might be the first to conceptualize to start off, but there are other people looking at these issues and I'm very hopeful that in the next two years we'll see an aggressive evolution of the way libraries deal with document delivery and how we'll incorporate this into our service matrix. So overall I don't think this is risky. It might even be considered behind the times, especially from the perspective of the user.

The question is, how do we measure user satisfaction? To me that means how we match our service offering to the client needs. One of the reasons we decided to do this project is that we've been trying to determine and meet user needs all along in several different environments. TRLN's Council on Library Resources grant, for example, was supposed to examine how we do cooperative collection development through a client-based approach. The CLR project's model copyright policy was designed to encourage or to examine how authors can retain copyright and still distribute documents. So we've been looking at the basic issue of user needs and user satisfaction all along. But nevertheless right now we don't have an articulated way to solicit the user information on the design of the system or how we'll get feedback on it. That's one of the things that the policies and the technical design group will work together on.

This next question... is that suppliers and publishers have drawn a line in the sand; and what I am saying here is that libraries need to look closely at whether they should step over the line. I'm not a copyright expert. There surely are people who could talk to this issue more intelligently than me. So I encourage someone to do that and in the meantime, I'll say just my brief little answer. First of all, I don't think that publishers have drawn a line in the sand

and I think they're are confused as anyone. I think there is still a lot of work that's being done, but there is an evolution in position and thought on the issue. There is an awareness of what's at stake, and also a sense that we have to somehow come out with an approach that will satisfy both sides. Right now I still believe that libraries have taken the most conservative stand and it may not be the right one to take. So I don't think that there's a line in the sand that has been drawn, but people are considering where to draw such a line right now, and libraries need to be involved in that consideration.

Statement from audience:

The most conservative view of copyright is the stand taken by the American Association of Publishers which says there is no such thing as fair use.

Speaker:
Well, they are only one voice. They're a major voice but they're only one voice. There are other publishers with whom we've had open conversations about how to implement a system where the client retains copyright, and those publishers anxious to encourage that, particularly society-based publishers who ·are willing to accommodate that kind of model. There's a good deal of writing and research and talk about this and we could go on forever and ever about it but I advise you to monitor those discussions. I think it's a real interesting prospect.

The question is how do we reconcile the high-fluting management ideas that we've been talking about the reality of contemporary inter-library loan. Yes, I agree with you that inter-library loan in many of our institutions is principally a clerical operation and apparently leagues removed from what we've discussed. It is a high production, high pressure operation that is labor intensive. But I believe that our profession is in the process of rethinking what inter-library loan means. It's our responsibility to give some leadership to that change because it is unquestionably true that inter-library loan will not be what we think of as inter-library loan in five years. Without doubt the whole complexion of interlibrary loan will change. So our role as librarians is to think about the intellectual side of it, and our role as managers to manage the people side, the migration side of this. But the changes will happen. We're simply not going to be able to just sit around and not let it happen.

The question is, what is the life expectancy of this system given technical developments in communications technologies and the like, such as frame relay? Probably six months. A problem and a blessing in working with technology is that it changes real fast. My boss can ask for budget projections for equipment and I'll give it to her, but when it comes time to do the purchase ·it has gotten cheaper so we buy more. That's one of the blessings. One of the drawbacks is that we will develop things that quickly become out of date. Good system developers plan for this and I would expect that the technical foundation for this project is something that is robust and supple enough to accommodate changes. The software technology for this project won't be produced by an acre of programmers but by two very, very skilled programmers, for instance, with an eye to the future. And we won't draw on acres of communications equipment, but we can draw on two or three very skilled communications people so that we build something that's flexible and something that's open. I have no better answer than that. I think all of us start out with something like that as our hope.

SHOWCASE PRESENTERS

User Initiated Document Delivery

Like all libraries with a significant investment in scientific journals, the TCU Library has been battling forces in scholarly publishing that have sent journal prices skyrocketing. Resorting to a wide range of palliatives in an effort to slow the rate of growth in that volatile sector of the library budget, TCU has nevertheless doubled its expenditures for library materials in five years. Yet, the larger budget is buying a smaller portion of available material than before. Projecting trend data forward, we feel that, while purchasing a steadily declining share of the published literature, TCU's $450,000 journal budget of 1987 could approach $3,000,000 in 2003. This condition of spending more and getting less is common among academic libraries.

In an effort to reverse the situation, library staff have engaged faculty, members of the governing board, and administrators in discussions about consciously changing the culture of scholarship at TCU. Through dialogue we have resolved to fashion a solution from the resource side of the equation by directing a larger portion of our funds toward the information technologies. Building upon the library's considerable electronic superstructure, board and administrators have agreed to allocate $100,000 in FY 1993-94 to fund electronic document delivery for faculty, postdoctorates, and graduate students. For their part, the faculty and library staff will attempt to cool the rate of budget growth by selecting lightly used European subscriptions for replacement with transaction access. While providing additional funds for the renewal of the bulk of the approximately $1,000,000 journal budget, some $60,000 of European titles have been initially targeted for cancellation.

Our belief is that TCU's strong core collection and the relatively small size of its faculty and graduate program make it possible to substitute "just in time" access for "just in case" subscriptions. Pilot projects have established the feasiblilty of unmediated activity. Researchers have individual accounts set up with the vendor of electronic information whose profile most closely matches

253

their research interests. Staff provide initial training and monitor activity. Over-the-horizon projections suggest that while improving access, the mixture of subscriptions and document delivery could mean a savings of as much as $500,000 per annum over the current means of doing business by 2003.

Fred M. Heath
Library Director
Texas Christian University
Box 32904
Fort Worth, TX 76129
Heath@Lib.IS.TCU.EDU.
(817) 921-7106

Electronic Document Delivery via Campus Networks

Researchers at North Carolina State University were able to request and receive library research materials via campus telecommunications networks as part of a demonstration service carried out by NCSU Libraries during the early part of 1992. Using the Electronic Document Delivery Service (EDDS), researchers submitted their document requests via the campus electronic mail system to the Libraries' interlibrary loan department. Requests were filled through the Digitized Document Transmission Project sites by obtaining scanned electronic versions of the article or an original electronic article. Filled requests were received and stored by a computer, which automatically notified the researcher that the digitized article was available and provided retrieval instructions for electronic pickup by the researcher. EDDS represented the second stage of the national research initiative led by NCSU and the National Agricultural Library and entitled the NCSU Digitized Document Transmission Project. This showcase session will describe the service and report on the technical and management issues related to implementing and managing an electronic document delivery service.

Carolyn Argentati
Branch Librarian
Natural Resources Library
NCSU
(919) 515-2306

*The NCSU Digitized Document Transmission Project:
An Experiment in Electronic Document Delivery*

The North Carolina State University Libraries and 14 land-grant institutions engaged in the testing and evaluating of a full-scale, computer-based document delivery system using the Internet combined with commercially available hardware and software. The demonstration project builds on a pilot study conducted jointly by the NCSU Libraries, the NCSU Computing Center, and the National Agricultural Library to study the electronic delivery of scanned and digitized research literature. Digitized scientific research materials were delivered to researchers via a central fileserver either as high-resolution printed output or on diskette. This showcase session will demonstrate the DDTP system software and describe the design and findings of the study.

Tracy M. Casorso
Project Manager
NCSU DDTP
NCSU Libraries
Tracy—Casorso@NCSU.edu
(919) 515-3339

Networked Information Discovery and Retrieval Tools: The Next Generation

This poster session will be a live demonstration of widely used public domain software tools for discovering and retrieving information published in networked computer environments. Information about the evolution of the tools, the influence of the library community on their development, and the need for continuing collaboration between the technical, library, and user communities will be available through handouts and discussion with the presenters.

Information retrieval over distributed wide-area networks like the Internet is becoming increasingly common. For example, over 300 online public access catalogs (OPACS) of academic, public, and special libraries can now be accessed and searched by connecting to the OPACs and then using the search software installed at each site. Numerous public access and commercial database services are also accessible, but again the user relies on the software interface at each site.

The emergence in the last couple of years of networked information discovery and retrieval (NIDR) tools such as WAIS, the Internet Gopher, and WorldWide Web have added a new dimension to information access and availability. Using public domain client and server software, individuals have become information providers or "publishers" for a large and diverse information consumer community. With these tools an individual can browse through vast "infospaces" of diverse resources located on networked computers. Through a single interface requiring only a few keystrokes, users can search and retrieve without learning specialized command syntaxes or formulating complex queries. Though NIDR tools are still in their infancy and the information collections available for access are sometimes of questionable quality, we are witnessing a radical change in the way information is provided and accessed. As the tools and information collections are evaluated by the rapidly growing Internet community, they will undergo an evolutionary process leading to improved utility and adherence to standards.

The Clearinghouse for Networked Information Discovery and Retrieval (CNIDR) has been funded by the National Science Foundation to facilitate this evolution by encouraging collaborative development and interoperability of NIDR applications. CNIDR considers the experience of the professional library community critical to guaranteeing the successful deployment and use of the "infospace" created by network publication and access.

George H. Brett II	Jane D. Smith	Robin Braun
Director	Assistant Director	Community Outreach
(919) 248-1886 (Brett)	(919) 248-9213 (Smith)	Coordinator
George.Brettþcnidr.org	Jane.Smithαcnidr.org	Robin.Braunþcnidr.org

Clearinghouse for Networked Information Discovery and Retrieval
Center for Communications at MCNC
PO Box 12889, 3021 Cornwallis Road
Research Triangle Park, NC 27709-2889
Phone: (919) 248-1499
FAX: 919-248-1405

"Exploring the Internet": A Cooperative Effort

Burgeoning campus interest in the Internet presented a challenge to the staffs of the NCSU Computing Center and NCSU Libraries. In response to this interest, a course has been developed and taught jointly by the Computing Center and the Libraries.

This two-day workshop, called "Exploring the Internet," made its debut in February of 1992. Through discussions, demonstrations, hand-outs, and hands-on exercises in the Information Technologies Teaching Center (ITTC), workshop participants become familiar with the history of networks, Internet resource access tools such as Telnet and File Transfer Protocol (FTP), Listservs, Newsgroups, Campus-Wide Information Systems (CWIS), Online Public Access Catalogs (OPACS), and electronic mail. Also covered are the various guides to the Internet and how to retrieve them.

Staying abreast of changes in this dynamic resource is a challenge in itself. Course instructors encourage participants to consider "Exploring the Internet" beyond what is covered in the ITTC sessions.

Liese Tajiri	and	Sarah Noell
Reference Department		Academic Computing
NCSU Libraries		NCSU
Liese'tajiri@NCSU.edu		noell@unity.ncsu.edu

The North Carolina State University Computing Center

The Computing Center provides academic computing support to the students, faculty, and staff of North Carolina State University. This support includes connections to the networks that link academic and commercial institutions throughout many industrialized countries. The center provides accounts on several computer systems—including a network of Unix computers, an IBM mainframe, minicomputers, and Local Area Networks (LANs) in the Computing Center—and maintains an extensive communications network connecting them with other sites on campus. The center also provides data entry operations, hardware maintenance, short courses, publications, and extensive consulting services for users.

The center operates a help desk that is available Monday through Friday from 8:00 a.m. to 5:00 p.m. for the NCSU community. Clients can call, send electronic mail, or stop by the Information Center with questions or problems that they are unable to solve themselves.

As part of its education program, the center offers a variety of short courses to the campus free of charge. Working with the NCSU Libraries, the center has codeveloped a course titled "Exploring the Internet," which is designed to introduce the campus community to the rich and vast array of information available over the Internet. This course is now taught five times a year by the staffs of the Computing Center and the Libraries.

The center also maintains *Happenings!*, NCSU's campus-wide information system, and InfoPoint, a gopher server. Both of these are accessible via an anonymous log-in and are accessible 24 hours a day.

Sarah Noell
Academic Computing
NCSU
noell@unity.ncsu.edu

Matching Technology to the Reader:
Implementing the Electronic Journal of Statistics Education

The *Journal of Statistics Education* (*JSE*) is a new electronic journal on postsecondary statistics education. The *JSE* will publish high-quality articles on a variety of topics related to the teaching of statistics, as well as reviews of software, books, and teaching materials. The short-term technical goals of the *JES* are to: (1) reach as wide a readership as possible, (2) provide both textual and graphical information, (3) provide an easy-to-use retrieval system, (4) educate readers concerning network resources, and (5) provide tools to allow readers to exploit those resources.

The *JES* information system will be flexible enough to accommodate different technological levels. For example, readers with minimal technology

may retrieve an article presented in plain text only with
no graphical inclusions; simultaneously, readers with a higher technological
capability may request the article presented with graphics and typeset text. We
are currently working to achieve this goal.

A parallel electronic discussion forum, the ability to access articles and other
related materials as they become available, and the capability to search the
entire archived journal are unique features of the electronic medium. As *JES*
evolves, we will discover new capabilities and possibilities of electronic
publishing that we cannot imagine today.

J. Tim Arnold
Director, Instructional Computing
NCSU, Dept. of Statistics
Campus Box 8203
Raleigh NC 27695
919-515-2584

The Mountain College Library Network: The Small College Alternative

The Mountain College Library Network (MCLN) was established in 1989 to
provide expedited document delivery of journal articles to students and
faculties of member institutions. It now includes rapid article delivery (24
hours) as well as coordinated collection development. The MCLN consists
primarily of small college libraries in western North Carolina.

Articles are requested by and delivered to member libraries via fax.
Coordinated collection development, begun in 1991, has broadened the range
of journals available to system members with no increase in cost. Members
are under no obligation to add or cancel subscriptions but are obligated to
maintain their holdings in their chosen subject fields.

From 1989 to 1993 the Mountain College Library Network has grown from
four to 10 members. The number of annual transactions has climbed into the
thousands. The members of the MCLN believe that this is a model for
document delivery and cooperative resource development that could be used
successfully in a large number of small- to medium-sized library environments.

Kelly R. McBride
Assistant Director for Public Services
John Cook Wyllie Library
Clinch Valley College
Wise, VA
(703) 328-0159
likrm3e.poe.acc@virginia.edu

Digitizing Local History Collections

Funded by grants from the Ford Foundation, IBM, and Virginia Commonwealth University, we have been working with Virginia Union University, the Black History Museum and Cultural Center of Virginia, and the Black History Archives Project Advisory Board to develop an electronic MultiCultural Archives. Planning for an imaging and optical character recognition center began in 1990 and installation was completed in April of 1992. Documents are loaned to us so that they can be scanned, processed using ocr, and housed in an optical WORM drive. The MultiCultural Archives database is accessible through a research station located in a public area and in the future will be open to researchers through Internet. An overview of the technology and politics of the project is provided.

By scanning documents and then processing them using ocr, we create new opportunities for access:

- archives has a better opportunity for securing access to the documents because the holder of information is more willing to lend it for a short time than to make a formal deposit or donation
- digitized files can be shared via telecommunications networks, thus providing researchers with greater access because the documents are not site specific and subject to availability depending upon the business hours of the facility
- scanned documents can be processed by optical character recognition software to develop lists of keywords for retrieval, thus giving the researcher greater depth of access to the information
- with keyword retrieval, the owner of the physical documents has greater access to the contents of the files loaned to the archives for scanning

John H. Whaley, Jr.
Head, Special Collections and Archives
Virginia Commonwealth University
901 Park Ave.
Richmond, VA 23284-2033
(804) 367-1108
J.=H.=Whaley%JBC%ULS@lib.uls.vcu.edu
Fax: 804-367-0151

Clemson University Libraries' EDDIE System

As part of an ongoing effort to create a "Library Without Walls" and allow users access to information from remote sites, Clemson University Libraries developed the EDDIE (Electronic Document Delivery Information Exchange) system in 1990. Not only can a faculty or staff member check for information in the online periodical databases in DORIS (Document Online Retrieval System) and check the online catalog (LUIS) to see if the needed item is in the CU collections, but through EDDIE a researcher can request that the book or periodical article be delivered to his or her office. If the faculty or staff member desires a book or an article not in the CU collections, another EDDIE screen can be used to request an interlibrary loan. This, too, is delivered when the ILL transaction is complete. These services—LUIS, DORIS and EDDIE— are also available to faculty, staff, and students located at remote research and/ or teaching sites in the state.

Requests filled from the CU collections are delivered within 24 hours for books and 48 hours for photocopies of journal articles. Delivery of books is provided at no charge, while photocopies of articles are billed at 10 cents a page. Staffing for this function consists of one full-time person and several hours of student labor per week. One run a day for delivery and pickup is done using a van leased from the motor pool. University sites both on and off the campus are served, allowing those at the computer center (which is 15 miles away) or those at the research sites of Apparel Research and Environmental Toxicology to have the same access to the collections as their colleagues with much closer proximity to the library.

The service has been popular since its inception and the use has been growing. Since January of 1991, the service has filled 6,682 requests. In 1992 the number of requests through November was 33 percent ahead of the requests for the entire year of 1991.

EDDIE is an integral part of CU's goals of continuous improvement and responding to the needs of our customers. Electronic access coupled with the physical delivery of materials facilitates access to information in a timely fashion to our busy faculty and staff.

Deana L. Astle
Assistant Dean of Libraries
R. M. Cooper Library
Clemson University
(803) 656-4782
DLAST@CLEMSON

Trinity's Knowledge Network

The campus-wide computer network links dorms and faculty offices to information and library services available on both PC and Macintosh platforms. In addition to services specific to Trinity, there is access to other libraries, databases, and information servers worldwide via the Internet.

Networked computers adhere to a standard configuration that makes access to these services easy and consistent. Mac users find icons on their desktops or access them through the Chooser. PC users can type MENU at a DOS prompt for a list of available options and commands. Terminal emulation is used only when required by a host system.

Elements of the Knowledge Network are:

- TRINFO: A Campus-Wide Information System. Calendars, phone and e-mail directories, info about colleges organizations, offices, and services.
- BANTAM: A shared area containing various applications programs ("freeware") for both Macintosh and PCs, as well as documentation on computer applications, services, and the Internet.
- NETWORK NEWS: Access to all newsgroups plus electronic editions of the *Los Angeles Times* and the *Washington Post*, delivered daily.
- LIBRARY RESOURCES: A number of familiar and new services, including:
  - LIBRARY CATALOG: Catalog of the Trinity, Wesleyan, and Connecticut College libraries, plus six Wilson indexes, *Reader's Guide* (with abstracts), and *Current Contents*.
  - OCLC FIRSTSEARCH: Free access to 23 databases.
  - OTHER LIBRARIES: Internet addresses for libraries frequently used by faculty or recommended for additional searching.
  - CD-ROM DATABASES: Additional locally mounted databases (accessible to Mac users only).
  - HYTELNET: Loaded automatically on PCs; used as HyperCard stack on Macs.
  - DOCUMENTATION: README files for most services, plus full-text documents and guides (St. George, Farley, Kovacs, etc.).

Alfred C. Burfeind
Computer Operations
  Manager
Trinity College Library

Angela L. Wolf, Computing Resource
  Specialist
Trinity College, Hartford, Connecticut

300 Summit Street, Hartford, CT 06106
al.burfeind@mail.trincoll.edu
(203) 297-2334

ABC Express: Resource-stretching in the Mountains

ABC Express has made it possible for thousands of students, staff, and faculty at Appalachian State University, UNC—Asheville, and Western Carolina University to borrow materials from each of the three universities' collections at a cost that compares favorably to conventional ILL but at a speed usually expected only from high-tech commercial suppliers. Fax transmission of requests and location checking by the patron rather than staff are among the "quick and dirty" procedures that make it possible to offer a turnaround time of one to three days. While the ABC Express van's route between Asheville, Boone, and Cullowhee (hence the name of the service) and its three-times-a-week delivery schedule have varied little over the past four years, a look at statistics points out the real change in the service. Between November 1988 and November 1992, the monthly total for books and periodicals exchanged by the three institutions grew from 298 (1988) to 1,749 (1992). With more and more patrons becoming familiar with the service and with budget cuts further reducing the periodicals collections in all three libraries, we can only expect continued growth in the coming years.

Pat Prieto
Reference/Interlibrary Loan Librarian
Hunter Library
Western Carolina University
Cullowhee, NC 28723
(704) 227-7274

Automated Patent System (APS)

The Automated Patent System (APS) is a full-text database covering U.S. patents from 1971 to the present. The D. H. Hill Library at North Carolina State University is one of 14 libraries selected by the U.S. Patent and Trademark Office to participate in a pilot project offering remote online access to U.S. patents. In addition to being full-text, another unique feature of the APS is the frequency of database updates, which is done every Monday night for patents to be issued the following day.

The system allows keyword, inventor, assignee, classification, and various combinations of search terms using boolean logic.

Jean Porter
Government Documents Department
The Libraries
NCSU
Jean—Porter@NCSU.edu

Geographic Information Systems Literacy Project

The NCSU and Duke libraries have been selected to participate in a project that seeks to introduce, educate, and investigate use of Geographic Information Systems (GIS) in research libraries and the campus community. The Association of Research Libraries (ARL), aware of the potential use of GIS in libraries and in the research community, is cosponsoring the "GIS Literacy Project" with the Environmental Systems Research Institute (ESRI) of

Redlands, California. ESRI is interested in fostering access to GIS technology and assisting libraries to move into the future of managing geographic information. ESRI has donated copies of its access software, ArcView, and prepackaged databases to participating project libraries. This showcase session will describe GIS technology, illustrate uses of the technology, and demonstrate GIS mapping software packages.

Lisa T. Abbott
Social Sciences/Data Resources
  Librarian
Reference Department
NCSU Libraries
Lisa—Abbott@NCSU.edu

Margaret S. Brill
State Documents & Maps Librarian

Perkins Library, Duke University
Durham, NC
919-660-5850

Finding Our WAIS Through a Gopher Hole

The NCSU Libraries, which is beginning to explore the use of WAIS and Gopher technologies, has implemented an organizational scheme using these technologies to store Internet resources in a way that mirrors a traditional library. There is a "reference desk," 'study carrels," and the stacks. We have been adding Internet resources containing pertinent information for the faculty, staff, and students of NCSU. When a resource is identified, it is inserted into the organizational structure. Then anyone with Gopher client software and access to the Internet can use the new resources.

We have also begun exploring the use of WAIS to create our own indexes of electronic journals. When new issues are received, the mail headers are deleted and the text is automatically saved and indexed with WAIS. Access to these journals is available through FTP, WAIS, or Gopher clients. Using WAIS, it is possible to create a master index. By searching this index we can find articles from a number of electronic publications. We propose libraries cooperate in collecting electronic journals and providing access to them the "WAIS" we have.

Try gopher by pointing your Gopher client to dewey.lib.ncsu.edu on port 70.

Eric Lease Morgan
Systems Librarian
NCSU Libraries
Eric—Morgan@NCSU.edu

Gelman Library Information Service: Turning "NO" into "YES"

The Gelman Library Information Service (GLIS) was proposed in 1986 as a more appropriate channel for responding to the information needs of the hundreds of daily library users who are not affiliated with the George

Washington University, a private, nonprofit institution located in the heart of the nations's capital. The disproportionately high level of service demanded by nonaffiliated users collided with the necessarily low service priority granted them. This led to frustration for both library staff and patrons. Establishing a separate unit that offers fast, personalized research and document delivery for a fee changed "No, I can't help you with that" to "Yes, we can do that for you."

GLIS enhances the degree and convenience of access to the library's collections for patrons who otherwise are limited to on-site use of materials. The fees charged for the special service cover the unit's costs and minimize the drain on library resources by those who do not directly support the library's collections and services. This showcase session will describe the planning behind GLIS: how the service was promoted to users and how it has evolved.

Lee Anne George
Head, Document Delivery Services Department
George Washington University
2130 H. Street, NW Room B07
Washington, DC 20052
(202) 994-6973

Image-In That! Great Images Sent 'Or Ere Your Pulse Beat Twice

Marilyn M. Roche
Senior Program Officer
Research Libraries Group, Inc.

The CICNet/OSU Network Fax Project:
Cooperative Library Network Document Delivery

Robert J. Kalal
Associate Director
Academic Computing Services,
Ohio State University

ABOUT THE EXHIBITORS

Adonis

An "in-house" document delivery system on CD-ROM covering 430+ biomedical journals. Identify and print articles in seconds. Includes all halftones and graphics. All copyright issues have been cleared with all publishers.

Contact: Paul Ashton, Regional Sales Manager
Adonis
3 Cambridge Center
Cambridge, MA 02142
(617) 547-8427 or (800) 944-6415

Article Express International, Inc.

Article Express provides full-text copies of virtually any article, conference paper, or technical report published in engineering and technology. Delivery options include mail, FAX, courier, or Internet; rush service is also available. Come see a demo of XpressNet—a family of software products that allows for the scanning, transmission, browsing, viewing, and printing of documents received via the Internet. Article Express International is a document services company jointly owned by Dialog Information Services and Engineering Information.

Contact: Michael G. Gannon, President
Article Express International, Inc.
Castle Point on the Hudson
P.O. Box 1808
Hoboken, NJ 07030-9998
(210) 216-8540 or (800) 238-3458

CARL Systems, Inc.

UnCover is an index to 13,600 English-language periodicals dating from 1989 to the present. Approximately 3,400 article citations are added to the database nightly. UnCover is current with the newsstand issue and is the largest, most comprehensive, and up-to-the minute article delivery service available today. Articles may be requested online for fax delivery within 24 hours. Payment is made via credit card or special deposit account. Uncover can be accessed by public dial-in or via the Internet.

Also being featured during the showcase program will be the Journal Graphics Online, a new CARL Systems service providing a free online index to news and public affairs programming with the capability of online ordering of full transcripts of programs.

Contact: Martha Whittaker
CARL Systems, Inc.
3801 E. Florida Ave., Bldg. D. Suite 300
Denver, CO 80210
303-758-3030

Data Research Associates

Data Research automates academic, public, and corporate libraries and provides comprehensive documentation, training, and support for all its customers. Today it is an industry leader in the national and international information standards. Data Research has more than 200 installations worldwide representing more than 800 libraries.

Contact: Linda Hendrix
Data Research Associates
1276 North Warson Road
St. Louis, MO 63132
314-432-1100

Digital Equipment Corporation

Digital Equipment Corporation is one of the world's largest suppliers of networked computer systems, software, and services, and it is a leader in multivendor systems integration. Digital has become a recognized leader for networked and interactive systems and has occupied a prominent role in computing and library automation for higher education.

Contact: Bill Drake or Michael Michaels
Sales Representative

Digital Equipment Corporation
4709 Creekstone Drive Suite 200
Morrisville, NC 27560-9772
Phone: (919) 367-4420
Fax: 919-941-1956

The Faxon Company

Faxon is the world's leading supplier of serials subscriptions and integrated systems, linking publishers to libraries around the world. Faxon's document search-and-delivery services provide convenient access to thousands of serials titles.

Contact: Michael Markwith
The Faxon Company
15 Southwest Park
Westwood, MA 02090
(617) 329-3350

Oxford University Press Electronic Publishing

Oxford University Press has recently launched an ambitious electronic-publishing schedule in four major areas: science, medicine, reference, and the humanities and social sciences.

Oxford currently publishes a full range of software, including *The Oxford English Dictionary* [*Second Edition*] on compact disc. The *Oxford Reference Shelf* series gives computer users on-screen access to Oxford's "little" dictionaries. The *Oxford Writer's Shelf* launched the collection, which will include titles for businessmen, scientists, and other professionals.

Other electronic publications include *Desktop Molecular Modeller; Microfit*, used by economists for time-series analysis; the *Oxford Electronic Text Library* (electronic editions of standard literary works); and several medical databases.

Oxford recently became the publisher of *Postmodern Culture*, a peer-reviewed electronic journal featuring essays on contemporary literature, theory, and culture, as well as postmodern creative writing. The journal is distributed fee of charge as electronic mail. Paid subscriptions are available on disk and microfiche.

Contact: Matthew Bedell
Oxford University Press
Journals Department
2001 Evans Road
Cary, NC 27513

Phone: (919) 677-0977
Fax: 919-677-1714

SOLINET

SOLINET—a not-for-profit library cooperative located in Atlanta, Georgia—provides resource sharing for the educational, cultural, and economic advancement of the southeastern United States and the Caribbean. SOLINET's main programs are OCLC Services, Library Automation Services, Preservation Field Services, Preservation Microfilming, Member Discount, and Workshops and Training.

OCLC is a nonprofit membership organization offering computer-based services to libraries, other educational organizations, and their users. Located in Dublin, Ohio, OCLC provides online and CD-ROM services for reference, cataloging, interlibrary loan, collection development, and bibliographic verification.

Contact: Joanne Kepics
SOLINET
1438 W. Peachtree St., Suite 200
Atlanta, GA 30309-2955
1-800-999-8558

Chemical Abstracts Service/STN International

CAS Document Delivery Service (CAS DDS) can provide documents from the CAS collection, including journal articles, conference proceedings, symposia, and edited collections published since 1975, with documents from the former Soviet Union since 1970. CAS can also provide patents issued by twenty-seven patent offices around the world. Copies of articles are registered with the Copyright Clearance Center. Product literature is available at the conference registration area.

Chemical Abstracts Service/STN International
P.O. Box 3012
2540 Olentangy River Road
Columbus, OH 43210
(614) 447-3731 or (800) 753-4CAS

Heckman Bindery

Heckman provides efficient personalized service designed to meet special customer requirements. Heckman's reputation for superior quality and service has continued for generations. Heckman Bindery offers compliance with LBI standards, guaranteed pickup and delivery schedules prepared one year in advance, a complete line of conservation services, plus many other options. Since 1931 Heckman has been a leader in the industry by combining quality craftsmanship and innovative technology.

Contact: Steven J. Sonafrank or Linda Kling
Heckman Bindery, Inc.
1010 N. Sycamore
P.O. Box 89
North Manchester, Indiana 46962
(219) 982-2107

ABOUT THE SPEAKERS

John E. Ulmschneider is assistant director for Library Systems at North Carolina State University Libraries. In addition to information systems management for the NCSU Libraries, he is project director for a research and development effort undertaken by the Triangle Research Libraries Network (TRLN)—comprised of Duke University, North Carolina State University, and the University of North Carolina at Chapel Hill—to create a model integrated electronic document delivery service for library constituencies. Ulmschneider's background includes training and experience in software design, development, and implementation; project management; systems management; network design; and library administration. Before his current position, Ulmschneider was systems manager at the College of William and Mary and systems librarian at the National Library of Medicine. Ulmschneider received the B.A. from the University of Virginia and the M.S.L.S. from the University of North Carolina at Chapel Hill.

Marilyn Roche, senior program officer for the Research Libraries Group (RLG), has managed Ariel, RLG's image transmission system; developed and analyzed the ARL/RLG ILL Cost Study model; managed SHARES, RLG's resource-sharing program; and led other major RLG initiatives. Prior to joining RLG, Roche was a member of the Connecticut House of Representatives from 1981 through 1987, where she was chair of numerous committees including the Education Committee; she has also worked as a systems engineer at IBM. Roche received her M.A. from Stanford University and her B.A. from Cornell University.

Robert Kalal is associate director of Academic Computing Services (ACS) at Ohio State University, focusing on distributed computing support and UNIX workstation support. He is also the ACS liaison to OSU University Libraries and co-chair of the state-wide Ohio LINK Library Document Delivery Subcommittee. At OSU Kalal has worked with mainframe scientific and

271

engineering computing, electronic mail and text-processing development and support, and CAD/CAM/CIM and computer graphics. He managed the project team responsible for the OSU/CICNetwork FAX project, led the design and implementation of the MAGNUS computer system (a cluster of small UNIX servers providing news, mail, and information services to over 10,000 campus users), and worked with OSU University Press and Libraries to develop an online version of a traditional print journal. He is also an associate of OSU's Center for Advanced Studies in Telecommunications (CAST) and is currently working to build a free public-access computer information system for the Columbus community. Prior to joining OSU, Kalal worked at OCLC and Ohio Bell.

Tracy M. Casorso is project manager of the NCSU Digitized Document Transmission Project. She was directly involved in the initial demonstration study on the transmission of digitized images conducted in 1989, a collaborative effort in conjunction with the *National Agricultural Library's National Agricultural Text Digitizing Project* [*NATDP*]. Before joining the NCSU Libraries in 1989, Casorso was chief architect and manager of INQUIRE, an on-demand, fee-based research and document delivery service at George Washington University in Washington, D.C. She received her A.M.L.S. from the University of Michigan and a B.S. in business administration from Aquinas College, Grand Rapids, MI.

Malcolm Getz, associate provost for Information Services and Technology at Vanderbilt University, is the director of libraries for the Jean and Alexander Heard Library (which includes the collections and facilities of all the university's libraries, the Computer Center, and initiatives in academic computing and other information technologies). He has been a faculty member in the Department of Economics at Vanderbilt since 1973, director of libraries since 1984, and associate provost since 1985. He earned his B.A. in economics from Williams College and his Ph.D. in economics from Yale University. Getz's recent publications address economic issues in libraries, academic computing, computing in instruction, information storage, and electronic publishing.

Sheila Creth has been university librarian at the University of Iowa Libraries since 1987. She previously held administrative positions in the libraries of the universities of Michigan and Connecticut and at Columbia University. Creth, on the board of the Research Libraries Group, is active in the Association of Research Libraries, serving on its Committee on Scholarly Communication. She is also active in the Coalition for Networked Information and the Strategic Visions Steering Committee, a group of library leaders interested in defining a vision for librarianship into the next century. Creth has published extensively on organization and administrative issues related to research libraries, including assessing the impact and integration of new technologies into library organization, the future of academic librarianship, and collection development. A frequent speaker at national conferences, she has designed and conducted numerous management and organization development programs and acts as a consultant on administrative and organizational issues. Creth holds an adjunct faculty appointment in the Department of Communication Studies at the University of Iowa and recently taught a course entitled "Information Technology and the Organization." Her undergraduate degree is from Columbia University with honors in anthropology, and she received the M.A. in communication studies from the University of Connecticut.

I. T. Littleton served as director of the D. H. Hill Library from 1964 until his retirement in 1987. During Littleton's 28 year tenure at the library, which began in 1959, NCSU's collection reached more than one million volumes and the library's physical space expanded three times, including the nine-story addition to the bookstack tower. Littleton chaired a committee to organize the Capital Area Library Association (CALA), an association for librarians in Wake County and the surrounding metropolitan area. As its president (1985-86), he appointed the Task Force on Research Facilities for Middle and High School Students in Wake County. The task force's report raised public awareness of the needs and problems of library service for middle and high school students and led to greater funding for public school libraries. Because of I. T. Littleton's efforts, the NCSU Libraries is known for its service to people.

The I. T. Littleton Seminar Series was instituted in 1987 to honor the contributions of Littleton. It is designed to be a professional development conference that studies major library issues.

Suzanne Striedieck is associate director of Technical Services and Collection Management, NCSU Libraries.

Charles Gilreath is associate director of Public Services, NCSU Libraries.

Susan K. Nutter is director of the NCSU Libraries.

ABOUT THE CONTRIBUTORS

Mark J. Bandera is at Temple University and is also a doctoral candidate in the Department of Slavic and East European Studies, University of Alberta. Recently, he served as a contract historian for the Department of Culture for the Province of Alberta.

Sheila S. Intner, professor in the Graduate School of Library and Information Science of Simmons College, returned recently from Israel where she was a Fulbright professor at the University of Haifa and the Hebrew University in Jerusalem. Dr. Intner also published a paper in volume 8, 1989 of this annual.

Murray S. Martin was born and educated in New Zealand, where he worked for 13 years in the then National Library Service. He moved to Canada where he worked in the University of Saskatchewan. In 1967 he moved to the United States, where he has held positions at the Pennsylvania State University and Tufts University. He is currently Professor of Library Science and University Librarian Emeritus from Tufts University. He is active in ALA, consults with libraries and speaks and writes for library science and literature associations. He is also managing editor for the series *Advances in Library and Information Science*.

Willie Mae O'Neal, Assistant Professor, Waldo Library, is a Continuing Education Librarian for off-campus study at Western Michigan University in Kalamazoo, Michigan.

Verna L. Pungitore is Associate Dean and Director of the Ph.D. Program at the School of Library and Information Science at Indiana University. She teaches in the areas of library management and public libraries, and is the author of *Public Librarianship: An Issues-Oriented Approach* (Greenwood Press, 1989).

Cordelia W. Swinton is the Head of Lending Services and the Acting Chief of Access Services at the Pennsylvania State University Libraries at University Park.

INDEX

Abbott, L., 200
Academic library in transition, 85
Access (definition), 5
Access to storage, 116; bibliographic, 117
Access, to information and library services, 88
Access to versus ownership of library materials, recommendations, 31-35
Accessibility, 78
Accessibility guidelines, 79
Accommodations, 79
Acquisition of material by format or type, 22
Americans with Disabilities Act, meaning for the nondisabled, 81
Adult services task force, 51
Agents, scholarly communication, 215
Aluri, Rao, 89
American Library Association, 39
Andersen, Axel, 130, 131, 132
Anderson, Carol Lee, 86
Anderson, Kathryn H., 205
Andre, Pamela O.J., 190

Architectural barriers common to accessibility, 78
Architectural concepts of the library, 97
Ariel, 167
Arrangement of materials in storage, 118
Association of College and Research Libraries, Slavic and East European section, 129
Author, 215
Authorware, (software), 217
Automated storage and retrieval system, 110
Auxiliary aids for handicapped, 79, 81

Babijcuk, R., 133
Ballard, Thomas H., 71
Bandera, Mark J., 128
Barriers common to accessibility, 78, 79
Beasley, Kenneth E., 50
Beckman, Margaret, 86, 90, 101
Ballanti, Claire, 115
Benne, K. D., 42
Benshoff, J.J., 77

277

Bhola, H.S., 41
Bibliotekar, 133, 134
Bingham, Karen Havill, 128
Blassingame, Ralph, 50, 52
Bloss, Meredith, 52-3
Bolt, Nancy, 49
Book and megabyte, 206
Books, interlibrary loan costs, 169-
    170
Boss, Richard W., 86, 91
Bowen, William G., 205
Bowker, R. R., 235
Boyer, Ernest L., 153
Brine, Jenny, 131, 132, 133, 134
Brodskii, M., 133
Brown, Roland C. W., 102
Browne, Michael, 86
Budget, 152
Butcher, Karyle E., 105

California State University, North-
    ridge, storage facility, 110
Campbell, Jerry, 158
Carnegie Foundation, 153
Casorso, Tracy, 191, 196, 200
Chambert, Ingrid, 128
Chandler, George, 132
Change Agent, 41
Change, professional, 156-8
Chepesiuk, Ron, 135
Chiang, J. T., 132
Childers, Thomas, 45
Chin, R., 42
Choldin, Marianna Tax, 131, 133
Chornovil, Vyacheslav, 134
Chubaryin, O.B., 130
CICNET, 177
"Client-centered Academic Library",
    155
Client/server, document delivery,
    245
Cohen Aaron, 91, 92
Cohen, Elaine, 91, 92

Collection development, (definition),
    5; study methodology, 6
Collection development survey, anal-
    ysis, 10; collection of data,
    9; conclusions, 26; findings,
    11; methodology, 6; sum-
    mary, 25
Common barriers to accessibility,
    78, 79
Communication, 207; scholarly, 206,
    215
Communication, significant features,
    231-2
"Community library services-", 51
Compliance, with the ADA, solu-
    tions and suggestions, 82;
    steps to, 80
Computer-assisted instruction, 158
Conquest, Robert, 127
Conroy, Barbara, 60
Cooperative storage, 114
Copyright, electronic material, 214-5
Costs of interlibrary loan, 20, 177-8,
    205
Creth, Sheila, 91
Cummings, Anthony M., 205
Curzon, Suzan, 85

Damanpour, Fariborz, 45
Data collection methods, 6, 47
Daugherty, Allen, 97
Difinitions, 5
DeProspro, Ernest R., 49, 52, 87
Design for diversity, 52
Designation of materials for storage,
    116
DIALOG, 2, 3
Diffusion, 41; Techniques, *43*
Diffusion Models, 43, 55, 68; link-
    ages, 68
"Dissemination", 41-2; activities, 59-
    65; plans, 56; strategies, 42
Dix, William, 86

Document assistant, 198
Document delivery project goals, 192; interlibrary loan process steps, 196; motivation, 240
Dougherty, Richard M., 152
Dowling, Kenneth E., 85
Drucker, Peter F., 154
Du, David H.C., 209
"Duel", 234
Dziuba, Ivan, 134

Eaton, N. L., 190
Editor, 220
Ekman, Richard H., 205
Electronic databases, costly, 25
Emerging virtual research library, 151, 152
Employee benefit plan review, 77
Environmental concerns, 100
Erastova, N., 133
Ergonomics, 92

Farewell to Alexandria, 85
Fee based services, 29
Fischer, Ken, 60
Fletcher, M., 77
Foundations of Slavic Librarianship, 127
Fraley, Ruth A., 86

Gawdiak, Natalie, 134
Genieva, Ekaterina, 131
Getz, Malcolm, 205, 228
Gigabyte, 207
Gorodinsky, Victor, 129
Graham, Barbara, 114
The Great Divide: Challenges in Remote Storage, 114
Griffiths, Jose-Marie, 46, 53, 56
Guidelines for accessibility, 79
Gunde, M., 78
Gurevich, Konstantin, 132

Harty, S. J., 77
Havelock, Ronald G., 43, 44
Higginbotham, Barbra, 29
High Performance Computing Act, 1991, 208
Horecky, Paul L., 130, 132
Hughes, Carol, 152

Ilnytzkj, Oleh, 127
Information brokering, 19, 20; low esteem for, 29, 128
Integrated planning for campus information systems, 91-92
Initiatives, 232
Innovation, 41
Interlibrary loan, betatesting, 180; costs, 20, 177-8, 205; document delivery process steps, 196; fax transmission, 176-7; (as) gatekeeper, 151; internet, 180; loan shark, 198; user initiated, 151
Internet, 206

Jenson, Mary Brandt, 236
Jokic, Maja, 127
Jones, William G., 97
Just-in-case, 1, 2
Just-in-time, 2

Kapp, David, 101
Kaser, David, 85
Kasinec, Edward, 132
Katz, E., 41
Keen, Peter G. W., 154
Keller, John J., 208
Kemp, Evan J., Jr., 76
Kennedy, James R., 111, 114
Kennedy, William H., 45
Kinch, Michael P., 105
Konn, Tania, 128, 132
Kountz, John, 119
Krol, Ed, 235

Kiz'min, Evgenii, 133
Layton, Daphne N., 91
Lazarus, Lauro O., 205
Levine, Marvin, 95
Librarian, permanent assignments, 154
Librarians, as teaching team members, 157; visibility to institution, 156
Libraries and librarians, 21st century, 150
Libraries, partnerships, 156
Libraries sharing operations and services, 156
Library, 227
"Library," as a concept, 156
Library change literature, 44
Library organization, 153; study, 155
Library Performance, 87
Library Space Planning, 86
Linkage model, 44
Lipow, Anne, 158
Lisson, Paul, 131
"Loan shark", 198
Logistics for information, 210
Lorkovic, Tanja, 132
Lougee, Wendy Pradt, 113
Lynch, Beverly, 85
Lynch, Clifford A., 191
Lynch, Mary Jo, 40, 50, 52, 53
Lyman Peter, 92, 104

Malia, Martin, 127
Market failures, 228
Market power, 228
Martell, Charles, 155
Martin, Allie Beth, 50
Martin, Murray S., 88
McGarty, Terrence P., 234
McClure, Charles R., 40
McManus, Neil, 235
Measuring Academic Library Performance, 88

Megabyte and book, 206
Mills-Fischer, Shirley, 54, 58, 61
Modifications for reasonable accommodation, 77-8
Modular planning, 100
Monopsony, 229
Morgan, E., 196
Muller, Claudya, 62
Musmann, Klaus, 45
Myths (affecting the handicapped), 81

National Research and Education Network, (NREN), 208
"Natigation," in a network, 213
Noll, Roger, 235
Northridge California, 110
Novak, Gloria, 101

OARNET, 177
Online Computer Library Center, 2
Oringdulph, Robert E., 99, 102
Output measures, 55
Ownership (definition), 5

Palmer, Mickey A., 86
Palmour, Vernon E., 40
Parcell, Elizabeth, 128
Patron awareness of location change for storage materials, 117-8
Petabyte, (definition), 207
Pierce, William S., 92
Pipes, Richard, 127
Planning, automated library services, 91-92
Planning for storage, 115
A Planning Process, 57, 62
Print products and library budgets, 205
Professional position, permanency, 154
Project Janus, 206
Property rights, 230

ProQuest, 205
Public Library Association, 39; planning process, 40; standards, 49
Public Library Development Program, 40
Public Library Inquiry, 50
Publisher, 223
Pungitore, Verna L., 41

Quality of the workplace, 92
Ramirez, Anthony, 234
Rawlings, Gregory J. E., 224
Raymond, Boris, 130
Reader, 218
Reference service, new models, 158
Research Libraries Group, 206
Research Libraries Information Network, 2
Rochester, Maxine K., 131, 132
Rodger, Eleanor Jo, 40
Rogers, Everett M., 41
Rogers, Sally, 128
Rohlf, Robert, 51
Ruggles, Melville J., 131
Rutgers University, 149
Rutland, Peter, 127

Sahaydak, Maksym, 134
Said, Caroly, 235
Scanning, of materials, 206
Schneid, T. D., 75, 76, 80
Schoeder, S., 81
Selection of materials for storage, 116
Shelf capacity percentage, 110
Shelving costs, 119
Shoemaker, F., 41
Siegfried, John J., 205
Slavic Librarians Electronic Mail Forum, 129
Slavic librarianship in the west, 126
Social and behavioral concerns, 105

Souheaver, H. G., 77
Soviet ideology and library practice, 130
Spatial relationships, 95
Standard generalized mark-up language, 213
Standard for university libraries, 87
Stein, Nancy Helburn, 42
Steinfeld, E., 81
Steinmueller, W. Edward, 235
Stereotyping, of handicapped people, 76-7
Stockton, Gloria, 111-114
Storage and access, bilbiographic, 117
Storage arrangement of material, 118
Storage, of information, costs, 206; logistics, 210
Storage facilities-four types: 110; new, 111; offsite, 111; onsite, 110; staffing, 113; used, 112
Storage shelving costs, 119
A Strategy for Public Library Change, 50, 52
Study design and procedures, (for planning) 46
Swank, Raynard C., 131
System design for document delivery, 192

Taubes, Gary, 235
TCP/IP, 176, 207
Teaching library, 157
Technology, 94; in east European libraries, 132; scholarly communication, 206
"Teledesk", 158
Terabyte, 207
Thompson, Godfrey, 86
Tompkins, Phillip, 85, 104
Training of library users, 89

Turchyn, Andrew, 127
Turner, Ann, 89

Ukrainian Legal Foundation, 134
Ulmschneider, John, 200
Uniform Federal Accessibility
      Standards, 79
University of Iowa Libraries, reor-
      ganization, 155
Iporova, V., 133
User, of libraries, 87
User satisfaction, 250
User-staff interactions, 99-100

Van House, Nancy, 40
Veatch, Lamar, 55
Velleman, Ruth, 95
Vetter, Ronald J., 209
Virtual collection, 164

Wagon wheel conference, 58
"What Presidents Need to Know",
      150
Whitby, Thomas J., 132
White, Herbert, 125, 136
Williams, Patrick, 52
Wireless communications, special
      report, 234
Witte, Marcia, 205
Working relationships, 103
Workplace quality, 92
Workstation (definition), 233

Z39.50, 170, 171, 205
Zweizig, Douglas L., 40

Advances in Library Administration and Organization

Edited by **Gerard B. McCabe**, *Director of Libraries,Clarion University of Pennsylvania and* **Bernard Kreissman,** *University Librarian Emeritus,* University of California, Davis

REVIEWS: "Special librarians and library managers in academic institutions should be aware of this volume and the series it initiates. Library schools and University libraries should purchase it."

-- Special Libraries

"... library schools and large academic libraries should include this volume in their collection because the articles draw upon practical situations to illustrate administrative principles."

-- Journal of Academic Librarianship

Volume 11, 1993, 320 pp. $73.25
ISBN 1-55938-596-0

CONTENTS: Introduction, *Bernard Kreissman.* Cost Analysis of Library Reference Services, *Marjorie E. Murfin.* Libraries, Technology and Quality, *Miriam A. Drake.* Transformational Leadershipfor Library Managers, *J. Fred Olive III.* Library Technology Transfer: Beyond the Cultural Boundaries, *Kenneth J. Oberembt.* Volunteers in Libraries: An Update, *Rashelle S. Karp.* Libraries: Improving Services to Non-Traditional Students, *Ray Hall.* National Technical Information: The Red October Problem, *Steven M. Hutton.* Examining Innovative Applications of Technology in Libraries, *Virginia Tiefel.* Automated Collection Analysis and Development: Business Collection, *Jane A. Dodd and Suzanne D. Gyeszly.* The Two-Year M.L.S.: Answer or Anathema, *Ahmad Fouad M. Gamaluddin and Jane Rogers Butterworth.* Speculations on Social Epistemology: Specialization in Society, Reflections on Emile Durkheim and Adam Smith, *Steven M. Hutton.* A Bibliography of Sub-Sahara African Librarianship, *Glenn L. Sitzman.* Bibliography of Sub-Sahara African Librarianship, 1990, *Compiled by Glenn L. Sitzman.* Biographical Sketches of the Contributors. Index.

Also Available:
Volumes 1-10 (1982-1992) $73.25 each

Foundations in Library and Information Science

Edited by **Thomas W. Leonhardt,** *Holt Library, University of the Pacific, Stockton, California*

Librarians and library school faculty members are becoming accustomed to finding the volumes of this series among the most useful studies of their subjects.

-- Journal of Academic Librarianship

Volume 30: A Guide to Library Service in Mathematics: The Non-Trivial Mathematics Librarian

1994, 402 pp. LC 93-43482 $73.25
ISBN 1-55938-745-9

Edited by **Nancy D. Anderson,** *Mathematics Librarian, University of Illinois at Urbana-Champaign* and **Lois M. Pausch,** *Geology Librarian, University of Illinois at Urbana-Champaign*

CONTENTS: Introduction. Mathematics Library Service in Academic libraries, *Nancy D. Anderson and lois M. Pausch.* Mathematics Library Service in Public Libraries, *Robert Thornhill.* Mathematics Library Service in Special Libraries, *Gary Davidoff.* References and Further Readings. Reference Materials for the Mathematics Library, *Willis F. Cunningham, Mary B. Harper, and Alice D. Merry.* Books for a Contemporary Mathematics Collection, *Nancy D. Anderson.* About the Contributors. Author Index. Subject index.

Volume 32: Diversity and Multiculturalism in Libraries
1994, 254 pp. LC 94-28566 $73.25
ISBN 1-55938-751-3

Edited by **Katherine Hoover Hill,** *Dry Memorial Library, Erie Community College*

CONTENTS: Introduction, *Katherine Hoover Hill.* Leading the Way to Diversity: The Academic Librarys Role in Promoting Multiculturalism, *Rush G. Miller.* Voices of Diversity in University of California Libraries: Impact, Initiatives and Impediments for Cultural and Racial Equality, *Carol J. Yates, Rafaela Castro, and Lillian Castillo-Speed.* Cultural Diversity Staff Training: The Challenge, *Cheryl Gomez.* Cultivating Workplace Diversity and Empowering Minorities by Fostering Mentor-Protege Relationships, *Edward D. Garten.* The Many We Are: Guidelines for Multicultural Collections Based on the Boomfield College Project, *Danilo H. Figueredo.* Rethinking Theoretical Assumptions About Diversity: Challenges for College and University Library Planning, *William C. Welburn.* Cultural Awareness and Bibliographic Instruction in Academic Libraries, *Scott B. Mandernack, Poping Lin, and David M. Hovide.* The International Student in the U.S. Academic Library: Building Bridges to Better Bibliographic Instruction, *Kwasi Arkodie-Mensah.* Library Services in an Asian American Context, *Julie Tao Su.* La Lectura es un Placer/Reading is Fun, *Adan Griego.* Transforming Academic Libraries for Employees and Students with Disabilities, *Donna Z. Pontau.* Library Services for Older Adults, *linda Lou Wiler and Linda Marie Golian.* Gay and Lesbian Library Users: Overcoming Barriers to Service, *Ellen Greenblatt and Cal Gough.* Living Diversity: Making it Work, *Cheryl Laguardia, Christine K. Oka and Adan Griego.* Positioning for Change: The Diversity Internship as a Good Beginning, *Linda Debeau-Melting and Karen M. Beavers.* About the Contributors. Index.

Volume 33: For the Good of the Order: Essays in Honor of Edward G. Holley
1994, 370 pp. LC 94-17405 $73.25
ISBN 1-55938-752-1

Edited by **Delmus Williams,** *University of Akron,* **John Budd,** *University of Missouri, Columbia,* **Robert E. Martin,** *Louisiana State University,* **Barbara Moran**, *University of North Carolina, Chapel Hill,* and **Fred Roper**, *University of South Carolina, Columbia*

CONTENTS: Preface, *Delmus E. Williams.* Richer For His Honesty: A Personal Memoir of Edward Gailon Holley, *James V. Carmichael, Jr.* The Future of the American Research University, *William Friday.* The Founding of Libraries in American Colleges and Professional Schools Before 1876, *Haynes McMullen.* What Lies Ahead for Academic Libraries? Steps on the Way to the Virtual Library, *Barbara B. Moran.* Somewhere Over the Rainbow: Organizational Patterns in Academic Libraries, *Irene B. Hoadley.* More Hortatory than Factual: Fremont Riders Exponential Growth Hypothesis and the Context of Exponentialism, *Robert E. Molyneux.* Andrew Carnegie and the Black College Libraries, *David Kaser.* Change and Tradition in Land-Grant University Libraries, *Donad G. Davis, Jr. and John Mark Tucker.* The Urban University and Its Library, *Delmus E. Williams.* Diversity and Democracy in Higher Education, *Charles W. Churchwell.* Scholarly Communication and Libraries: Contemporary and Future, *John M. Budd.* Academic Library Literature, *Donald E. Riggs.* The Old Scholarship and the New: Reflections on the Historic Role of Libraries, *Phyllis Dain.* Catalog of A.L.A. Library (1893): Origins of a Genre, *Wayne Wiegand.* Theories of Collection Development in the Early Years of the Graduate Library School at University of Chicago, *Robert N. Broadus.* The State of Library and Information Science Education, *John Richardson, Jr.* Future Directions for Programs of Library and Information Science Education, *John N. Olsgaard and Fred W. Roper.* OCLC: Past and Future, *K. Wayne Smith.* Edward G. Holley: A Select Bibliography, *E. Jens Holley.* An Edward Gailon Holley Chronology, *James V. Carmichael, Jr.* About the Authors, *Delmus E. Williams.*

J A I P R E S S

Advances in Library Automation and Networking

Edited by **Joe A. Hewitt,** *University of North Carolina, Chapel Hill*

The purpose of this series is to present a broad spectrum of in-depth, analytical articles on the technical, organizational, and policy aspects of library automation and networking. The series will include detailed examinations and evaluations of particular computer applications in libraries, status surveys, and perspective papers on the implications of various computing and networking technologies for library services and management. The emphasis will be on the information and policy frameworks needed for librarians and administrators to make informed decisions related to developing or acquiring automated systems and network services with special attention to maximizing the positive effects of these technologies on library organization.

Volume 5, In preparation, Fall 1994
ISBN 1-55938-510-3   Approx. $73.25

Edited by **Joe Hewitt**, *Associate Provost for University Libraries, The University of North Carolina at Chapel Hill and* **Charles Bailey, Jr.** *Assistant Director for Systems, University of Houston.*

CONTENTS: Introduction, *Joe A. Hewitt.* Next-Generation Online Public Access Catalogs: Redefining Territory and Roles, *Carolyn O. Frost.* Full-Text Retrieval: Systems and Files, *Carol Tenopir.* What can The Internet Do For Libraries, *Mark H. Kibbey and Geri R. Bunker.* Electronic Document Delivery: An Overview With a Report On Experimental Agriculture Projects, *John Ulmschneider and Tracy M. Casorso.* Campus-Wide Information Systems, *Judy Hallman.* Use of A General Concept Paper As RFP For A Library System Procurement, *Mona Couts, Charles Gilreath, Joe Hewitt, and John Ulmschneider.* Research On The Distributed Electronic Library, *Denise A. Troll.* Notes on The Contributors.

Also Available:
Volumes 1-4 (1987-1991) $73.25 each

J A I   P R E S S

J
A
I

P
R
E
S
S

The Journal of Academic Librarianship

Executive Editor: **Peter Hernon**
Associate Editor: **Charles Martell**

The Journal of Academic Librarianship, an international and
referred journal, publishes articles that focus on problems
and issues germane to college and university libraries. JAL
provides a forum for authors to present research findings
and, where applicable, their practical applications and significance; analyze policies, practices, issues, and trends;
speculate about the future of academic librarianship;
present analytical bibliographic essays and philosophical
treatises. JAL also brings to the attention of its readers (college and university librarians, academic administrators,
educators and students in programs of library and information science, and others interested in academic
librarianship) information about hundreds of new and
recently published books in library and information science,
management, scholarly communication, and higher education. JAL, in addition, covers management and discipline-
based software and information policy developments.

Subscription Rates:
(all subscriptions are for the calander year only)

Volume 21 (1995)   **Published Bimonthly**
                                        Institutions: $125.00
ISSN 0740-624X   Personal: $50.00

Volume 20 (1994) $125.00 per volume
Outside the U.S.A. add $19.00 for surface mail or $39.00 for airmail

JAI PRESS INC.
55 Old Post Road # 2 - P.O. Box 1678
Greenwich, Connecticut 06836-1678
Tel: (203) 661- 7602   Fax: (203) 661-0792